The
CBT
Toolbox

Second Edition

A Workbook for Clients, Clinicians & Coaches

185 Tools To Manage Anxiety, Depression, Anger, Behaviors & Stress

Jeff Riggenbach, PhD

Copyright © 2021 Jeff Riggenbach

Published by
PESI Publishing
PESI, Inc.
3839 White Ave
Eau Claire, WI 54703

Cover: Amy Rubenzer
Layout: Amy Rubenzer & Bookmasters

ISBN: 9781683732792
Printed in the United States of America

PESI Publishing
pesipublishing.com

 **Jeff Riggenbach, PhD,** is an internationally recognized trainer in CBT and an award-winning author. Dr. Riggenbach trained with the prestigious Beck Institute of Cognitive Therapy and Research, is certified with the Academy of Cognitive Therapy, and has used CBT in individual and group settings in psychiatric hospital clinics for over 20 years. He has trained clinicians in all 50 states, and is on faculty with educational institutes in Canada, UK, Australia, and South Africa, and his trainings routinely receive high evaluations from workshop participants.

After 20 years of clinical practice developing and directing CBT-based programs for depression, anxiety disorders, addictive behavior disorders, and personality disorders, he has devoted his recent years to teaching, training, coaching/consulting, and writing. He is known for equipping clinicians and coaches with practical tools to empower clients in their everyday lives. You can see his entire clinical toolbox series, resilience journal, and other publications and resources at jeffriggenbach.com.

TABLE OF CONTENTS

INTRODUCTION

Why a Second Edition and What Is Different?

A friend of mine asked me the other day, "Jeff, why are you doing a second toolbox?" My initial response was, "Nobody read the first one, so I thought I'd try again." He laughed (I think he believed me.)

The reality is that is untrue. The first edition sold over 50,000 copies, and I received messages from people all over the world testifying as to how helpful it was for them or their clients. Perhaps one of the things I was most pleased to hear was its scope of reach. It is being used in primary care settings, master of social work programs, domestic violence shelters, community mental health settings, university counseling centers, as well as both inpatient and outpatient hospitals and treatment settings.

However, as pleased as I was with the success of the first toolbox, an honest answer to my friend's question would address a few areas:

Advances in the Field

First of all, things have changed in the field. There is a greater emphasis on so-called "third wave" approaches. Dialectical Behavior Therapy (DBT), Acceptance and Commitment Therapy (ACT), and other mindfulness-based approaches have become all the rage. Whether it is necessary to modify content of thoughts and beliefs has become a topic of much discussion. While on one hand this notion challenges the very fabric of traditional Cognitive Behavioral Therapy (CBT), these approaches do involve "doing something different" with cognitions, and their ability to change mood and behavior is worthy of consideration.

In addition to third wave or other metacognitive approaches, a more concentrated attempt has been made in recent years to become more inclusive of other modalities and to draw and pull from a variety of therapies. While being "eclectic" for the sake of being eclectic has no doubt harmed many clients, incorporating strategies from different modalities can help professionals get where they want to go with their clients. As long as clinicians work consistently within their conceptualization of the case and continue to use that as their guiding "road map," drawing from a variety of modalities can be a powerful way to help clients reach their goals. New techniques have also been developed to enhance traditional CBT work as well.

Tools for a Broader Range of Diagnosis and Symptom Sets

An additional new element to this edition includes tools for new conditions not addressed in the first book. CBT now has over 26 discrete cognitive models to address different symptom sets. It is no longer just for depression and anxiety.

Some exciting developments within "traditional" CBT show promise as well. Bob Leahy's *Emotional Schema Therapy* adds an extra layer of depth to traditional CBT approaches. Irismar Reis de Oliveira's *Trial-Based Cognitive Therapy* (TBCT) provides an interactive way for clients to "put their beliefs on trial" so as to examine their validity in a fun and nonthreatening way. Also, Tullio Scrimali and others have helped the CBT community pay increasing attention to the interaction of CBT and the latest advances in neuroscience. Christine Padesky's Strengths-Based CBT and David Burns' TEAM-CBT highlight a myriad of new "spins" on an old model.

While this manual is, as is its predecessor, a guide full of practical tools to help clients living in the real world, the scientific and theoretical basis of these tools should be acknowledged. This edition explores some practical applications derived from these new approaches as well as new and improved tools using the traditional approach.

Adapting CBT for Different Settings and for Use with a Broader Range of Practitioners

It is impossible to ignore the emergence of the use of CBT in other disciplines, including by alternative medicine practitioners, clergy, and in life and corporate coaching settings. Some topics relevant to these settings are addressed as well in the final section, which uses less clinical language.

Although the book was primarily intended to be used by clinicians with their clients, I learned that more clients purchased this book than I ever imagined. While I have a book for clients only in the pipeline (stay tuned!), this second edition represents a step in that direction in that it uses less clinical and more client-friendly language, particularly in the personal growth and coaching sections.

HOW TO USE THIS WORKBOOK

The following tools are skills and activities you can add to your toolbox of resources to be better equipped to deal with issues that clients may present. Some people may struggle in all of these areas, while other users may find only one or two chapters to be relevant to them. For example, some may only deal with depression, whereas others may fight depression, anxiety, anger, and battle addictive behaviors as well. Others may just need stress management for a particular work environment.

This edition is broken up into three sections:

Section 1 addresses core competencies, socialization, and starting well with clients.
Section 2 covers issues of clinical concern.
Section 3 deals with brand new content completely, venturing into application of CBT techniques in corporate and coaching environments.

Similar to the previous book, you will notice some of the same tools show up in multiple chapters. You will have evidence logs, thought logs, and a number of other tools in each chapter. Note, however, that they may be used differently with different symptom sets and you may be working with different cognitive content.

Thus, it is still important that if you find that a tool in Chapter 8 appears to be the same as a tool you've worked with in Chapter 3 not to assume, "I've already seen that in a previous chapter" and just skip it. The tools are laid out strategically to ensure that you have what you need for each symptom set discussed. Also, questions within a given tool may sound similar, but have been modified to fit the particular problem being addressed. For instance, the relationship circles tool shows up in many chapters. Although the exercise is the same, people who struggle with depression may have different themes in the types of relationship problems than people who struggle with anger management. So, the circles themselves look the same, but the questions asked to help address those particular problems are different. By organizing the book this way, people can read it cover to cover or just flip to the chapter they are interested in and be able to access what they are looking for easily.

Finally, be cognizant that in addition to the tools that are used in a cross-cutting manner, each chapter has its own specific tools as well.

The first 15 tools in each clinical chapter help you work across the sequence of the basic cognitive chain. Tools 16 and beyond offer additional strategies to specifically target the symptom set addressed in that particular chapter.

Here are the tools for the chapters addressing clinical concerns:

Tool 1 is devoted to **identification of triggers.** This is an important starting place regardless of symptom set. This helps clients identify the "event" that set off the chain to give them a better understanding of their symptoms. Triggers may be internal (bodily sensations, hallucinations, or other physiological symptoms) or external (environmental events). Triggers activate beliefs by tapping into the specific content area of vulnerability. They activate the belief (or "push people's buttons") thus setting off the sequence.

Tool 2 helps facilitate **awareness of feelings.** Some people are very good at expressing their feelings. Others have difficulty recognizing feelings, giving names to feelings, or even acknowledging that they have feelings at all. This section in each chapter offers a **Feelings Face Sheet** for aiding people in giving terminology to the emotions in that particular "feeling family" they are experiencing.

Tool 3 deals with **identification of distorted thoughts.** Some therapists may use the term *irrational thoughts* (Ellis, 1975). Others prefer the term *dysfunctional thoughts* or *maladaptive thoughts*. (A. Beck, 1987) The advantage of considering thoughts to be dysfunctional is recognizing that thoughts that were functional or helpful in one setting may become dysfunctional or hurtful in other settings. For instance, someone who grew up in a violent family might have learned through experience, "If I speak up, somebody gets hit or yelled at, so it's best that I just keep my mouth shut." If while growing up one really did get hurt every time he opened his mouth, it would have been adaptive to keep his mouth shut as long as he was in that environment. But, if that person adopts that way of thinking ("It's best that I just keep my mouth shut") even after he has grown up and left that home, it is no longer adaptive to never speak his mind, especially when he is in safe settings to do so. Thus, what is functional in one setting is not necessarily helpful in others. Other professionals use the terms *distorted, or unhealthy thinking*, which are the terms this book uses.

Tool 4 helps people identify their **"autopilot" coping skills** (initial reactionary behaviors). Most people develop a set of standard go-to coping skills when they feel certain emotions. Perhaps you have heard the phrase "on autopilot," referring to falling back on the same old behaviors that in some way feel comfortable but usually don't help. Again, these behaviors often "worked" in the past but no longer work in the present. Also, some may continue to work in the short term but make problems worse in the long term. For example, alcohol, drugs, promiscuity, spending, or over-working are coping skills people use to avoid feeling negative feelings about themselves. These behaviors do serve that purpose but create longstanding problems that are almost always worse. Before figuring out healthy skills to use when these feelings creep up, it is often useful to generate a list of behaviors that may present a temptation to engage in but that have proven themselves to be *unhelpful* in the long run.

Tool 5 addresses **awareness of consequences.** Some people have little to no awareness as to how their past coping choices have impacted their present life circumstances. Others fully recognize that their present choices may cause future consequences but continue to choose that quick, "feel-good" choice regardless. Tool 5 helps increase people's awareness of these consequences by asking them to consider a variety of areas in life in which autopilot behaviors may have created problems and write them down.

Tool 6 takes people through the step-by step process of completing a **Cognitive Behavior Chain Analysis.** This tool asks them to take the information they have accumulated from the previous tools and enter them into a CBT chain analysis tool. This will help them "connect the dots" from their previous work and get a bird's-eye view of an entire situation.

Tool 7 asks clients to visualize their **desired results.** Asking "what would you rather experience?" gives people something to strive for rather than something to stay away from. In essence, it asks what they would like to increase in their life rather than what they want to decrease, which, for some, is a more effective motivator. If people know what they are striving toward, then they are more likely to do the work of changing their thoughts and behaviors.

Tool 8 asks clients to consider **new coping skills.** Once clients have identified what they don't want as well as what they do want, this tool guides them in identifying what types of alternative behaviors they may need to engage in to achieve more of their desired results.

Tool 9 promotes generating **new thoughts.** Once clients have identified more healthy behaviors to strive for, tool 9 helps them generate new ways of thinking that will facilitate the desired behaviors.

A central idea in traditional cognitive therapy has always been that once someone recognizes a thought that may be unhelpful they need to do something about it. That "something" traditionally has been change the content of the thought in some way. Challenge it with logic. Conduct a behavioral experiment. Examine the evidence. Many different cognitive techniques have the aim of restructuring content, and this book will cover many of them. But as chapter 4 speaks to, newer approaches suggest that challenging thought content directly may not always be best. Distraction, mindfulness, and other acceptance and attention-based approaches offer alternatives for what people can do with their thoughts one they notice them.

Tool 10 addresses **new feelings with intensity ratings.** This tool asks clients to pay attention to the types and intensity of their feelings and to compare mood states before and after new thinking. CBT doesn't make terrible feelings go away completely, but it can often lessen the intensity of unpleasant emotions, making it easier to cope. CBT can also serve to increase positive emotions as well.

Tool 11 revisits the **Cognitive Behavior Chain Analysis with rational responses.** This modified version of the initial chain analysis tool walks clients through how to plug their new thoughts, feelings, and behaviors identified in the previous tools into a new comprehensive chain. This breaking down of specific episodes can be helpful for suggesting new behaviors as well as analyzing larger patterns.

Tool 12 introduces the **downward arrow to help clients identify core beliefs.** You may have informally heard the phrase "beliefs drive behavior." This phrase is common in the coaching world, although few coaches have more than a surface level understanding of how this process works. But the reality is that every behavior is *a schema (belief) driven behavior.* Different conditions, symptom sets, and problematic ways of relating with people can all be traced to specific core beliefs, conditional assumptions, and "rules" that accompany them. This tool helps clients identify exactly which beliefs are responsible for their behaviors.

Tool 13 facilitates the **identification of an alternate belief.** Once clients have identified their unhealthy beliefs responsible for the problem, they can construct more healthy beliefs that can drive them toward solutions. Tool 13 helps explain how to begin this process.

Tool 14 helps break down the **components of beliefs.** Beliefs are formed based on the meaning we assign to experiences. Tool 14a helps clients identify some key experiences that led to the formulation of their unhealthy beliefs. Tool 14b then helps lay the groundwork for constructing new healthy ones.

Tool 15 introduces **evidence logs.** Constructing new beliefs is not an easy process. It requires intentional and repetitive work. Part of this involves helping clients to focus on aspects of experiences their autopilot thoughts would "miss" due to existing beliefs. As one pays attention to evidence supporting new beliefs being constructed, logging this evidence can help in the process of internalizing new beliefs.

Additional Tools

All clinical chapters have these same 15 basic CBT related tools adapted to their particular problem area. Beginning with Tool 16, each chapter then offers additional tools helpful for that particular symptom set.

I hope you enjoy and get maximum benefit from these tools. They have changed many lives. I hope they at least help enhance yours.

1

Basic Tenets, Core Competencies, New Trends

CHAPTER **1**

CBT 101

One day, while on my way to a speaking engagement, there was some confusion with my plane ticket, which had been purchased some three months in advance. After doing some scrambling, the airline accommodated me and got me in one of the last seats on the flight. Having received one of the last tickets on the entire flight, of course I was assigned one of those highly coveted middle seats. Not a petite individual myself, I was less than thrilled to discover my assigned seat was in between two other adults.

There I was, jammed in between these two individuals with no room to move at all. It didn't take long before the person on my right began sweating profusely. With no room to move, her sweat began dripping on me—if you fly much, you know they don't start circulating the air until the plane begins taxiing toward the runway for takeoff. Then we had some minor mechanical difficulty. So I was sandwiched in, no room to move at all, and, as if it couldn't get any worse, a lady in front of me started changing her baby's diaper! I was jammed in there, no room to move at all, accumulating sweat by the moment, with a horrible stench emanating throughout the cabin. Any guesses how I felt? Wouldn't everyone in that situation feel the same way? As I turned my head, I noticed the lady on my left smiling, laughing, and saying things like, Goo-goo, ga-ga and playing with the baby through the space between the seats. She was trying to help the mother out. She was trying to get the baby to stop screaming. If you had taken a picture of this woman's face, you might have guessed she was having the time of her life! Although she was in virtually the same situation as I was, she was experiencing it in a much more enjoyable way. Why? Because she was obviously having different thoughts!

I now have a confession to make. When I wrote this in the first edition, although it was a good example of what I wanted to illustrate, and 100 percent true, I still found it a little far-fetched at the time. Why? Perhaps because I did not have kids when I began to write the first edition and I do now. I have to admit that the me of today would be naturally much more sympathetic to the woman's plight. It would be much easier for me to be the "goo-goo, ga-ga" onlooker now than it was eight years ago. This highlights the role that our experiences play in shaping our thinking, both our initial thoughts and our ability to generate alternate thinking.

This story remains a good illustration that I have used with my clients in the initial psychoeducation phase that should (I know…a cognitive distortion…we all do them) accompany any CBT in the early stages. Specifically, it reminds me of the importance of helping the individual understand what CBT is and what it is not. This book devotes the majority of its contents to what CBT is. But there are a few things CBT is **NOT**.

1. CBT is not "don't worry be happy" therapy. Many people mistakenly believe CBT is just about positive thinking. This is untrue. Sometimes CBT is about thinking more positively. But sometimes it is about getting clients to actually think more negatively. I know it sounds strange, but you probably know at least one of those "sunshine pumpers." They are annoying, right? I know, pump the brakes a bit. We enjoy being around people who are happy to be alive and fun to be with. They brighten our days and encourage us. They help us to stay grounded and remain thankful. So they are much needed. But, to an extreme, this "positive" thinking can actually be harmful. The person who just says "Oh, I'm fine—I know I feel a little different, but it will pass, it always does," and doesn't go in to get their chest pains evaluated, is putting themselves at greater risk of a heart attack. The person who says to her friend "just hang in there and keep your head up—things will get better," but does not ask her to consider the role of her daily marijuana smoking and abusive boyfriend is likely leading her friend astray. And the coach who encourages her client, "I'll send good vibes your way—keep your energy positive and you will live a transformed and abundant life," but does nothing to address the client's unemployment or other practical strategies for paying his bills is leading the person off the cliff.

Many well-meaning people say things like "pull yourself up by your bootstraps and you will be fine." Pretending things are ok when they are not couldn't be farther from the goal of CBT.

2. CBT is not surface-level symptom management that is incapable of treating complex conditions. "Just refer him to CBT for symptom management." I can't tell you how many times I have heard this phrase from biologically oriented psychiatrists (and others). CBT does offer effective symptom management. CBT lends itself well to anger management, anxiety management, and depression management. But the uninformed clinician does not realize that if symptom management is all CBT had to bring to the table, CBT would not do so well in all of the relapse prevention studies. Cognitive therapy has been repeatedly shown to not only help people get well in the short term but stay well in the long run. This phenomenon would not occur over and over again if CBT were not able to **treat** conditions rather than just "manage symptoms." Moreover, cognitive and behavior-based approaches now have empirically supported protocol for PTSD, panic disorder, suicidality, personality disorders, hallucinations, and delusions, just to name a few. This isn't your grandfather's CBT. The claim of CBT doing only symptom management for depression and anxiety is a good 50 years old.

3. CBT must not always be delivered by a disgruntled clinician with anger management problems in clients' faces with a highly confrontational approach. I am being a bit facetious here, but I continue to be amazed that this is still many potential clients' notion of what they are signing up for. The style of the therapist can vary dramatically. In the same way you can have a physician or a plumber or an accountant with different personalities, the same will be true of a cognitive therapist. Some are more direct. But the reality is the politically correct posture these days is to be "person-centered," and "strengths-based." So it is really fairly unlikely you will get someone who is "in your face." I actually hear more clients complaining that they wish their therapist was more directive. The important thing is to find a clinician who is a good fit with the client.

4. CBT must not always involve a person with schizoid personality disorder behind a computer entering data asking about therapeutic drift. Ok, I am being a bit sarcastic again. But this is a *very* common complaint among patients and clients. Part of this, I believe, has to do with the move to electronic medical records. Most mental health professionals are not overly proficient with technology—that's why we went into mental health! The excessive technical demands overwhelm some clinicians, and it's all they can do to get client information submitted in the correct box so as not to get an error screen and have to reenter all the data. While I am certainly sympathetic to the clinician, I also feel terrible for the thousands of clients who are pushing themselves to be vulnerable about challenging and personal situations in their lives, some of which they may not have ever shared with anyone before…only to have a clinician not making eye contact with them poking at a keyboard say, "Could you say that again—the computer wouldn't take what I typed."

Finally, CBT, has some language that is less than user friendly. One of my clients told me she left her most recent cognitive therapist named Jane when she made the statement, "Sally, I don't want to create a rupture in our therapeutic alliance, but the protocol dictates that we stick strictly to your cognitive conceptualization map, and I am going to have to politely interject to prevent any therapeutic drift." Perhaps one of the funnier parts about this is that I agree completely with the notion of not letting clients stray away to topics not central to addressing their problems. But many clinicians don't even come across as a real person. As a professional, it is important to know the lingo to converse intelligently with colleagues in the field. But many clinicians do not appear to be breathing human beings. The good news for clients? While they are out there, most CBT practitioners are *not* Jane. If you think they are, be encouraged! There is hope!

5. CBT does not take a person going through a horrible situation and help them to feel fabulous about it. This is unrealistic. CBT is about realistic thinking. So it is important that people know up front what CBT can and cannot do. In a world of empty promises, such honesty is refreshing to most people.

To that end, it may not have been realistic for me at the time of that flight to have had the attitude of the lady in the seat behind me. But now having the experience of attempting to travel with 18-month-old twins to Hawaii (one of the poorer decisions I have made in my life), I have to say my natural reactions are much different. Now my response to the many screaming babies I encounter on planes is in fact quite different. Although I am not as eager to help as the lady in the seat next to me on the plane that day, I do now automatically have sympathetic thoughts of genuine compassion for the stress they are under, having a greater personal understanding of what they are going through. Regardless, this illustrates the point that *our* past experiences inform our ever-evolving beliefs that drive how we experience everything else. Psychoeducation about how this process works is an important early component of treatment and part of that is helping the client to set realistic expectations.

The Thoughts-Feelings Connection

CBT is based on the principle that thoughts influence feelings, feelings influence actions, and actions influence our results (A. Beck, 1967). In other words, situations don't *make* us feel certain ways. People don't *make* us feel certain ways. It's how we interpret (or think about) situations or things people say or do that influences how we feel.

A simplified, linear version of the general model of CBT looks like this:

Event ➧ Thoughts ➧ Feelings ➧ Actions ➧ Results

We all experience events in life that "trigger" this entire process. How we think about, process, or interpret those triggers affects what type of emotions we experience *and* how intensely we feel them. Feelings often influence actions. How we choose to respond influences the outcomes of specific situations which, over time, shapes our life circumstances.

You may see this model taught in a variety of ways. Some use the "cognitive triangle."

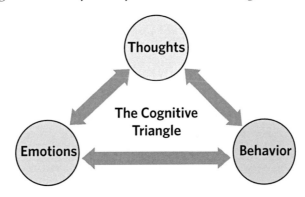

While accurate, this model is incomplete and less helpful for most people attempting to understand how to use this approach. Others use complicated charts with three-way bidirectional arrows that have clients seeing stars. While it is true that life rarely happens in this simplistic linear format, I have found that teaching the sequence in this five-part way is effective in helping most people learn to use it. As clients get comfortable, you can expand on the model with them slowly so they can continue to develop increasing levels of mastery. Although we are constantly processing information ("thinking"), many people *experience* feelings before they are able to consciously identify their thoughts. Also, people can have thoughts about those feelings…which create new feelings…and you can have thoughts about each of those…so you see how this can get a little complicated.

When working with clients, one can also start anywhere in the sequence. For instance, with an 18-year-old boy who got suspended from school and certainly didn't want to be in therapy, I simply started by saying very directly, "Ok, let's get this over with quickly. You got suspended from school. How did that happen?" (starting with results). Alternatively, with my highly anxious female client who easily gets emotionally flooded, I started at the "feelings" stage. As she improved her self-monitoring, awareness of anxiety-related emotions and bodily sensations now cue her to ask herself, "What negative thing am I predicting will happen in the future that I won't be able to cope with?" This helps her identify some of her thoughts involved in creating the distress.

I had one "big name" in the field refuse to write a recommendation for my first edition because he said, "This clinician oversimplifies the relationship between thoughts and feelings." While the reality is that CBT has a depth to it many are unaware of, the skilled clinician presents it to clients in a way that makes sense to them. If we can't meet people where they are at, they will never be able to harness the power of CBT to improve their lives.

Socialization to the Model

Beyond the basic framework, another important principle of CBT is that all behavior makes sense. That is, we all come to think the way we do for specific reasons—all behavior serves a purpose. We can learn from Padesky who says people do things for good reasons. However, the ideas we have learned over the years aren't always healthy—some may have worked in one setting but not in another. Some may have worked at one point in life but not anymore. So ideas that don't work aren't necessarily crazy, irrational ideas. They helped at one point in one setting in life but are no longer helpful. The point, then, is to identify ways of thinking that are in some way distorted or dysfunctional and test and modify them over time. The clinical term for changing the way you think is *cognitive restructuring*. The good news is that over time, anything that is learned can be unlearned. Notice the phrase *over time*.

In my conferences worldwide when I start to talk about socialization, I often get eye rolls. I have heard "Oh, socialization, that's so elementary–I came here to get the more advanced stuff." Yet, when we discuss how to educate people about the model in a way that creates buy-in, those same clinicians often have little to say, or the dialogue gets vague or confusing. Although this seems "basic," I believe this is one of the most important parts of treatment. Namely, because if we don't do this well, it will be difficult to engage clients in a meaningful way. In studies that review things like mechanisms of change and potential reasons for positive treatment outcome, important factors always include the client's beliefs about the clinician and the approach. Doing socialization well plays an important role in initiating both of these.

Having said that, there is no "right" way to socialize. There are certainly some "wrong" ways, but different approaches can be effective with different clients. Some clients may be more formal and prefer a more detailed socialization—perhaps even using some of the fancy words I gave a good-natured poke at earlier. Analytically inclined individuals may be interested in knowing about outcome studies. Some patients couldn't care less about outcome studies; they just want to know how the professional will help them find some relief. Many other variables may be involved. Regardless, quality socialization helps client's "sync" their life problems with the treatment model that you are about to offer them. If this is accomplished, it can instill some confidence at an early point and provide the foundation for an enjoyable therapeutic experience and a positive outcome. It also likely contributes to decreased treatment dropout.

Some basic starter questions might include:

❓ Which comes first, a thought or a feeling?

Let clients share with you what *they* experience first. This gives clinicians a good idea of what stage it may be most effective to start with when working with this particular client.

❓ What is the difference between thoughts and feelings?

Thoughts are not feelings. A lot of people say things like, "I felt like he was scheming against me." That is not a feeling—it is a thought. That type of thought often leads to feelings of *fear, hurt,* or *betrayal*. We teach our patients, "If it's a full sentence, it's a thought." Feelings are one word and are expressions of emotion. Examples include *angry, sad, mad, happy, excited, fearful, anxious, overwhelmed, panicked,* and *annoyed*. Some people do not get the importance of this, but for a person to learn to use the tools this workbook provides, it is important to understand the difference. As we discuss in the paragraphs that follow, it is the *content* of our thoughts that determines what *types of emotions* we feel.

❓ Is it possible for two people to go through the same event and come out with a different experience? If yes, how?

Identifying someone in their life, such as a grandparent, friend, or mentor to use an example can be helpful in illustrating this point.

❓ Where in this sequence can people intervene directly to impact the end result in a positive way?

I usually walk people through the sequence asking about each point of potential intervention.

❓ Do I choose or can I influence events in my life?

Sometimes. Sometimes we put ourselves in situations that make us vulnerable to certain triggers. For example, we choose whom we date, whom we marry, whether we go to certain parties or hang out with certain people, whether we stay at a job or leave it, whether to engage in substance use. And sometimes we do not.

We don't choose our parents, our siblings, the situations our caretakers put us in when we are young, who is driving on the road when we are, or natural disasters. We have a say regarding some of the events (triggers) we experience, and others are completely out of our control.

❓ Do I choose my thoughts and feelings?

To answer this question, let's try a brief exercise. Close your eyes. Picture a giraffe. Can you do it? Picture a snowflake. Can you see it? Picture yourself in your best friend's house. Can you conjure up these images? Of course you can. Now *feel* enraged. Just feel it. Can you do it? What did you have to do to feel enraged? You had to *think* about something that would get you there. Maybe you thought about an ex. Some of you perhaps thought about an issue that ticks you off. Clients will often think about an abusive situation that happened many years ago or "the jerk who cut me off in traffic" that very morning. Regardless of *what* you thought, the point is that it's impossible to command our feelings. Has anyone ever said to you something like, "Oh, come on, there's no need to be depressed—you have so much to be thankful for"? How many times has that been helpful? How many of you have said, "Oh, thanks for the feedback—I'll now choose to be happy"? It is worth noting that well-meaning people can say hurtful and invalidating things. Sometimes people want to help but just don't know how. The point here is that we don't have direct access to our feelings; we only have access to our feelings through our thoughts. So if you have been frustrated when someone told you to just "be happy," you're not alone!

However, if feelings are influenced by thoughts—and as our exercise just illustrated, we do have some control over our thoughts in life—then we do have the power to influence our feelings by learning to slowly retrain the way we think. Does that mean we choose all of our thoughts? Absolutely not. We all have thoughts that just come. Sometimes we know exactly where they came from, and sometimes it seems as though they came "out of left field." The clinical term for these is *automatic thoughts*. We all have these thoughts, some of which we will never be able to keep ourselves from experiencing. However, although we don't always have a choice about whether these thoughts "appear," once they do, we can get better at increasing our awareness, paying attention to them, and working to change them through the tools this workbook teaches!

? Do I choose my actions?

Occasionally, this question gets some people fired up. The short answer is that we almost always choose our actions. (There are a couple of clinical conditions in which someone literally does things outside their awareness, but these are rare.) Some people say things like, "He made me do it," or "I didn't have a choice," or "What about fight or flight?" Some decisions are made instantaneously, and the thought process behind them is less conscious, but to determine whether thinking was involved, helpful questions to ask include:

- Would it have been possible *not* to do the action in that situation?
- Would someone else in my life have reacted differently?

? Do I choose my results?

Our actions *influence* our results. *Influence* is an important word to understand, because it doesn't mean *dictate*. Thus, it is not accurate to say we *choose* our results. It is possible that when we make healthy decisions, bad things still happen. It is also possible to make a certain number of poor choices and get away with it. But, generally speaking, the healthier choices you make, the better chance you have of a positive outcome, and the unhealthier choices you make, the better chance you have of running into trouble in some area of your life (relationally, occupationally, financially, legally, etc.).

Workshop participants often ask me if I have a handout or an article that I give clients to explain to them what CBT is. Many are surprised to hear that I never have. I have simply explained the model in my own words using situations the clients bring into session, writing on the whiteboard as we talk. While working in the moment is crucial and using client's own experiences can help them connect the model to their personal lives, an initial handout can be helpful. It can be less threatening for people to work with somebody else's dysfunctional thinking as they do the intellectual learning. Then once they start to understand the concepts, they can begin to apply them to themselves.

Refer to the **Socialization Tool** (Tool 1.1) if you would like a detailed explanation of the model in client-friendly language using my chapter opening story as an example. Use it to guide your discussions about how to work from this modality. The **Function of Feelings Form** (Tool 1.2), and the **I Felt, Because I Thought Log** (Tool 1.3) can also aid you in your conversations about working from this perspective. Once your client has been able to identify some thoughts to work with, a **Thought Log** (Tool 1.4) and **Mini-Chain Analysis** (Tool 1.5) are also provided.

It took our whole lives thus far to learn to think the way we do, so retraining the way we think takes time. Since CBT is not "don't worry, be happy" therapy, it takes a critical look at how we process information and attempts to test and modify this over time. Eventually, responding to life circumstances in healthier ways comes more naturally.

? How can two different people go through the exact same life event and come out with a vastly different experience?

People are different. We have each gone through unique experiences in life. Some of us may actually have endured strikingly similar experiences but assigned different meanings to those experiences. It is the meaning that we assign to our life experiences that contributes to the development of our *core beliefs*, or *schemas*. Although technically these two terms don't have exactly the same meaning, this workbook uses the terms interchangeably. The definition for both is "a mental filter that guides how people interpret events."

Judy Beck, the director of The Beck Institute of Cognitive Therapy and Research, created a visual of a schema that looks like this:

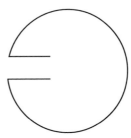

The most common negative core belief in the general population is believed to be that one is not good enough in one area or another; that or they are a failure.

Picture this imaginary structure in your brain.

When someone who has this belief has experiences in life that are consistent with this theme, it reinforces that the belief is true. These experiences can be represented in the schema diagram by rectangles. Examples might include the following:

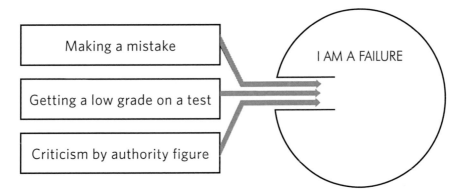

Conversely, when someone with this belief experiences something that is contradictory to his or her core beliefs, we represent these with triangles.

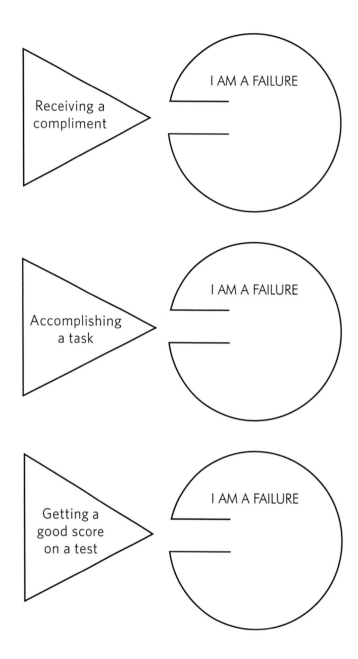

When life events are inconsistent with one's particular belief, the "triangles" will bounce off the structure and the person often comes up with reasons the data doesn't count. This is how low self-esteem (or any negative emotional state connected to identity) is maintained. This book provides tools designed to help with this.

Another way to think about beliefs is that they make us pay attention to some things more than others. Although these beliefs are typically unconscious, we can, through awareness exercises, become more in tune with them and how they are being reinforced. Politicians use this process purposefully to manipulate the public. In this context it is often referred to as "spin."

As an example of the ways in which beliefs shape how we interpret events, I often remember the television commercial featuring Michael Jordan in which he said, "I missed more than 9000 shots, lost 300 games, missed 26 game-winning opportunities the team trusted me with…. I have failed over and over and over in my life."

Would we view him as a "failure"? Of course not. He is the undisputed best basketball player of all time. From a marketing perspective this was a creative approach. However, it serves as an excellent example of how information is processed. Beliefs filter what we pay attention to in life and what we don't.

Identifying what specific beliefs or filters we have is an important part of recovery, as these are what drive our thinking and behavior.

Drs. Aaron Beck (1987) and Jeff Young, (1993) have identified a number of early unhealthy beliefs or schemas common in people with mental disorders. It might even be said that we all fall somewhere on a continuum with each of these beliefs.

Spend a few minutes reading this list. Make sure you have a clear understanding of each. Ask your practitioner if you need help. Some of the tools later in this book will target change at this deeper level. Each chapter will also contain a face sheet that will identify which of these beliefs are most commonly present in the area of focus in that particular chapter.

Abandonment: The belief that significant others in one's life will leave or won't be there for them and that they will not be able to tolerate being alone. People with this belief may go to extreme measures to keep from being alone.

Approval seeking/Unlovable or Unlikable: The belief that one is not likable or lovable, that nobody cares about them, and that they can't make or keep friends or romantic relationships, and they are bothered by these thoughts. If someone is a "people pleaser," this is the belief that is involved.

Emotional deprivation: The belief that one will not get emotional needs met, so they often don't try. Some people with this belief will say, "I don't have needs," "Your needs are more important than mine," or "It's weak to have needs."

Emotional inhibition: The belief that one must inhibit one's emotions—not speak up or not share thoughts or feelings—because to do so would be unacceptable or harmful in some way.

Entitlement: People with this filter believe that they are special or in some way better than or more deserving than others. Often this serves to cover up an underlying insecurity (defectiveness, emotional deprivation beliefs). Most people with this belief feel insecure but do not want to be seen as fragile, so they put on a "tough guy" or "tough girl" facade. However, some were raised with no limits growing up and really do view themselves as better than others.

Failure: The belief that one isn't good enough, can't do anything right, is a loser.

Helplessness: The belief that one is powerless or can't cope—with a particular situation or with life in general. This core belief leads to feelings of inadequacy and anxiety.

Insufficient self-control: The belief that produces the cognition, "I have to have it now." People with this filter believe that they have no self-control, no ability to restrain themselves or delay gratification. Impulsive substance abuse, sexual promiscuity, binge eating, temper tantrums, and shopping sprees may be products of this belief.

Mistrust: The belief that others are untrustworthy, out to get one, or otherwise not looking out for one's best interest. This is a core belief that leads people to become overly suspicious or outright paranoid.

Punitive: The belief that one deserves to be punished. Punishment can be directed toward self or others. Our society has become quite litigious due to this belief. Some psychiatric patients and inmates just can't wait to file a grievance. Sadistic, masochistic, and self-harming behaviors may also be products of this belief.

Subjugation: This belief is related to control. Some people believe they must turn control over their lives to others, while others make efforts not to be controlled or even become controlling. If someone has "control issues", this belief is involved.

Vulnerability: There are different versions of this belief, as it can show up in different areas of life, but in general, this is the belief that one is unsafe and, in some way (relationally, medically, financially) overly susceptible to being hurt. People with this belief interpret triggers as more threatening than they really are.

Worthlessness/Defectiveness: The belief that one has no value, is unworthy, or that there is something inherently "wrong with them." It is a much more deep-seated and debilitating belief that the surface level "failure" belief, which is more performance oriented. People with defectiveness beliefs often view themselves as "damaged goods."

Remember that core beliefs *feel* true, but just because they feel true doesn't mean they are. *That is what core beliefs do: They make things that aren't facts feel like facts.* Clients will often say, "I feel like such a loser," to which I will always reply, "Just because you feel like a loser doesn't mean you are one." Labeling beliefs as beliefs and not accepting them as global facts about ourselves is vital for getting better. This book contains tools designed to help in this process of testing beliefs.

Different beliefs produce the different types of thoughts referred to above. Alcoholics Anonymous is famous for the term *stinkin' thinkin*; basically, thoughts that don't serve us well. CBT has a more specific way of categorizing these types of thoughts that are unhelpful and lead to different types of unpleasant or unnecessarily intense emotions. In other words, every time you feel angry, you are experiencing a certain type of thought. Every time you feel anxiety, certain types of thoughts are going through your mind, and so on.

The following tool contains a list of types of thought processes that don't serve people well, known as cognitive distortions. Many versions of this list are floating around out there using different terminology. Much of this can be attributed to the work of David Burns (1999) in his initial work, *The Feeling Good Handbook*, which does an excellent job of breaking down in everyday language the work of Drs. Aaron Beck, Albert Ellis, and others who are considered pioneers of this field. The list that follows the diagram is my adaptation. The aforementioned **Feeling Face Sheet** in every chapter refers to this list as well. Learn these well. This is not an area to skim.

Cognitive Distortions

Events: Internal or external triggers that initiate or redirect thoughts.

Thoughts: You interpret events with a series of thoughts that flow through your mind.

Mood: Your feelings are influenced by your thoughts.

Our emotions are largely influenced by how we *perceive* events in life. Before we can experience any feeling, our minds must process the event and give it meaning. The way you understand what is happening influences how you *feel* about it. To the degree that your thinking about a given event is biased in any way, your feelings may be that much more intense, which will make it that much harder to act in a way that is helpful.

What follows are ten types of biased thinking that are often referred to as *cognitive distortions,* which form the basis of emotional difficulties (adapted from Burns, 1999). I give a brief explanation of each.

1. All-or-nothing thinking. This refers to a tendency to see things in black-and-white categories with no consideration for gray. You see yourself, others, and often the whole world in only positive or negative extremes rather than considering that each may instead have both positive and negative aspects. For example, if your performance falls short of perfect, you see yourself as a total failure. If you catch yourself using extreme language (best ever, worst, love, hate, always, never), this is a red flag that you may be engaging in all-or-nothing thinking. Extreme thinking leads to intense feelings and an inability to see a middle-ground perspective or feel proportionate moods. A more technical cognition term you may hear is dichotomous thinking.

2. Discounting the positive. You reject positive experiences by insisting that they don't count for some reason or another. In this way, you can maintain a negative belief that is contradicted by your everyday experiences. The terms *mental filter* and *selective abstraction* basically describe the same process.

3. Emotional reasoning. You assume that your negative feelings reflect the way things really are. "I feel it, therefore, it must be true."

4. Fortune-telling. You anticipate that things will turn out badly and feel convinced that your prediction is already an established fact based on your experiences from the past. Predicting a negative outcome before any outcome occurs leads to anxiety and other negative emotions. A lot of people call this way of thinking the "what ifs."

5. Magnification. You exaggerate the importance of things, blowing them way out of proportion. Often this takes the form of fortune-telling or mind reading to an extreme. This way of thinking may also be referred to as *catastrophizing* or *awfulizing.*

6. Mind reading. Rather than predicting future events, engaging in this distortion involves predicting that you know what someone else is thinking when in reality you don't. This distortion commonly occurs in communication problems in many types of relationships.

7. Overgeneralization. You categorize different people, places, and entities based on your own experiences with each particular thing. For example, if you have been treated poorly by men in the past, "all men are mean," or if your first wife cheated on you, "all women are unfaithful." By overgeneralizing, you miss out on experiences that don't fit your particular stereotype. This is the distortion on which all of those "isms" (e.g., racism, sexism) are based.

8. Personalization. You see yourself as the cause of some external negative event for which, in fact, you were not primarily responsible. You make something about you that is not about you and get your feelings hurt.

9. Rationalization. In an attempt to protect yourself from hurt feelings, you create excuses for events in life that don't go your way or for poor choices you make. We might call these *permission-giving statements* that give ourselves or someone else permission to do something that is in some way unhealthy.

10. Should statements. You place false or unrealistic expectations on yourself or others, thereby setting yourself up to feel angry, guilty, or disappointed. Words and phrases such as *ought to, must, has to, needs to,* and *supposed to* are indicative of "should" thinking.

Now that you have the basic CBT framework, you are ready to learn specific tools to add to your therapeutic toolbox that will equip you or your client on a journey toward recovery!

TOOL 1.1: SOCIALIZATION

CBT has had many forefathers who contributed to our present understanding of the relationship between thoughts and emotions. However, many consider Dr. Aaron Beck the father of modern CBT. His model suggests, in short, that we experience some kind of an event in life (often referred to as a trigger). How we think about, process, or interpret that event will affect what **type of emotions** we experience as well as **how intensely we feel them.** Feelings often influence actions. The choices we make then influence the outcome, or the circumstances in which we find ourselves. You may hear more in-depth explanations, variations, or nuances of this model, but these are the basics you need to understand to get you started.

Cognitive Behavioral Model of Therapy and Coaching

A simplified, linear version of the general model of CBT looks like this:

Event ➡ Thoughts ➡ Feelings ➡ Actions ➡ Results

Let's start with a few commonly asked questions about CBT:

? **Do I choose the events I go through in life?**

Sometimes. Sometimes we put ourselves in situations that make us vulnerable to certain triggers. For example, we choose whom we date, whom we marry, whether we go to certain parties or hang out with certain people, whether we stay at a job or leave it, whether to engage in substance use. And sometimes we do not.

We don't choose our parents, our siblings, the situations our caretakers put us in when we are young, who is driving on the road when we are, or natural disasters. We have a say regarding some of the events (triggers) we experience, and others are completely out of our control.

? **Do I choose my feelings?**

To answer this question, let's try a brief exercise. Close your eyes. Picture a giraffe. Can you do it? Picture a snowflake. Can you see it? Picture yourself in your best friend's house. Can you conjure up these images? Of course you can.

Now… feel enraged. Just feel it. Can you do it?

What did you just have to do to feel enraged?

You had to **think** about something that would get you there. Maybe you thought about an ex-partner. Some of you perhaps thought about a current issue that ticks you off. Some of you likely thought about an abusive event in your past that has wounded you so deeply you still have not recovered from it twenty years later. Or maybe you thought about the jerk that cut you off in traffic on the way to your appointment less than an hour ago.

Has anyone ever said to you something like, "Oh, come on, there's no need to be depressed—you have so much to be thankful for"? How many times has that been helpful? How many of you have said, "Oh, thanks for the feedback—I'll now choose to be happy"?

It is worth noting that well-meaning people can say hurtful and invalidating things. Sometimes people want to help but just don't know how.

The point in this exercise is that doesn't matter **what** you think about. The takeaway is that **no human being can command a feeling.** No human being has direct access to our feelings. We only have access to our feelings through our thoughts.

? Do I choose my thoughts?

Likely some of you answered this question "yes," and some of you answered it "no." You are both right. If feelings are influenced by thoughts—and as our exercise just illustrated, we all do have some control over our thought life—then we do have the power to influence our feelings by learning to slowly retrain the way we think.

However, we all have thoughts that just pop into our minds. Sometimes we know exactly where they came from, and other times it seems as though they came "out of left field." The clinical term for these is **automatic thoughts.** We all have these thoughts that are immediate responses to triggers that we don't choose to have. However, although we don't always have a choice about whether these thoughts appear, once they do, we all have the ability to get better at increasing our awareness, paying attention to them, and working to change them through CBT tools.

? What is the difference between thoughts and feelings?

Thoughts are not feelings. A lot of people say things like, "I felt like she was trying to backstab me." That is not a feeling. It is a thought. That type of thought often leads to feelings of *fear, hurt,* or *betrayal.* If it's a full sentence, it's a thought." Feelings are one word and are expressions of emotion. Examples include *angry, sad, mad, happy, excited, fearful, anxious, overwhelmed, panicked,* and *annoyed.* There are obviously many others. Some people say, "Oh, it's not a big deal." It is a really big deal if you are interested in doing effective cognitive therapy.

? Isn't rational thinking the same thing as positive thinking?

No. A lot of different terms are used to describe unhealthy thinking (e.g., *irrational, dysfunctional, maladaptive, distorted*), but positive thinking focuses only on the positive. Rational thinking focuses on probability, likelihood, patterns, and evidence. So there is such a thing as rational thinking that is negative. The reality is that there are a lot of negative aspects to life that require acceptance. There is also a sort of positive thinking that is irrational. In extreme forms, this may be called delusional thinking. It is often helpful to focus on positives but not to ignore the reality of negatives in our lives. Several tools have been designed to help you in this process and are discussed in this chapter.

? Do we choose our actions?

Occasionally, this question gets some people fired up. The short answer is that we almost always choose our actions. (There are a couple of clinical conditions in which people literally do things outside their awareness, but these are rare.) Some people say things like, "He made me do it," or "I didn't have a choice," or "what about fight or flight?"

Some decisions are made instantaneously, and the thought process behind them is less conscious, but to determine whether thinking was involved, helpful questions to ask include:

- Would it have been possible to *not* do the action in that situation?
- Would someone else in my life have reacted differently?

The reality is, 99 percent of the time, we do choose our actions.

❓ Do we choose our results?

Our actions *influence* our results. *Influence* is an important word to understand, because it doesn't mean *dictate*. Thus, it is not accurate to say we *choose* our results. It is possible that when we make healthy decisions, bad things still happen. It is also possible to make a certain number of poor choices and get away with them. But, generally speaking, the healthier choices you make, the better chance you have of a positive outcome, and the unhealthier choices you make, the better chance you have of running into trouble in some area of your life (relationally, occupationally, financially, legally, etc.).

In my experience, many people are able to look retrospectively at how they might be able to view major events in life differently such as a divorce, a rape, or some other kind of traumatic situation. CBT certainly can bring healing to victims of these atrocities. But I think many people miss the power that CBT has to influence our smaller day to day emotions, interactions, and choices. People who develop some mastery of these tools are able to, even in the moment, identify those automatic thoughts that just pop into their minds and use cognitive tools and techniques to improve their day-to-day experience of life.

Consider the following example from my life: I shared a version of this in my first book, *The CBT Toolbox: A Workbook for Clients and Clinicians:*

One day, while on my way to a speaking engagement, there was some confusion with my plane ticket, which had been purchased some three months in advance. After doing some scrambling, the airline accommodated me and got me in one of the last seats on the flight. Having received one of the last tickets on the entire flight, of course I was assigned one of those highly coveted middle seats. Not a petite individual myself, I was less than thrilled to discover my assigned seat was in between two large adults.

So there I was, jammed in between these two individuals with no room to move at all. It didn't take long before the person on my right began sweating profusely. With no room to move, her sweat began dripping on me—if you fly much, you know they don't start circulating the air until the plane begins taxiing toward the runway for takeoff. Just when I thought the time couldn't have gone any more slowly, the pilot makes an announcement that the plane is having some minor mechanical difficulty, and that there would be a delay.

So I was sandwiched in, no room to move at all, and, as if it couldn't get any worse, a lady in front of me started changing her baby's diaper! At this point, I am not able to move left or right, start accumulating sweat by the moment, and am forced to deal with the horrible stench that begins emanating throughout the cabin.

Any guesses how I felt?

Wouldn't everyone in that situation feel the same way?
As I turned my head, I noticed the lady on my left smiling, laughing, and saying things like, "Goo goo, ga ga" and playing with the baby through the space between the seats. She was trying to help the mother out. She was trying to get the baby to stop screaming. If I would have pulled out my cell phone and taken a picture of this woman's face, you might have guessed she was having the time of her life! Although she was in virtually the same situation as I was, she was **experiencing** *it in a much more enjoyable way.*

Why?
Because she was obviously having different thoughts than I was!

This happened to me fairly recently, and I often share this or similar stories at my seminars. Although it has a bit of a humorous element, it also highlights, in practical terms, **the role that one's thought process plays in influencing emotions**, behaviors and, ultimately how they experience life. Start by using this event from my life to apply, in practical terms, how CBT applies to our everyday lives.

Mini-Chain Analysis Questions

1. What was the event, or trigger?

2. What thoughts would you guess I had in response to the trigger?

3. What feelings might you guess I could have experienced as a result of having those types of thoughts?

4. What behaviors could I have engaged in?

5. What might have been some of the results of those thoughts, feelings, and behaviors?

Event ➡ Thoughts ➡ Feelings ➡ Actions ➡ Results

Once one has identified some of the automatic thoughts they are having that seem to be contributing to the unpleasant or overly intense feelings, it is important to do something to change them. Martin Luther famously said, "You can't stop a bird from landing on your head—but you can keep it from building a nest in your hair!" Here is where you have the power!

Many clients like the imagery of the little devil character tapping you on one shoulder or whispering into one ear to represent these unhealthy automatic thoughts they are having—coupled with the angel character tapping on the other shoulder or whispering into the other ear to represent more rational, positive, or realistic thoughts they can use to combat them with. This initial strategy is known as **challenging unhealthy thoughts.** This is the most basic of CBT tools to put in your repertoire.

If you had a thought that sounded something like this: You could then counter with something like this:

Use the thought log provided to (1) list some of the *automatic thoughts* you identified that I might have had on the plane, and (2) come up with some *challenges*, or ways you think it might have benefitted me to think about it differently.

Automatic Thoughts	Rational Responses

Once rational responses have been generated on the thought log, you can plug them into the sequence below, sometimes referred to as a mini-chain analysis, to see the impact of the changed thinking in response to the same situation (in this case, the trigger on the plane).

Event ➡ Thoughts ➡ Feelings ➡ Actions ➡ Results

Now that you have generated some hypotheticals for practice, I thought I would show you a version of some of the automatic thoughts I actually had, and some of the challenges/rational responses I used. I also included examples of what this would look like plugged into a thought log (Tool 1.4) and a mini-chain, using a version that looks at the effects of my changed thinking on the situation (Tool 1.5) as well.

Automatic Thoughts
- "That mother shouldn't change the diaper here."
- "She is being so inconsiderate of others."
- "The smell is hideous."
- "I am going to be miserable this whole flight!"

Rational Responses
- "The reality is that she is."
- "Maybe she had nowhere else to change it."
- "Maybe she is at the end of her rope."
- "Even if she could have changed it somewhere else, it doesn't do me any good to be angry with her."
- "Even though the smell is bad, I won't be miserable the whole four hours. The smell is bound to dissipate over time and I can find other things to focus on. I can even leave my seat if I need to."

Initial Mini-Chain

Event ➡ Thoughts ➡ Feelings ➡ Actions ➡ Results

Event
- Lady in front of me changing baby diaper

Thoughts
- *"That mother shouldn't change the diaper here."*
- *"She is being so inconsiderate of others."*
- *"The smell is hideous."*
- *"I am going to be miserable this whole flight!"*

Feelings	**Actions**	**Results**
▪ Irritation	▪ Sit and stew	▪ Elevated blood pressure
▪ Anger		▪ Continued anger
▪ Dread		▪ Diaper still stunk
▪ Stress		

Mini-Chain with New Thinking
New Thoughts:
- *"Maybe she had nowhere else to change it."*
- *"Even if she could have changed it somewhere else, it doesn't do me any good to be angry with her."*
- *"Even though the smell is bad, I won't be miserable the whole four hours. The smell is bound to dissipate over time and I can find other things to focus on. I can even leave my seat if I need to."*

Feelings:	**Actions:**	**Results:**
▪ Less Stress	▪ Tried to put myself in her shoes	▪ Smell stayed horrible
▪ Compassion	▪ Shifted my focus to my work	▪ Felt less upset
		▪ Started being productive

Now that you have had a chance to practice with some of my thoughts, try one on your own! Pick a recent situation in your own life. Use the following **Mini-Chain Tool** (page 26) to identify some thoughts and feelings you might have had in response to the event. List some behaviors you did and some of the consequences (results) of your behavior.

Then transpose your initial automatic thoughts that fueled your instantaneous feelings and initial behaviors onto the left column of the **Thought Log Tool.** Then spend some time generating some rational responses. Use logic. Look at evidence against the thought. Enlist others to offer alternative explanations. Write down all of the information you can opposing the initial automatic thoughts on the right column of the thought log.

Finally, plug the new thinking into another mini-chain. Note the change in feelings, behavior, and results that are possible when employing new thinking.

TOOL 1.2: FUNCTION OF FEELINGS FORM

I have heard it said, "emotions are neither good nor bad...they just are." I have never believed that. Who wouldn't prefer to feel happy versus sad? Who in their right mind would say "I don't like feeling calm and at peace? I'd prefer to be a nervous wreck?" Nobody, right?

Now I certainly get behind the idea that feelings are part of normal human experience. It is natural for all people to feel angry at times, down at times, worried about certain situations, etc. Although it is natural for all humans to feel these feelings in certain situations, the degree of intensity with which they feel it may differ from person to person. A healthy perspective on emotions would assert that they all serve a purpose, and when certain emotions are felt with strong intensity, they can be unpleasant.

Use the following **Function of Feelings Form** to:
- Identify the emotion.
- Label the situation.
- Rate the intensity of the emotion (1–10, with 10 being most intense).
- Identify what purpose the feeling could be serving.
- Decide if you believe it is hurtful, helpful, or neutral.
- Problem solve action steps for regulating your emotions.
- List what you learned.

Example:

Emotion: Anxiety, Fear

Situation: Saw a shadow moving outside the tent

Purpose of Emotion: To warn me that I could be in danger if it is a bear outside

Intensity: 8—Very Fearful

Helpful or Unhelpful: Helpful. If I didn't feel this way, I would not be prompted to assess my safety.

Action Step: Look carefully out the screen to see what is causing the shadow.

What I Learned/Result: I saw it was just a tree branch blowing in the wind. My fear level went down to 1. I learned that I have a tendency to feel fearful a lot of the time, even when there is no real danger.

MY FUNCTION OF FEELINGS FORM

Emotion: _____

_____

Situation: _____

_____

Purpose of Emotion: _____

_____

Intensity: _____

_____

Helpful or Unhelpful: _____

_____

Action Step: _____

_____

What I Learned/Result: _____

_____

_____

TOOL 1.3: I FELT, BECAUSE I THOUGHT LOG

I felt ...	Because I Thought...

TOOL 1.4: I THOUGHT LOG

Automatic Thoughts	Rational Responses/Alternative Explanations

TOOL 1.5: MINI CHAIN ANALYSIS

Event	Automatic Thoughts	Feelings	Actions	Results
	Rational Responses	**New Feelings**	**Alternative Actions**	**Results**

My Conclusions:

_____

_____

_____

CHAPTER **2**

Cognitive Conceptualization

While giving conferences around the world, the most common question I get from workshop participants who purchased the first edition of this book was "Is there a tool for the cognitive conceptualization diagram you talk about?" The answer to the question was "no." I did not include a conceptualization map in my initial CBT Toolbox book.

One reason for not including it was that I did not actually consider it a tool in the same way I did the others that were included. By that way of thinking, a tool was something you used to work on or complete a project. However, no one starts the "project" of building a skyscraper before they have a blueprint. That is how I viewed the cognitive conceptualization map. I have actually heard Dr. Aaron Beck refer to the cognitive conceptualization map as a person's internal "architecture." I have always emphasized having a client-specific understanding and a corresponding map to guide our actions **before** implementing any tools.

The literature certainly supports the efficacy of interventions that are not considered explicitly "CBT strategies." However, there is a big difference between being eclectic for the sake of being eclectic (or "integrative") and strategically choosing alternative strategies that we hypothesize might be useful in helping our clients achieve their goals. I believe there should always be a rationale for why we are doing what we are doing when we are doing it. As long as we are working within the framework of the clients' cognitive conceptualization, CBT clinicians have a wide variety of techniques and strategies at our disposal to pick and choose from to help our clients achieve their goals.

Another common statement I often encounter at training events is "I thought cognitive therapy was not concerned with the client's past." While it is true that with what were formerly considered "Axis I conditions," focus is primarily on the present day, treatment of individuals with personality disorders or more complex conditions actually requires more exploration of the past. Regardless of the focus, development of initial conceptualization diagrams does require taking at least a peek in the rearview mirror but only with the purpose of keeping eyes focused on the road ahead.

Note the term "initial" in the previous sentence. While an initial conceptualization session lays out the map for the client and the clinician, sometimes original routes need to be altered. It is at times necessary to make a hypothesis before you have all the data to support it. Thus, these conceptualization diagrams can be fluid throughout treatment as new information is revealed or new life events unfold.

Having said that, this second edition includes a few words about cognitive conceptualization. Whether you consider it a "tool" or not, it is an integral part of cognitive therapy. I always share in my trainings that I believe it is next to impossible to do effective cognitive therapy without working from a thorough and accurate case conceptualization.

This topic is addressed in depth in a number of other publications. Padesky (2009) perhaps has done the most comprehensive work on the subject to date. Since this is a toolbox for clients and clinicians rather than an academic text, only a brief and practical walk-through will be provided.

Note: Most tools (although most effective in conjunction with a practitioner) can be used by clients alone. **This tool almost always requires clinician guidance.**

Significant Historical Experiences

This is called different things on different diagrams. The version I learned from called this top box "childhood data." Personally, I use the phrase "significant historical experiences" when working with clients.

First, the use of the word "significant" may seem unnecessary to explain. However, I have encountered many therapists whose need to be "thorough" compels them to include minute details from the client's childhood that, though they did occur, have no relevance to the presenting problem(s). Thus, the word "significant."

Secondly, I eliminate the word "childhood." While the most common historical events that are relevant to conceptualization do occur during childhood, using the term "historical" also leaves the door open for significant later life experiences to be included in the blueprint. Getting fired from a job, moving back in with one's parents as an adult, going through a divorce, and experiencing a traumatic event of some kind are just a few of the many common experiences people have that occur after childhood and affect present day thinking and behavior.

Finally, the term "data" always seemed a bit impersonal and cold to me and to many clients I have worked with. While I may, even if out of habit, use this term in clinical consultations or even in my trainings for clinicians, when collaboratively exploring these with clients I have come to use the term "experiences." Every human being has experiences. In my experience, this is usually received more positively by clients.

This section goes by different names but its purpose is to identify any events in the client's past life experiences that are contributing factors in the development and maintenance of the client's problematic thinking and behavior.

A couple of tips for filling out the historical experiences box: First, if you are familiar with DBT, use your "Describe" skills language. That is, record this information in a "just the facts" manner without labeling, name-calling, or clinical jargon. Second, be specific.

While it is important to list behaviors in a way that is specific to client experience, general areas to consider for this box include but are not limited to the following:

- Physical abuse
- Sexual abuse
- Verbal abuse
- History of substance abuse in client or family
- History of mental illness in client or family
- Significant medical conditions in client or family
- Specific family dynamics

- Educational background
- Religious and cultural beliefs and practices
- Academic achievement
- Developmental milestones and social skills
- Relevant socioeconomic factors
- Other

Of course, not all areas will be relevant for every client. Remember that we are identifying only information that, in the clinician's judgment, is *relevant* to the client's presenting problems.

Core Beliefs

As discussed in chapter 1, core beliefs are deeply ingrained beliefs that all human beings have. Dr. Aaron Beck identified that we have these beliefs in three different areas: beliefs about self, beliefs about others, and beliefs about the world.

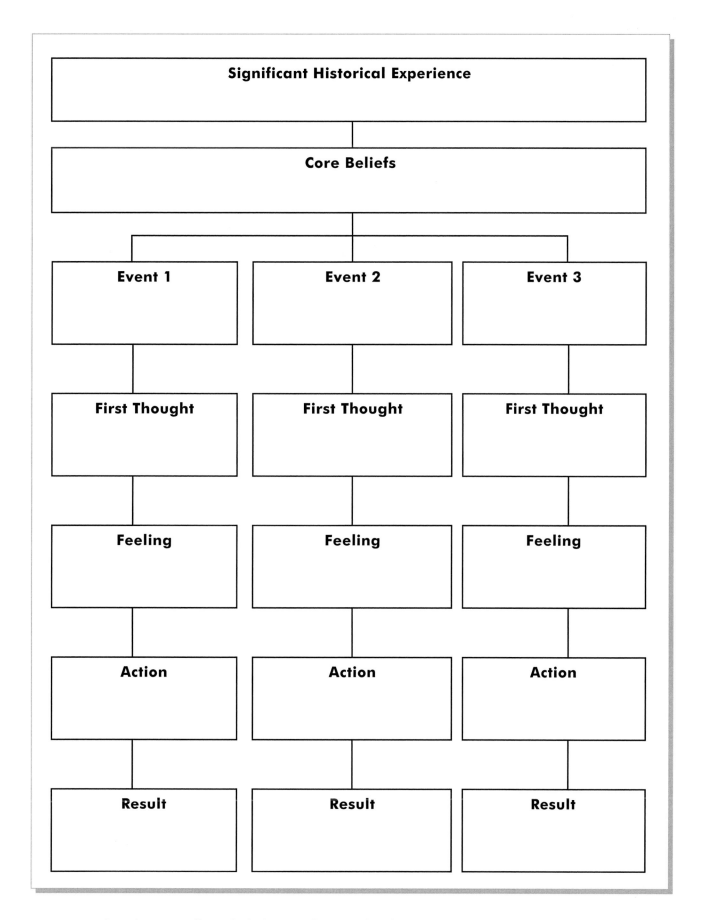

Significant Historical Experience		
Core Beliefs		
Event 1	Event 2	Event 3
First Thought	First Thought	First Thought
Feeling	Feeling	Feeling
Action	Action	Action
Result	Result	Result

In this box, we hypothesize what core beliefs may be involved: That is, what beliefs did the client formulate based upon those prior experiences and the meaning they attributed to them? See Jeff Young's *18 Early Maladaptive Schemas* (1993), or use Dr. Aaron Beck's *dysfunctional beliefs* if you prefer that language. These beliefs play a central role in the client behavior patterns that you will help bring into their awareness throughout the process.

Events

Once you have identified relevant historical experiences and hypothesized about the beliefs that might have been formulated, it is time to help clients start viewing events in their life through the lens of those core beliefs. I usually start by identifying some events that occurred in the recent past. If possible, incorporate an event that led them to treatment.

Thoughts ➜ Feelings ➜ Actions

This is basically retrospective CBT: Identify thought processes they had in response to those specific events/triggers and show them how those thoughts, which are products of the activated belief, fueled their feelings, drove their choices, and influenced the results in that given situation. The more examples clients are able to see over time (historically or moving forward), the better they will be able to see the themes in their choices, which can then be targeted in breaking behavioral patterns later in treatment.

Results

Most clients initially have difficulty making connections between thoughts and their feelings as well as their behaviors and direct consequences. For many clients, this connection must be continually emphasized. Until one can make a connection between their actions and their consequences, the development of new coping skills is extremely difficult to facilitate.

Now that you have a sense of the *why* and the *what* of conceptualization, let's use the case of Terri as an example:

Terri is a 34-year-old married female. She has two sons Derek and James Jr. ages 10 and 12. She reports having been "fairly happily married" to her husband Jim for 16 years, although she is presenting with "some mild depression."

She has no family history of psychiatric or substance use disorders. She describes her parents as "overprotective but loving." She reports that her life changed forever at age 11 when her older sister Tammy drowned in a swimming accident. At that point she reports that her mom quit her part time job at the post office and her father "did everything within his power to make sure I was safe." She was not allowed to participate in any extracurricular activities, was required to be home immediately after school, and her curfew remained 10 pm even her senior year of high school when she had a serious boyfriend. She reports being a compliant child for the most part stating "the few times I did voice being upset about not being able to spend time with friends, I was punished." While she wished she could try more things, she states she also felt a safety in knowing her parents would always be there for her. She states she had no prior formal treatment but states the one time in high school she asked her parents about some counseling her father said, "Well, I can be your counselor. You share everything with your old man anyway." She states, "it wasn't that big of a deal though... I think I was just a little depressed feeling left out; you know because I did not get to do the things other kids got to do... I never had many friends, but I always did pretty good in school and my parents were certainly proud of me for that."

When Terri graduated from high school with a 3.8 GPA, she had multiple scholarship offers. She states that "The thought of going to college excited me... you know I thought maybe I could make a difference in the world... but I ended up being too scared and just decided to get married." After all, I did love him and being a good wife and a mom is all I ever thought I was supposed to be." Terri was an especially good writer but was discouraged from taking a class or joining a group because "that artistic stuff doesn't help your family any."

Terri states that her relationship with her parents has remained "pretty good all these years as long as I check in with them every day and they know I am being a good wife and mom." She has struggled to make friends. They attend church somewhat regularly & even joined a bunco group "but I've just never had my own friends, so it's hard to open up and really talk to people you know."

At the initial session, Terry verbalized uncertainty regarding her treatment goals. "My family is not the most supportive of me being here and to be honest I am a little skeptical myself, but my little bit of sadness has just lasted too long, and I wanted to see if there was something I could do."

As you read Terry's background, hopefully you were able to identify some relevant information that contributed to her presenting problems.

The therapist at our clinic that worked with her identified the following:

Significant Historical Experiences

▪ Sister drowned at age 11.

▪ Parents became overprotective (limited free time, extremely early curfews for developmental stage in life, limited her social interaction, particularly with the opposite sex).

▪ She was given few responsibilities. Did not learn basic skills such as how to do chores, household tasks, and other necessities for taking care of oneself.

Much more depth could have been provided here, but this information definitely provides a basis for the way Terri "filters" events she encounters throughout her life to this point and some of the patterns the therapist helps her uncover and eventually change.

Core Beliefs

▪ Dependent

▪ Helpless

▪ Subjugation

It's likely others exist as well, but these do seem to be significant drivers in her pattern of behaviors.

Events

Here the therapist opts to highlight two specific events from Terri's childhood, as well as an event that happened only last week and one that occurs on a regular basis. One important note: It is important to identify specific instances of events occurring. Clients may say, "It doesn't matter which one—it happens all the time." However, it is important to pick specific events, even if the trigger involved is identified as a recurring theme in the person's life. They are then worked through one at a time.

Event 1: Requested to go to counseling

Thoughts ➡ Feelings ➡ Actions ➡ Results

The next step was to identify the "thoughts," "feelings," "actions," and "results" boxes by using her notes taken in the initial assessment when Terri described each of these occurrences in the first place.

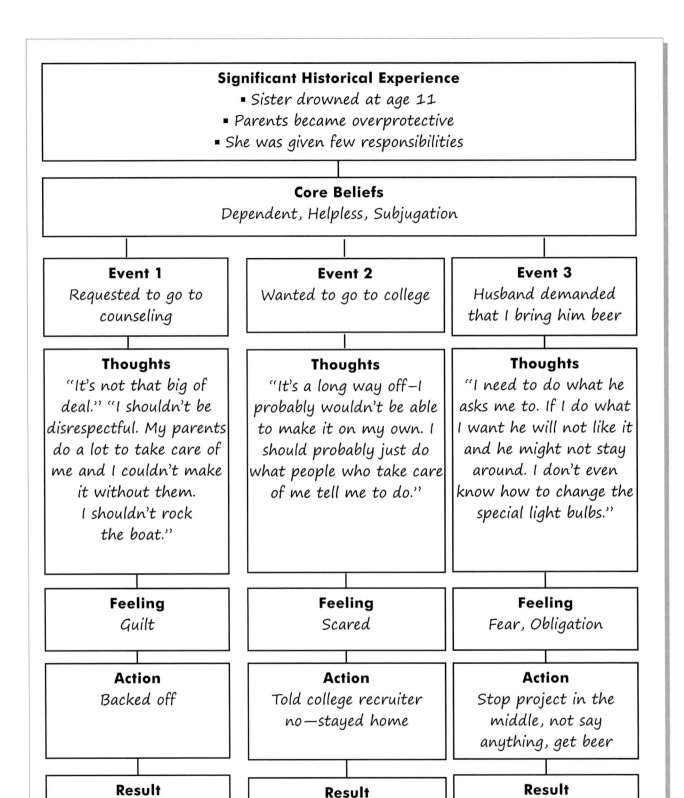

Significant Historical Experience
- Sister drowned at age 11
- Parents became overprotective
- She was given few responsibilities

Core Beliefs
Dependent, Helpless, Subjugation

Event 1 Requested to go to counseling	**Event 2** Wanted to go to college	**Event 3** Husband demanded that I bring him beer
Thoughts "It's not that big of deal." "I shouldn't be disrespectful. My parents do a lot to take care of me and I couldn't make it without them. I shouldn't rock the boat."	**Thoughts** "It's a long way off—I probably wouldn't be able to make it on my own. I should probably just do what people who take care of me tell me to do."	**Thoughts** "I need to do what he asks me to. If I do what I want he will not like it and he might not stay around. I don't even know how to change the special light bulbs."
Feeling Guilt	**Feeling** Scared	**Feeling** Fear, Obligation
Action Backed off	**Action** Told college recruiter no—stayed home	**Action** Stop project in the middle, not say anything, get beer
Result Did not get needed help	**Result** Did not get to develop talent and pursue dreams	**Result** "Losing my voice"

Strengths

The initial idea was simply incorporating client's strengths as resources to utilize in promoting recovery. More recently, these CBT approaches have not only used existing client's strengths but also helped to build new strengths. Further, CBT has been proven effective in the facilitation of resiliency, which will be addressed later in the book.

Cognitive conceptualization provides a way to synthesize the cognitive approach with actual client experiences. The conceptualization diagrams not only provide a roadmap that guides treatment, they also serve as a powerful propellant for the development of rapport early in the process.

The next chapter will demonstrate how to use the cognitive conceptualization maps to drive goal setting, treatment, and even documentation.

CHAPTER **3**

Goal Setting

Traditionally, cognitive therapy has primarily viewed goals in terms of *decreasing symptoms*. Most clinicians have traditionally thought this way, and required treatment plan verbiage has reflected this. Although I see benefits to this traditional medical model, certain drawbacks exist. This is one of them: If clients are thinking only in terms of decreasing depressive symptoms "or "managing anger outbursts," they inevitably remain problem-focused rather than solution-focused.

When I went to see my physician for a severely sprained ankle, my motivation for doing so was to return to my tennis team. My physician never once asked me *why* I wanted my ankle to heal, or what I would be able to do once it did: he remained laser focused on the symptom: the sprained and swollen ankle.

While this standard approach has focused on the decrease of negative symptoms or behaviors, newer approaches are shifting the focus from removing obstacles toward an emphasis on actualizing the goals themselves.

I believe that some strengths-based advocates shift the pendulum too far in that oftentimes it is necessary to target problems, strife, or symptoms. However, I do believe that many clients can benefit from incorporating more strengths-based content into the treatment process and using actualization-based goals to promote long-term life satisfaction.

The reality is that we now see clinicians on both ends of this spectrum and everywhere in between. For a number of years now I have been paying attention to both. For clients who are overly problem focused, I will help them shift their focus toward achieving their goals and dreams. For clients who continue to talk about achieving these lofty dreams but continue to be ineffective in dealing with the symptoms that are preventing them from getting where they want to be, I will challenge them to shift their thinking accordingly.

As one of my clients once put it, *"Oh, you want to me to focus on less bad as well as more good."*

We have long used the language "arrows down" to help clients increase their awareness to behaviors and symptoms we want them to decrease, and "arrows up" to be constantly mindful of the behaviors we want them to increase. The following tool is often useful in helping clients identify these.

TOOL 3.1: GOAL SETTING: "ARROWS UP, ARROWS DOWN"

This tool can guide your thinking as you carefully consider very specific behaviors you would like to see decrease as well as specific behaviors you would like to see increase over the course of your work with your clinician. You can then use this tool regularly to monitor your behaviors.

Goals: _____

_____

_____

Three target behaviors I would like to decrease to help me achieve my goals are:

⬇ Behavior	Did I Engage in Today? Y/N	If Yes, How Many Times?
1. _____	_____	_____
2. _____	_____	_____
3. _____	_____	_____

Three target behaviors I would like to increase to help me achieve my goals are:

⬆ Positive Behavior	Describe
1. _____	_____
2. _____	_____
3. _____	_____

The motivational writer Stephen Covey famously said, "begin with the end in mind." An analogy I often use that many can relate with is a GPS. The first thing one does before starting a trip is identify a destination. When we don't know how to get somewhere, all we must do is enter the endpoint in the GPS. The "how to get there" steps will then be spelled out for us based upon traffic, road construction, or other obstacles, but when we are starting a journey, above all else, it is first necessary to know where we want to go.

I also like Steve de Shazer's famous "miracle question" as a way to help facilitate this type of future "dream big" thinking. I have seen several adaptations of this question. We typically asked it the following way: "Pretend that tonight while you are sleeping God grants you a miracle and when you wake up in the morning all your problems are gone. How specifically would your life be different?" This nudges clients to think very specifically about what success would look like for them.

One of the amazing things humans have been born with is an unquenchable desire to have a better life. Sadly, some have gone through life experiences that have temporarily quenched their ability to live out that desire. This is when a *helpless* belief is often developed. But we can help clients overcome this by rebuilding the cognitive ability to lay out a plan to achieve their dreams. It may take some prodding and poking, but it's possible. For some clients, it may have to be framed as, "even if..."

"even if you don't believe it is possible, what would it look like if it were?"

A final tip: Know your purpose. Values work will receive additional attention later in this toolbox, including a values inventory tool. In his best-selling book, *The Purpose Driven Life*, Rick Warren points out something that on the surface level seems rather obvious, but it remains a struggle for millions of people. The principle is simply that once we know what our purpose is, it provides a clarity to define goals that are in alignment with that. Think about your purpose in life and use this as a guide in the journey of completing the miracle question.

The following tool is an adapted version of that miracle question which gets clients thinking in the different areas of their life we emphasize throughout the course of treatment.

TOOL 3.2: MIRACLE QUESTION

Imagine that one night while you are sleeping, God grants you a miracle, and all of your problems are solved—how would your life be different? What would it look like?

_____

_____

_____

How will others know you are different? What will they say? What will they notice that is different?

_____

_____

_____

How will you be different physically?

_____

_____

_____

How will your emotions be different? What will you feel more of? Less of? Will you laugh more?

_____

_____

_____

How will your relationships be different? Will you have more relationships? Fewer? Different types of friends? Family? Will you be married or single? Children? How will others think of you differently?

_____

_____

_____

How will your spiritual life be different? Will you view God differently? Be more or less active? Have a stronger faith?

_____

_____

_____

How about your professional life? How will it be different? Different job? Co-workers?

_____

_____

_____

Where will you live? Who will you live with?

_____

_____

_____

What other areas of your life will the miracle have affected?

_____

_____

_____

Goal Setting

Different terminology can be used to describe different types of goals.

Some clients may need help understanding the difference between short-term, intermediate, and long-term goals. All play an important role in success with goal achievement. For the purpose of this exercise, a *long-term goal* will be anything that will take at least one year to achieve. An *intermediate goal* can be anything achievable in one day to one month. A *short-term goal* will be considered anything you can accomplish today.

For instance, one of my client's goal sheet looked like this:

Long-Term Goal: Run Tulsa Run in 6 months.

Intermediate Goal: Lose 8 pounds this month.

Short-Term Goal: Walk 1 mile in park and eat 2000 calories or less today.

There are a few important questions to ask when setting good goals. You may be familiar with the famous acronym **SMART** (Doran, 1981). Sometimes it is best to review this *before* setting goals. Others set goals first and then revisit their goals through the lens of the acronym and consider modifications. Use the **SMART Goals Tool** as you see fit.

TOOL 3.3: SMART GOALS

The acronym SMART means Specific, Measurable, Attainable, Realistic, and Time-Sensitive. Think about your goals in these ways. Write down if your goal "checks the box" as a "Yes" and write down why or why not.

Specific:

_____

_____

_____

Measurable:

_____

_____

_____

Attainable:

_____

_____

_____

Realistic:

_____

_____

_____

Time-Sensitive:

_____

_____

_____

MY SMART GOALS

Long-Term: _____

_____

_____

Intermediate: _____

_____

_____

Short-Term: _____

_____

_____

One small step I will take today to move toward my goal is:

_____

_____

_____

_____

TOOL 3.4: GOAL SETTING THOUGHT LOG

Some clients get stuck setting goals. One way to help them get "unstuck" is by using a thought log to identify which thoughts are in their way. This tool provides common automatic thoughts that are often barriers to successful goal setting and achievement. See if you can fill in the rational responses to each.

Automatic Thoughts	Rational Responses
"I will never be able to achieve that, so why even try."	

Automatic Thoughts	Rational Responses
"Change is scary—at least I know the misery I have now. What if I can't handle whatever is around the corner?"	

Automatic Thoughts	Rational Responses
"I don't deserve to be happy."	

Other:

Automatic Thoughts	Rational Responses

So now that we have asked the *"What do you want?"* questions, it is time to move to the *"What is getting in the way?"* part of this equation. This is where clinicians can help clients increase their awareness regarding the importance of the "arrows down" behaviors in order to achieve what their really want.

Consider Terri from the previous chapter. Some of her big picture goals included *more* positive interactions with her family members, *more* feelings of happiness, and *more* satisfaction related to her desire to "make a difference" in the world.

A quick side note: In some cases, clients will identify goals in terms of feelings (i.e. more happiness). These don't stand up as well to the **SMART** criteria, as feelings are less measurable. We can, and regularly do, have clients scale their emotions subjectively. There are many inventories available, such as the Beck Depression Inventory, Beck Anxiety Inventory, and many others. However, there is still a subjectivity to rating emotions that is not present in behaviors. For instance, clients may rate their anxiety a "7," on a scale of 0-10. They might then look back at their notes and observe rating their anxiety a "7" a year ago. From that information, it is easy to come to the conclusion "I am not getting any better." However, what clients fail to realize is that what they considered a "7" a year ago is nowhere near what they are considering a "7" today. They are so much better now that their frame of reference has changed. Having said that, I allow clients to state goals in terms of emotional states, but I want feelings to be one of several markers we are looking at in terms of goal achievement. Behaviors must also be included.

One look at Terri's conceptualization diagram helped her realize that her "backing down" (her words) behaviors were a theme in her life that was keeping her from doing some of the things that she believed would truly fulfill her. We started by identifying some shorter-term goals for her. She needed some guidance making them **SMART** goals. She eventually identified that she wanted to:

1.   Have some outside contact with friends
2.   Get connected with some people who do writing
3.   Take a class at the local community college

With some clients, we could just set up immediate short-term goals for accomplishing this and help guide them on a week-by-week basis move toward accomplishing them (with regular checks of how moving forward toward these goals was affecting her mood, pointing out when depressive feelings went down and happiness went up).

However, with Terri it was not that simple. She had family pressure not to do any of these things. Her parents didn't know why she needed to go to college and her husband was not supportive of her spending time or money with friends while he was at work and did not even want her joining a Facebook group of aspiring writers.

So, treatment for Terri needed to target the "arrows down" behavior of "backing down" *less* and arrows up" behaviors of having *more* assertive conversations with her mother, her father, and her husband. This required more than simple coaching. It required some deeper work modifying her core beliefs that she was dependent and helpless. Each session specifically consisted of:

1.   Reviewing homework from the previous session related to increasing social interaction with friends, working on developing her writing, and/or taking steps toward a college course.

2.   If the steps were taken, we would spend time affirming what she did well and devise a plan for the following week.

   If steps were not taken (which is common in the early stages of treatment), we would identify what got in the way. In Terri's case this usually involved thoughts about and behavior toward her mother,

her father, or her husband. We would make modifications we believed would help make it easier for her to succeed the following week.

3. Deeper belief/schema level work related to being dependent and helpless.

— ◆ —

Identify long-term goals and dreams. Identify shorter-term goals (or objectives) necessary to eventually meet those goals. Consider what regular behaviors need to increase in the short and intermediate term, label those "arrows up" behaviors and look for ways to increase them. Finally, identify what problems behaviors, thoughts and beliefs are preventing the goal achievement, label them "arrows down" and work to decrease them. Intense focus on a problem behavior can make it decrease or completely go away. And also keep your eyes on the bigger prize.

CHAPTER **4**

Acceptance, Mindfulness, Motivational Interviewing, and Other New Trends

There are many new trends in cognitive therapy. However, one of the things I am discovering as I travel and speak is that the word "new" is even relative.

So for some people, "What's new?" means "Has anything changed since the 1960s?" while others are wondering if there is anything new since last year!

The following highlights a few of the "newer" developments as CBT is a constantly evolving modality that now contains within its umbrella a number of approaches that may be classified as "cognitive" in some way.

Awareness of Biological Factors

A chapter addressing and offering a few tools from "what's new" in CBT would be remiss if it did not mention this area. Let's start with two terms that have become trendy in today's neuroscience-laden therapy world: *neurogenesis* and *neuroplasticity*.

Neurogenesis is the process of brain cells regrowing themselves. For many years, we believed that once brain cells were damaged, they couldn't grow back. We are learning that this was a false belief. Neuroscientists in Japan have been on the forefront of demonstrating that the environment can have powerful effects on neurogenesis. University studies are now demonstrating that psychotherapy specifically can also impact neurogenesis.

Neuroplasticity, on the other hand, has to do with the brain's ability to form neural connections, which we now know continues throughout life. We also know that cognitive factors including memory, recall, focus, and selective attention play key roles in this process. An increased role of focus and what one is paying attention to is among the many new trends on the therapy side, which is covered later in this chapter.

So the *Reader's Digest* version? The old notion that there are "psychologically based disorders" and "biologically based disorders" is really somewhat of a misnomer. Although certain conditions may lean more heavily toward being biologically influenced versus environmentally influenced in terms of etiology, the reality is that a more complex interaction exists between the two than we ever realized—and we continue to learn more about it every day. Also, it should be noted that just because a condition or state may be predominately biological in terms of etiology doesn't mean there can't be any helpful environmental interventions and vice versa.

We now have ample evidence to support the fact that traumatic events (environmental) can have significant adverse effects on one's neurobiology. On the flip side, multiple studies using pre- and post-treatment imaging have demonstrated that CBT can have significant positive impact on brain structure and function.

The bottom line is this: The CBT strategies that we use with clients are having biological effects. And I for one am excited to see what is yet to come in this area as we learn more about neurobiological responses to specific therapeutic interventions. Strategies such as monitoring and manipulating affect to maximize cognitive gains are now a routine part of what we do. The day we learn to modify stimulus environments to alter gene expression will surely help put an end to the dichotomous notion of *A* is medical and *B* is not.

For those interested, Tool 4.1 provides a *very* basic place to start in terms of further reading on this topic. It offers some titles as informal as blogs and others as scientific as peer-reviewed journal articles.

TOOL 4.1: BIOLOGY AND COGNITION: A BRIEF READING

- *Does Cognitive Behavioral Therapy Change the Brain?* Neuropsychiatry in Clinical Neuroscience

- *Change Your Brain with Cognitive Therapy*

- *For Anxiety Disorders, CBT May Restore Brain's Structural Balance*

- *Neuroplasticity in Response to Cognitive Behavior Therapy for Social Anxiety Disorder*

- *Brain Plasticity: You Can Actually Rewire Your Brain with CBT*

- *The Neurobiology of Trauma: Sexual Assault Awareness Handout (University of Michigan)*

- *Does Cognitive Behavioral Therapy Change the Brain? A Systematic Review of Neuroimaging in Anxiety Disorders*

- *Brain Changes After Cognitive Behavior Therapy*

- *CBT Changes the Brain! (Kings College, London)*

- *Depression: A Change of Mind*

Changes Within Traditional CBT

One "newer" aspect to how traditional CBT clinicians approach treatment has to do with the emphasis on the *point of intervention*. The original traditional Beckian model (see chapter 1) looked like this:

Event ➔ Thoughts ➔ Feelings ➔ Actions ➔ Results

In earlier days, standard practice emphasized intervening at the thought level first, using thought logs, dysfunctional thought records, evidence logs, and the like. In more recent years, it has been recognized that behavioral changes produce modifications to information processing. So in that sense, any behavioral intervention we use is actually a cognitive intervention as well (in a "back-door" sort of way.) Clinicians no longer must feel compelled to start with the trigger or even the thoughts. Initial discussion can start at the feelings, actions, or results stage. And "results," among other things, can be relational, emotional, environmental, and sometimes may even involve physiological symptoms. So clinicians can intervene anywhere in the sequence first, as they are all interrelated.

Increasing Role on Focus

Another newer development has to do with what the client is paying attention to. That is, in addition to being concerned with changing thought content, much more attention is being given to attention. I have even heard Dr. Beck in recent years teach conceptualization in a way that I had not previously heard with that very emphasis. He stressed that a quick initial hypothesis and conceptualization should consist of:

1. What are the problem behaviors?

2. What is the belief driving them?

3. What is the focus? In other words, what is the client paying the most attention to?

We now know that the more we focus on something, often a physical symptom, the more magnified the symptom will become. That is why focus plays an important role in the protocols for treatment of chronic pain.

Increasing Emphasis on the Role of the Therapeutic Relationship

In recent years, much more emphasis has been given to the role of the therapeutic alliance. I don't know that it was ever considered unimportant. However, I recently attended a training at a major university where the first four hours were devoted to the therapeutic alliance. We discussed the importance of therapeutic relationship, we covered ways to build a strong alliance, we role-played ways *not* to behave that could produce a rupture in the therapeutic alliance. We know that in general, a strong alliance is associated with positive treatment outcomes and decreases treatment dropout. And as Marsha Linehan is famous for saying "treatment has been shown to be highly ineffective for those who drop out."

Finally, there is trust. Not only is trust a bedrock of a secure attachment, the more that clients trust clinicians, the more credence they may be willing to give to alternative explanations offered in the cognitive restructuring process. David Burns and others have even started offering regular rating scales as a means of monitoring, in part, the strength of the alliance over time. Some clinicians assess the therapeutic relationship on a regular basis as part of their treatment process. Others may simply use tools of this nature when there is a perceived problem with the rapport. Some clients and clinicians find them cumbersome and tedious. Others consider them invaluable. The following tool offers clinicians a brief opportunity to assess the relationship post-session. If you are a client, it may be helpful to reflect on these questions as well.

TOOL 4.2: THE THERAPEUTIC ALLIANCE

On a scale of 1-10, how would you rate our relationship and how well we worked together in today's session?

_____

_____

_____

Was there anything I did as your therapist that caused you to feel uncomfortable working with me or trusting me?

_____

_____

_____

Was there anything I did as a therapist in this session that you helped feel more comfortable or trust me more?

_____

_____

_____

What do you think it would take from you or me or both of us to do differently in the next session to get that rating to a _____? (one number higher than the client originally rated the relationship).

_____

_____

_____

More Experiential Work

Repetition and experience seem to be important components of long-lasting belief change. With this knowledge, there has been a shift away from traditional thought logs toward more experiential work (or at least using experiential work to accompany the thought logs). Behavioral experiments (BEs) have always been a key strategy employed by CBT practitioners. These are constructed collaboratively by the client and the clinician and aim to test assumptions. These experiments can be creative in nature, but the experiment must be designed in such a way that the findings have direct bearing on the validity.

A socially anxious woman I treated had a belief "If I go in public places, I'll probably do something clumsy or awkward and people will laugh at me." I asked her on a scale of 0–10 how much she believed this. Her initial response was "10." We then collaboratively designed an experiment in which she agreed to go to a certain restaurant with her sister. Her sister was instructed to *purposefully* spill a drink. My client's only job was to observe and take notes as to the reactions of the people in the vicinity when it happened, paying particular attention to how many people laughed at them.

The results of the experiment? My client observed eight people who reacted in any way to the planned spill. Six of them glanced in their direction, and then continued what they were doing as if nothing even happened. One woman said in a concerned voice, "Are you all ok?" And one person actually found a waiter and came back to the "scene of the accident" with a towel to help clean up! So as we processed results, we identified that six people were completely indifferent, one was concerned, and one was even helpful! I then asked the client again, on a scale of 0–10, how much did she believe her assumption. Her response after one behavioral experiment was "5." So that one experiment that produced evidence contrary to her belief cut her believability rating in half.

It should be noted that beliefs fluctuate, so if I would have called her and asked her the next day how much she believed it, the cognitive fortification might have lessened over 24 hours, and I could have received a much different number by then. Thus, we continued doing additional experiments creating (1) more evidence to consider against her assumption, and (2) additional emotional experiences associated with them.

This experiential component can also play a powerful role in the "head-heart disconnect" many clients feel at a certain stage in treatment. Use the following **Behavioral Experiment Tool** to identify client assumptions, devise experiments to test them, and record the changes in believability that occur.

TOOL 4.3: BEHAVIORAL EXPERIMENT

Assumption	Initial Belief (0-10)	Experiment	Results	Final Belief (0-10)

In addition to behavioral experiments, experiential work is being incorporated in more simple, everyday ways as well. For instance, a client might make the statement "I'm too depressed. I can't do anything for more than a few minutes." In this case, the practitioner might define "few" and then, if there is a way to, get up and test the belief right there in session.

A male client of mine with depression made that exact statement. When I probed, he defined "few minutes" as "five to ten." He rated his depression at 8 on our 0–10 scale. He rated his energy as a 1 on a 0–10 scale. We then proceeded to set a timer and see if he could play frisbee for 15 minutes with me right there in session on the hospital grounds. Not only did he make it the entire 15 minutes, afterward he rated his energy level a 4, and his depression level a 6. His energy was slightly higher, his depression was somewhat lower, and he didn't want to quit playing! In addition to that obviously being good for him in that moment on that day, he was able to *experience* his belief being proved false. We then also had him do some writing about what it felt like, and he recorded for himself a short video on his smartphone of what it felt like for him to feel good.

There are many other powerful uses of experiential techniques in CBT, including David Edwards's seminal work on the use of imagery in cognitive restructuring.

Strengths-Based CBT

Strengths-based CBT was developed by Padesky over a number of years, but her publication *Strengths-Based Cognitive-Behavioural Therapy: A Four-Step Model to Build Resilience* was published in 2012. Her premise was that since CBT had been shown to be so effective at ameliorating symptoms, perhaps it could be used to build strengths as well. Her four-step model to developing resilience includes:

Step 1: Search for strengths.

Step 2: Construct a personal model of resilience (PMR).

Step 3: Apply the PMR to a problem area.

Step 4: Practice resilience.

If you want to incorporate strengths-based CBT into your practice, I highly recommend her work. In the meantime, **My Strengths Tool** can get you started.

TOOL 4.4: MY STRENGTHS TOOL

Although traditional therapy targets reducing symptoms (decreasing what is "wrong") with us, we can also benefit from increasing what is "right" with us to achieve our goals. Every single person has gifts, strengths, and talents. Strengths-based work may involve many aspects, including increasing our awareness of the strengths we already have, developing new strengths, and identifying how we might use specific strengths to help us in overcoming specific problems we are dealing with. Use the My Strengths Tool to help get your wheels spinning as to how you can harness strengths to empower you in your recovery. Many people have found it helpful to use the I AM, I CAN, I HAVE model.

I AM (or at least can be)—Here list all the positive personality traits you see in yourself. If you have trouble seeing these traits, ask someone who knows you well. Finally, note the words in parentheses. (Nobody IS something all the time. If someone tells you that you have patience, but your internal roommate wants to remind you of a time that you weren't, write it down anyway, because if someone else said it, there likely were also times that you were patient.) Anything we have demonstrated that we have the capability of being, we can harness and use.

_____

_____

I CAN—Here list all the skills you have. What are some things you can DO?

_____

_____

I HAVE—Here list resources that you HAVE at your disposal. These could involve community resources, family, or other people.

_____

_____

Strengths I don't believe I have yet that would be helpful for me to develop to deal with a particular problem, or that I think would serve me well in life in general include:

_____

_____

Now, pick three strengths and consider how you might use them to help you with a specific situation you are currently dealing with:

I could use my strength of _____ to help me

with _____.

I could use my strength of _____ to help me with

_____.

I could use my strength of _____ to help me with

_____.

Positive Psychology

Positive psychology was developed in 1998. Although it had other contributors, Martin Seligman is largely recognized by most as being the father of the movement. Extreme and perhaps distorted perceptions of this approach have criticized it for being out of touch with reality. After all, *rational* thinking is not the same thing as *positive* thinking. By many definitions, there is negative thinking that is rational. For instance, my client reported that the doctor told him that his grandmother likely had less than a week to live. That was, from his perspective, a "negative." It would be a huge loss for him. Mourning, crying, and grieving would be healthy reactions and certainly understandable given the situation. As negative as it was, he recognized the healthy thing was to accept the likelihood that she would not be with him on this earth much longer. This enabled him to take off work, leave the state, and spend as much time with her as possible before she passed.

This perspective, which could be viewed as "rational but negative" can be contrasted with my client who remained in denial when her aunt was in a similar situation. She had thoughts such as:
- "Doctors are often wrong about these things."
- "She is tough—she has bounced back from sickness before, she will again."
- "I know she will make it!"

Her insistence on "staying positive" resulted in her not being there for her aunt's death, a choice she has now regretted for over ten years.

There seem to be some misnomers about this approach. According to Peterson (2008), positive psychology is defined as "the scientific study of what makes life most worth living." To be brief, positive psychology focuses on aspects of CBT like:
- creating positive experiences and emotions, such as happiness and love
- emphasizing positive characteristics, such as compassion and thankfulness
- creating life satisfaction, hope, and a general sense of well-being

So this is more than just "thinking positive." It certainly seems to have some overlap with aspects of strengths-based cognitive therapy, Compassion-Focused Therapy (Gilbert, 2010), as well as some of Linehan's work on reasons for living (1983).

In terms of focus, however, it is possible to acknowledge the negative and also focus on the positive. There are psychological and emotional benefits to recognizing any small aspect of good in situations or events that strike us as "bad." This is a mindset I have worked to instill in my twins from an early age. When they were 5 we started playing "the bright-side game," in which every time something happened that was "bad," we acknowledged the current reality and then somebody (usually but not always me) would yell out "bright-side game," and each person had to come up with one current or potential positive aspect of what just happened.

Use the following tool to help facilitate this process. When something bad occurs, acknowledge it. Grieve. Mourn. Don't deny reality, feelings of hurt, loss, or sadness. Seek support if necessary. Then list at least one potential bright side you can see coming from the situation.

TOOL 4.5: THE "BRIGHT SIDE"

In *Hamlet*, Shakespeare writes, "There is neither good nor bad, but thinking makes it so." Some may argue with that, but what is undisputed is that part of what positive psychology has given us is a challenge to look for different types of "good" in situations our initial perceptions may deem to be "bad." Use the following tool to identify an event (or multiple events) where your initial perception was, or maybe still is, that the event was bad, and then try to see any small bright side. That is, look for *any* silver lining in the situation *now* or potential good you could see that might come of it in the future.

Event	Downside: Why I Perceived it as "Bad"?	Bright Side: What Good Could Come of It?

— ◈ —

Irismar Reis de Olivera's Trial-Based CBT, David Burns' TEAM-CBT, and a revamped Rational Emotive Behavior Therapy (REBT), originally from Albert Ellis, all represent newer approaches in the traditional CBT family.

"Third Wave" Approaches

The emergence of mindfulness, acceptance-based therapies, and other "third wave" approaches into the established mainstream of psychotherapy is perhaps the most significant of the changes in recent years.

The term "Third Wave" was coined by Steven Hayes in 2004 to describe newer CBT approaches that emphasize "noticing, observing, and even turning toward" thoughts rather than attempting to change their content, in the way that traditional cognitive restructuring and schema work do. Hayes's Acceptance and Commitment Therapy (ACT), Mindfulness-Based Cognitive Therapy (MBCT) Compassion-Focused Therapy (CFT), and Dialectical Behavior Therapy (DBT) are among the approaches that could be considered in this category.

This third wave movement has been somewhat controversial in the sense that this term almost seems to imply some kind of historical progress has been made (when compared to traditional or "second wave" approaches). Many would argue that these tenets are nothing new and don't represent any original contribution to the field. Ideas related to compassion and acceptance have been around hundreds of years. Morita therapy, which had the stated goal was of "accepting life as it is," was developed in the early 1920s by the Japanese physician Shoma Morita. In more recent years, these ideas have been built on by many others, including Adrian Wells, who has been pioneering metacognitive work for decades. His first book *Attention and Emotion* was published in 1994, and his *Metacognitive Therapy for Anxiety and Depression* has been a staple on many CBT therapists' bookshelves for years.

So while versions of these third wave approaches have existed for decades and, depending on your perspective, for centuries, there is no question that innovative minds in the field such as Linehan, Hayes, and many others have articulated new spins on these approaches that have catapulted them into the mainstream of the psychotherapeutic community, and the vastness of their impact cannot be denied. Some of these approaches are now considered evidence-based for certain conditions as well.

Although there were literally hundreds of exercises to choose from to represent the third wave, Richard Sears, the director of the Center for Clinical Mindfulness & Meditation Center in Cincinnati, Ohio, has given permission to reprint this following tool.

TOOL 4.6: MINDFULNESS

A simple but helpful mindfulness exercise that clients often find useful is called The Three-Minute Breathing Space, which comes from the Mindfulness-Based Cognitive Therapy protocol (Williams, Teasdale, Segal, & Kabat-Zinn, 2007). When a client hears that the exercise is only three minutes long, it doesn't sound very intimidating, so they are more likely to start practicing it. Because it is shorter than other formal mindfulness practices, it is easier to incorporate throughout the day. Also, as you will see, even though it is short, it contains a lot of different pieces to exercise the client's ability to be mindful.

The Three-Minute Breathing Space

Checking in with ourselves is the first step to dealing with our lives and our emotions more consciously and proactively. As the name implies, The Three-Minute Breathing Space is a short exercise, which allows you to do it several times a day to develop more self-awareness. Once you notice things as they are, you open up the chance to consciously respond instead of automatically react to what is happening.

Because this is a short exercise, you can do it almost anywhere—lying on a couch at home, sitting at a desk at work, or you can slip off to the bathroom if you don't want anyone to see you. By the way, if there are people around, and you think it might look weird to just sit still for three minutes, just hold your cell phone in front of you for three minutes—no one would ever question that!

To begin, you might find it helpful just to remind yourself, right now, there is literally nowhere else that you could be. You don't have to be doing something else more important for the next few minutes. Just give yourself permission to drop into this moment as it is.

First Minute

The first minute of this exercise is to just check in with yourself. We spend so much of our time thinking about or paying attention to other times, places, and people. Just check in with yourself to notice things as they are right now.

Start with your physical body. What sensations are you noticing right now? Do a quick scan from your head down to your toes. For just this moment, you don't necessarily have to analyze or fix anything—just notice. Become aware of the surface you are on, feel the clothing on your skin, and even notice if there is some tension or discomfort in your body. You can certainly move your body if you need to but see if you can just notice what is already here as it is.

Then check in with your emotional state. Right now, in this moment, how are you feeling? Are you a little bit tired, irritated, happy, or some combination of things? How do you know how you are feeling? Are there places in your physical body that give you a clue about your emotional state? Again, right now, you don't have to fix anything, analyze anything, or make it go away. Just give yourself permission to feel what you are already feeling.

At a more subtle level, see if you can notice what you are thinking. What thoughts or images are coming and going in your mind? Instead of getting lost in your thoughts, or carried away with them, can you just notice them as thoughts? You might even imagine you are watching your thoughts being projected on a movie screen. Instead of getting lost in the movie, with all the emotions and drama, can you step back and just notice the movie?

Second Minute

The second minute is just to feel your breath, as a way of gathering up the attention, to sort of collect yourself, to center yourself, by focusing on one thing, in this case your breath. Rather than thinking about, or imagining your breath, can you get in touch with the actual physical sensations? Feel your stomach as it rises and falls. Or maybe you notice the air as it moves in and out of your nose. It's a little bit cooler when you inhale, and it's a little bit warmer when you exhale.

Chances are your mind is going to wander off or get distracted by something. That's okay. That's just what minds do. See if you can notice when that happens, and without struggling with it, simply keep gently bringing your attention back to your breath.

Third Minute

For the third minute, expand your awareness out beyond your breath, to include the entire body, all at once. Instead of just feeling like you are a brain with something kind of dangling underneath, can you feel yourself inside your entire body all at once, with a broad awareness? Feel your embodied presence. And if you find it helpful, you can even remind yourself that whatever it is, or whatever is going on, it's already here anyway. I can let things be exactly as they are for just this moment.

Now, with a deep breath, let go of this exercise, and bring your attention back to the rest of the room.

At the end of this exercise, you might feel "better." Maybe the pause allowed your body, emotions, or thoughts to settle down, or you noticed that things are pretty good right now, and you have a sense of appreciation. Wonderful!

Maybe after doing this exercise, you feel "worse." Wonderful! No one wants to feel bad, but if that is your reality right now, it is best to notice it. If you became aware of lots of thoughts or feelings of stress, you might not have realized how stressed you were already feeling until you paused to check in. Maybe now you can choose to take a break. If you noticed muscle tension or pain, you can choose to go back to ignoring it, or you can do some stretching before it gets worse. Maybe you need to push through a work meeting first, but you can make a note to yourself to get more rest later. Noticing opens up a chance for you to do some self-care, or at least to relate differently to your experiences.

See if you can bring some of this awareness with you into the next few moments of your day. Ideally, you can practice this exercise several times a day to develop the habit of regularly checking in with yourself.

Reprinted with permission from Dr. Richard Sears

THE THREE-MINUTE BREATHING SPACE

Journal or process out loud, reflecting on the experience.

What was that experience like for you?

_____

_____

_____

Did you find it helpful? If so, How?

_____

_____

_____

How can you incorporate mindfulness into your recovery plan? (Some people have a daily mindfulness practice. Others just use it as one of many coping skills when they are emotionally overwhelmed.)

_____

_____

_____

If you want to add this to your toolbox, practice it this week and continue to log your reflections in your daily log or journal.

Reprinted with permission from Dr. Richard Sears

Incorporation of Other Approaches

I am often asked questions along the lines of "If I am going to use CBT, do I have to use strictly CBT, or can I still be eclectic?" Although different viewpoints exist regarding the question "What makes a cognitive therapist?", many of you know that I have strong feelings about this. The main reason for my opinion, as I share at most of my conferences, is the number of conversations I have had with clients after hearing their stories, which all sound a little something like this:

Me: "What I'd like to offer you is called cognitive behavioral therapy…"

And before I get my first sentence out:

Client: (interrupting) "Oh, CBT. I've had CBT; it doesn't work for me."

Me: "Oh, I'm sorry to hear that. Would you mind telling me about your experience?"

Client: "Well, she pretty much let me vent every week, taught me some deep breathing exercises, and got me involved in a yoga class."

You get the point. Often clients have been introduced to some helpful adjunctive strategies. But very rarely do they describe having gotten the nuts and bolts of CBT. So their thinking and coping skills have remained largely unchanged. Yet, because a practitioner self-identified as a "CBT therapist," or maybe even just said something like "I do some CBT," and that particular professional was not able to help them, they develop a belief that "CBT doesn't work for me."

This has become a pet peeve of mine as it keeps many from seeking treatment who could benefit and improve significantly from what is ailing them. Having said that, there are a thousand gradations of fidelity to the model. Actually, strict adherents to empirically supported protocol have accused me of practicing "watered down" CBT.

As I stated earlier, there is a big difference between being eclectic for the sake of being eclectic (identifying as "integrative" has become trendier than committing to a particular model) and drawing strategies intentionally from other modalities to accomplish your particular goal based on your specific case conceptualization.

For example, the transtheoretical model of change, motivational enhancement therapy, techniques from EMDR, and many other nontraditional CBT approaches can all offer helpful adjunctive therapeutic tools. I have even used gestalt-like empty-chair exercises with the explicit purpose of attempting to modify specific underlying schemas driving problem behaviors. Professor David Edwards has done some powerful work using imagery to modify schemas (Edwards, 2014).

The transtheoretical model of change, sometimes known as the "stages of change" model, was developed by Prochaska and DiClemente in 1984. It posits that when people make a change of any kind in life (substance, dietary, exercise, relationship) they do so in a series of stages. Their original five stages were as follows (my *Reader's Digest* version):

1. Pre-contemplation Stage—In this stage a person has not yet considered making a change.

2. Contemplation stage—Something has brought it to the person's attention that there *could* be a behavior worthy of changing.

3. Preparation stage—The balance tips. The person decides to make a change and starts taking initial preparatory steps.

4. Action stage—The preparation steps are put into action.

5. Maintenance stage—One considers contingency planning and looks for ways to make positive ongoing habits out of initial action steps.

Relapse prevention has since been addressed in this model as well. The transtheoretical model can be a helpful model to assess a client's readiness for change. Knowing which stage your client is in can inform how you engage them. Use Tool 4.7, **Readiness for Change**, to help make this determination.

This tool puts forth a new version of one of Prochaska and DiClimente's exercises designed to attempt to draw out clients who have little interest in being different. This will be applied later in chapter 8 specifically to substance use and addictive behaviors.

TOOL 4.7: READINESS FOR CHANGE

Pre-Contemplation ➡ Contemplation ➡ Preparation ➡ Action ➡ Maintenance

Area of life: _____

I know I am in the _____ stage because _____.

For me to move to the next stage of readiness, I believe it would take:

_____

_____

On a scale of 1–10, how ready am I to move to the next stage right now?

_____

_____

Why is my number not one number higher?

_____

_____

Why is my number not one number lower?

_____

_____

One small step I am willing to take to move in the right direction is:

_____

_____

TOOL 4.8: EXPRESSIONS OF CONCERN

Use the following tool to help you move clients forward to the next step in their journey. As you think about a particular client, ask yourself the following:

This particular tool asks you to embark on a two-step process:

1. Identify all people in your life who have voiced concerns about any of your behaviors. List the specific concerns and the reasons for them in the appropriate columns of the tool.

2. Revisit each of the above and ask the question "Can I see where this person is coming from at all, even if I disagree with them?" If so, write down what you see in their thinking and why they might view it as a concern.

Then process the exercise with your practitioner.

Person	Concern	Reason

One specific technique developed to help clients enhance the motivation many of them lack is called motivational interviewing (MI). MI was developed my Miller and Rollnick in 1991. Their hallmark text, *Motivational Interviewing: Preparing People to Change Addictive Behavior*, describes it as a person-centered approach that aims to elicit and harness strengths to help clients move through the stages of the change. Although it has some philosophical differences with CBT, MI offers some helpful adjunctive strategies.

One such technique involves use of the **RULE** acronym, which is more for the practitioner than the client. It piques the clinician's focus to resist the fighting reflex, understand the client's dilemma, listen authentically, and empower the client to move forward in life.

TOOL 4.9: MOTIVATIONAL INTERVIEWING

Clinicians - Use the following version of the RULE acronym to guide your thinking as you approach your clients considering making a change.

Resist the fighting reflex

In what way am I tempted to "fight" in working with this client?

_____

Understand the client's dilemma

From the client's perspective, what must be going through their mind? What concerns might they have? What might they view to be at risk?

_____

Listen

How can I be a better listener?

_____

Do I have the urge to interrupt? Is it triggered by any specific topics?

_____

What do I hear them saying are their pain points?

_____

What do I hear are the client's main goals?

_____

What seems to be their primary motivators?

_____

Empower

In what way can I empower this client today?

_____

TOOL 4.10: SCULPTING TO FACILITATE THE RESTRUCTURING PROCESS

Incorporation of techniques from psychodrama can also present powerful adjunctive strategies for making CBT work more experiential. Once such technique, family sculpting, can be used to create an experiential component in the cognitive restructuring process.

This tool is for clinicians. First, explain sculpting. If you aren't familiar with it, a brief explanation might sound something like this:

> "I want you to pretend like you are a sculptor, and the characters in the scene of this drama are made of clay. You can put them in any position you want to represent your relationship with them. Hands can be up or down; they can be touching each other or on the other side of the room. They can be facing each other or looking away. They can be standing on chairs. They can have different facial expressions. You are the director of this scene."

An introduction like that usually will suffice. Answer any questions, and then begin.

1. Identify who needs to be present in the session for this to be most effective and arrange a time when all parties can commit to be present.

2. Start by having the client identify a situation or event to sculpt.

3. Ask the client how they viewed their relationship to other people in the room during the identified event, as well as how they viewed the relationships of others in the room to each other. Guide them as needed. Questions might include:

   - Where would the client go in the room?

   - Which direction should they face?

   - What is their posture like?

   - Where would each of the others present go?

4. Once the client has placed everyone where they want them to represent their perception, ask the client questions to elicit underlying cognitions. Some starter questions might include these:

   - What was going through your mind as this happened?

   - What thoughts and feelings did you have as you re-created this scene?

- What thoughts did you have about different people in the room?

- What thoughts did you have about yourself?

5. Once you have identified the client's thoughts and feelings in the triggering scenario, you can have her/him change the sculpt by asking the question: "How would you like to change this scene? Where would you move each person in the room (including yourself)?" Then ask similar questions to elicit new thoughts and feelings.

- What is going through your mind now?

- How does that differ from what you were thinking in the previous scene?

- How does it feel to have yourself in a different place?

- How have your thoughts and feelings changed due to your being positioned differently?

6. If you believe it would be helpful, you can have others in the room script scenes from their perspectives as well. (This can be particularly helpful when the distortions of mind reading and personalization are involved.)

7. If you did step 6, follow up. Point out differences in perception of closeness. Ask the client questions like this:

- Did you have any idea the other person would script the scene like this?

- How does it feel that the other person has you in that position?

- What is different about your scene versus the other person's scene?

- Now that you have seen what your perception is versus what the other person's perception is, how would you like the scene to change?

2

CBT for Issues of Clinical Concern

CHAPTER 5

Depression

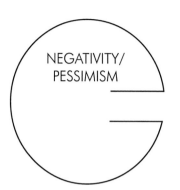

NEGATIVITY/
PESSIMISM

Common Beliefs
- Negativity/Pessimism

Common Distortions
- Discounting the positive/Selective abstraction/Mental filter
- Rationalization

Common Automatic Thoughts
- "I have always been depressed, and I always will be depressed."
- "There is no way out."
- "Things will never get better."
- "It's ok to stay in bed because I don't feel like doing anything."

Common Feelings
- Sad
- Depressed
- "Blue"
- Disappointed
- Lethargic
- Fatigued
- Unmotivated

Common Behaviors
- Stay in bed
- Skip class
- Isolate from friends
- Miss work
- Use substances

TOOL 5.1: IDENTIFICATION OF TRIGGERS

Depression has both biological and environmental components. Some people more than others seem to be predisposed to struggle with low mood. For some, it seems to take a major life catastrophe to affect their mood significantly in any negative way. Others may struggle with at least low-level feelings of depression despite minimal "reason to be depressed."

Wherever you fall on this spectrum, identifying triggers is an important first step. Even if you seem to be predisposed to feelings of low mood regularly, identifying triggers can help prevent downward spikes in your already low mood. Triggers for depression can be people, places, or things, and they are often related in some way to loss. Some triggers are much more obvious than others. Answer the following questions that may give you a window into your triggers for depression.

To me, depression is:

_____

I notice I am most depressed when:

_____

The last time I remember feeling this way was:

_____

Themes I notice include:

_____

Some things that I have observed happening right before I feel this way are:

_____

My Depression Triggers

1. _____

2. _____

3. _____

4. _____

5. _____

TOOL 5.2: IDENTIFICATION OF FEELINGS

Emotions have been described by some in terms of being in discrete "feelings families" based on different types of emotional states humans experience. Depressed mood is associated with decreased arousal, and a variety of feelings words have been used to describe emotions on that continuum. Pick from the following emotional expressions commonly thought of as being in the depression family or come up with your own words. Then list five of them on the continuum below with "1" being the least depressed and "5" being the most intense depression for you.

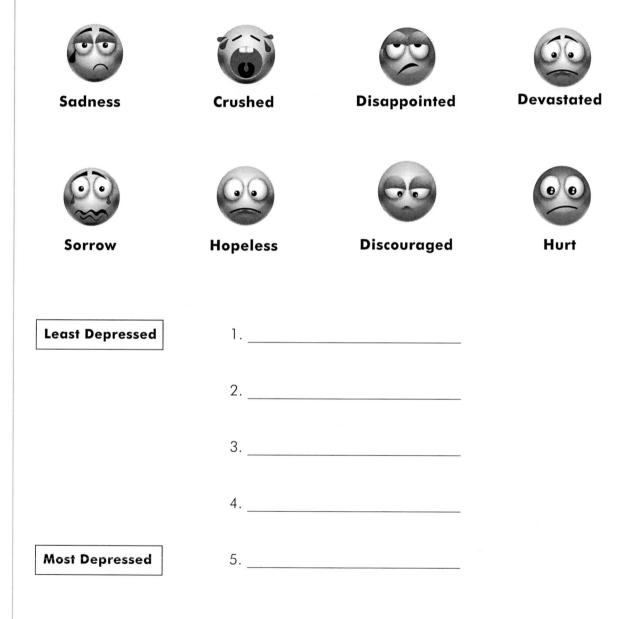

Sadness　　**Crushed**　　**Disappointed**　　**Devastated**

Sorrow　　**Hopeless**　　**Discouraged**　　**Hurt**

Least Depressed

1. _____

2. _____

3. _____

4. _____

Most Depressed

5. _____

TOOL 5.3: IDENTIFICATION OF DEPRESSIVE THOUGHTS

The following questions are designed to help you identify your distorted thoughts specifically related to depression. Remember, these thoughts will often be related to negativity, loss, or discounting some positive aspect of self, others, or the world.

When _____ happens, and I feel _____.
              (Trigger)   (Emotion)

What kinds of things am I often telling myself?

_____

_____

If I were in a cartoon, what would the bubble above my head be saying?

_____

_____

If there were a tape recorder in my head recording my every thought, what would it be saying if someone pushed "play"?

_____

_____

Use the table on the following page to log the thoughts you identify to be going along with your depression-related feelings.

Example

I felt...	Because I thought...
Sad	I can't live without her in my life.
Discouraged	They are taking so few people—I'll never get into medical school.
Hopeless	There's nothing to live for.

THOUGHTS/FEELINGS AWARENESS LOG

I felt ...	Because I Thought...

TOOL 5.4: UNHEALTHY "GO-TO" COPING SKILLS

"Autopilot" skills used to cope with depression can vary from person to person. Some people simply surrender to these feelings and shut down. Isolating, not returning phone calls from loved ones, laying around on the couch, calling in sick to work, and not taking care of basic activities of daily living can be manifestations of this coping style. Some people's go-to "skills" include attempts not to feel the unpleasant feelings by smoking pot, self-medicating with alcohol, promiscuous sex, gambling, or other instant gratification behaviors. Use the following tool to help you identify some of yours.

Some autopilot behaviors I have engaged in when feeling down or depressed:

1. _____

2. _____

3. _____

4. _____

5. _____

6. _____

7. _____

8. _____

9. _____

10. _____

TOOL 5.5: AWARENESS OF CONSEQUENCES

As Tool 5.4 touched on, coping mechanisms that worked in the past don't always work in the present, and attempts that work in the short term don't always work in the long term. Use this tool to increase your awareness by trying to identify some of the consequences of your unsuccessful attempted solutions to depression in the past.

Example

Autopilot Coping Skill (from Tool 5.4)	Current or Past Negative Consequences
Stay in bed all day	Expelled from college
Not answer phone calls	Lost many good friends

Autopilot Coping Skill	Current or Past Negative Consequences

TOOL 5.6: CBT CHAIN ANALYSIS

Here is where the rubber meets the road. This is where you get to put it all together. Now that you have mastered the skills covered in the previous tools, identify a specific situation/trigger in your life for your feelings of depression. See if you can identify specific thoughts that you had, feelings you experienced, choices you made, and consequences of those choices.

Use the following tool to help you follow the sequence to analyze your response in a particular episode. Also, when you identify your feelings, rate them on a scale of 0–10 with zero being "none" and 10 being "extreme intensity". For instance, if you identify "sadness" and it was as sad as you have ever felt, your entry would look like: "Sadness—10."

Once you have done enough of these, you will able to identify patterns, which can facilitate powerful insights for recovery.

Depression Chain Analysis

Event (Trigger)	Negative/ Discounting Thoughts	Depressive Feelings and Intensity	Coping Skills	Results

TOOL 5.7: DESIRED RESULTS

This one is pretty simple. When you look at the undesired consequences of choices in your life, what are some alternative outcomes you would have liked to have had? What desired results do you have for your future?

Results I would like to create in my future in similar situations:

1. _____

2. _____

3. _____

4. _____

5. _____

TOOL 5.8: NEW DEPRESSION COPING SKILLS

Now that you know how you would like situations to end in response to a given trigger, how might you need to change your behavior to create your desired result? This tool offers you an opportunity to brainstorm alternative coping skills you can employ in your battle against depression.

When I am experiencing feelings of depression, skills that have worked or might work for me include:

1. _____

2. _____

3. _____

4. _____

5. _____

6. _____

7. _____

8. _____

9. _____

10. _____

TOOL 5.9: CHALLENGING DEPRESSION-RELATED THOUGHTS

Challenging depression-related thoughts doesn't always make them go away, but it can put up enough of a "fight" that the feelings aren't quite so intense, and it can keep them from snowballing. Challenging the depressive thoughts may also make it slightly easier to use some of your depression-related coping skills. Use this tool to attempt to challenge or generate some more rational responses to your depression-related thoughts.

Example

Distorted Thought	Rational Response
I can't live without her in my life.	I will miss her in my life, so it's ok to feel some sadness, but she is better off now, and I can develop other meaningful relationships.
They are taking so few people. I'll never get into medical school.	My grades meet the requirements. I have a good resume. I have a decent chance of getting in. If I don't get in this time, maybe I can later. If I never get in, it's not the end of the world. There are other areas in which I can use my skills and help people medically without being a physician.
There's nothing left to live for.	A lot is going wrong in my life right now, but I still have a mother who cares, my faith in God, and my dog.

DEPRESSION THOUGHT LOG

Negative/Discounting Thoughts	Rational Responses

TOOL 5.10: REEXAMINING DEPRESSED FEELINGS

Now that you have attempted to challenge your thoughts, reflect for a few minutes on your feelings. Ask yourself if the feelings have changed? If so, how much has the intensity changed from before versus after the new thinking? Are you feeling any completely new feelings? Which new thoughts seem to have the most effect on your feelings? The least? Use this tool to examine the differences and then record your observations.

Automatic Thoughts	Initial Feelings	Intensity

Rational Responses	Current Feelings	Intensity

My Observations:

_____

_____

_____

_____

_____

_____

TOOL 5.11: CHAIN ANALYSIS WITH RATIONAL RESPONSES

Use the chain analysis tool below with your rational responses to see the impact that your new thinking had on your feelings. Be sure to rate the intensity of the new feelings. For instance, you may still be experiencing sadness, but recognize that if after your initial automatic thoughts your sadness was a "10," and after your rational responses your sadness was a "6," that means the new thinking made an impact. Scaling your feelings can help you not make the mistake of black-and-white thinking by saying "I was sad then and I am sad now—this didn't do anything." Scaling can help increase your awareness to incremental change. You will then be able to better see how changed thinking, feeling, and behavior affected current results and could affect future results.

Event	Automatic Thoughts	Feelings	Actions	Results
	Rational Responses	**New Feelings**	**New Actions**	**New Results**

TOOL 5.12: DOWNWARD ARROW TO IDENTIFY CORE BELIEFS

As a refresher, *core beliefs* are deeply ingrained beliefs that serve as filters through which we process information. All of our distorted thinking is the product of one or more harmful beliefs. This technique asks us to take a thought and continue to ask, *"What would that mean about me if it were true?"* until we get to the core belief at the bottom of the distorted thought. If necessary, review the chapter to note beliefs that often contribute to depression. Also remember that many people need a clinician's help to assist with this for a period of time. Note the example below and then try one on your own using one of your own automatic thoughts.

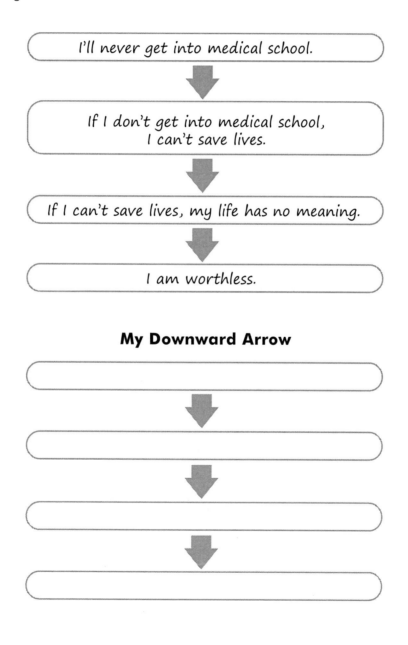

I'll never get into medical school.

↓

If I don't get into medical school, I can't save lives.

↓

If I can't save lives, my life has no meaning.

↓

I am worthless.

My Downward Arrow

TOOL 5.13: IDENTIFYING ALTERNATIVE HEALTHY BELIEFS

Remember, beliefs come in pairs. I teach in my workshops and conferences that it is kind of like a sheet of paper. It inherently has a front and a back side. For each unhealthy belief you identified, you also have an alternate opposite belief. This tool asks you to formulate in your own words what you would want your opposite belief to be. Then use percentages to rate how much you believe your core belief versus how much you believe your alternate belief. These will be used in a later tool to subjectively measure your belief change as you move forward in your recovery.

Believability Ratings
Example

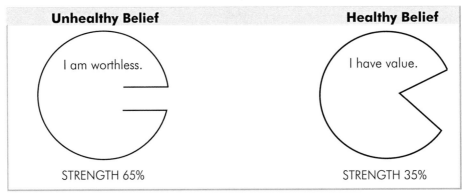

Rating the Strength of My Beliefs

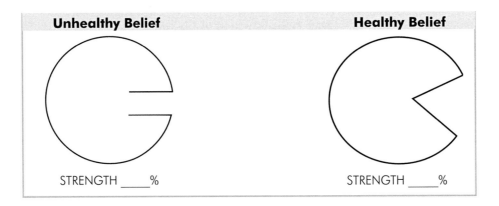

Identifying Components of the Beliefs

Now that you have identified at least one unhealthy belief and an alternate, healthier belief, the next step is to identify what are called the *components of the beliefs*. To identify the components of the unhealthy belief, it can be helpful to look back in time to see where these beliefs came from in the first place. To work on changing a belief moving forward, it is necessary to identify how you define the alternate belief today.

Beliefs are formulated by the meaning we assign to events or experiences in life. These experiences then become "evidence" to support our beliefs. "Evidence" is in quotation marks because some people count "data" as "evidence" that others do not. It is understandable that those who live through different types of life experiences are more likely to develop different beliefs. Although every person's life experiences are in some ways unique, another phenomenon practitioners encounter is that some clients have strikingly similar backgrounds but develop different types of beliefs. The explanation is that even though the experiences themselves may have been similar, the meaning assigned to them may have been quite different.

Leslie Sokol with the Academy of Cognitive Therapy shares a visual for a belief that compares it to a table. In the same way that a tabletop needs legs to support it, beliefs need similar supporting structures. Experiences in life serve as "evidence" to support these beliefs, based on the meaning that is attributed to them. So in this tool, the "legs of the table" represent evidence one internalizes to support a belief.

This visual can be used in a variety of ways. When working to analyze how you may have acquired an unhealthy belief (such as the one you identified in your downward arrow) this involves *looking back at past experiences* in life to examine the conclusions you came to in formulating the beliefs you currently hold. Then a different exercise will help you look at the alternate beliefs you are attempting to construct so you know what to look for as you are examining evidence moving *forward* in life.

Because different people can assign different meaning to strikingly similar events, it is not uncommon for two different clients who are looking back to examine historical evidence that led to the development of a belief that they are "worthless," to identify very different types of experiences or interpretations that led them to the same conclusion about themselves.

Similarly, if the same two people were working to construct an alternate belief moving forward that they "have value," they might be "counting" very different types of things as well.

Thus, it is important when doing these exercises to be honest about what your "legs of the table" really are. Not what your parents thought it meant. Not what your faith community or your friends tell you something means. But how you really define meaning. Failing to identify what "counts" *for you* will lead to you logging evidence that makes no difference in your beliefs and ultimately the mood state you are trying to change.

TOOL 5.14(A): ANALYSIS OF COMPONENTS OF UNHEALTHY BELIEF

Start by looking *back* in time. Use the table visual to identify the components of your beliefs; that is experiences that you went through that were important in contributing to an unhealthy belief you identified when doing the downward arrow. These will help you know specifically what types of experiences will be necessary to create or expose yourself to when modifying your beliefs going forward.

The following questions may be helpful in reflecting on different periods of time in your life to uncover some of the experiences you counted as evidence to support your unhealthy belief as it was being developed. You may need assistance from your clinician to get the most out of this tool.

The first time I ever remember feeling _____ **[belief] was** _____

_____

The people in my life who influenced me to feel that way were:

Family members _____

Friends/Peers _____

Other significant people _____

Experiences during my elementary school years _____

_____

Experiences during my junior high years _____

_____

Experiences during my high school years _____

_____

Experiences during my college/young adult years _____

_____

Significant experiences since then _____

_____

Legs of Table

Fill in the unhealthy belief you are analyzing in the tabletop portion of the structure. Use the exercise in Tool 5.14(A) to insert some of the "evidence" from your past that you have "counted" to support each belief in the legs below. "I am a failure" is a common belief with depression, so it will be used as an example. Consider the example and then use the blank table provided on the next page to identify your own components of your own unhealthy belief.

Example

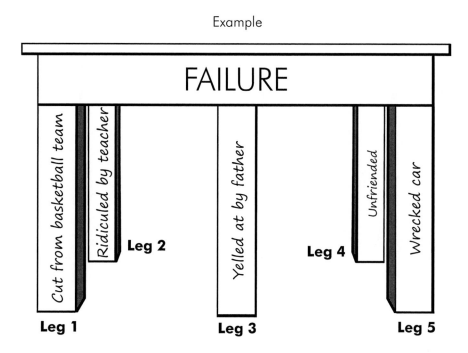

Evidence supporting the belief that I am a failure:

Leg 1: *Cut from 8th grade basketball team*

Leg 2: *Ridiculed by teacher for science project*

Leg 3: *Father yelled at me in garage for mistake on construction project*

Leg 4: *Was unfriended by classmate*

Leg 5: *Got into car accident while texting and driving*

MY TABLE WITH COMPONENTS OF BELIEF

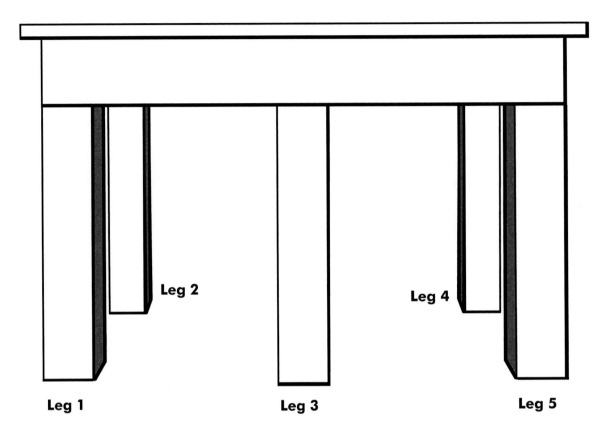

Leg 2

Leg 4

Leg 1

Leg 3

Leg 5

Evidence supporting my unhealthy belief:

Leg 1:

Leg 2:

Leg 3:

Leg 4:

Leg 5:

TOOL 5.14(B): ANALYSIS OF COMPONENTS OF HEALTHY BELIEF

Now that you have identified some of the experiences you assigned meaning to that contributed to formulating your unhealthy belief, take a few moments to consider what evidence might look like to support the alternate healthy belief. For instance, what might you be doing, saying, or being if you "had value" or were "succeeding?" What might others be doing, saying, or being? Consider the following example and then use the blank table provided to identify your own components of your healthy belief.

Example

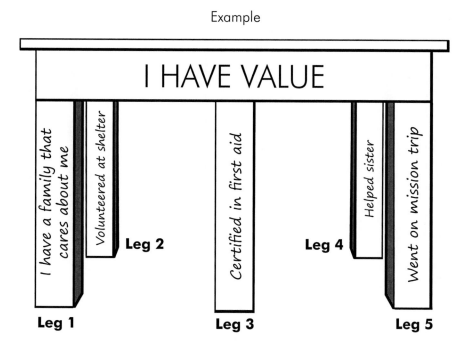

Evidence That I Have Value:

Leg 1: I have family that cares about me.

Leg 2: I volunteered at the animal shelter.

Leg 3: I am certified in first aid.

Leg 4: I helped my sister get out of a bad situation.

Leg 5: I went on a mission trip and helped disaster victims in Haiti.

MY TABLE WITH COMPONENTS OF BELIEF

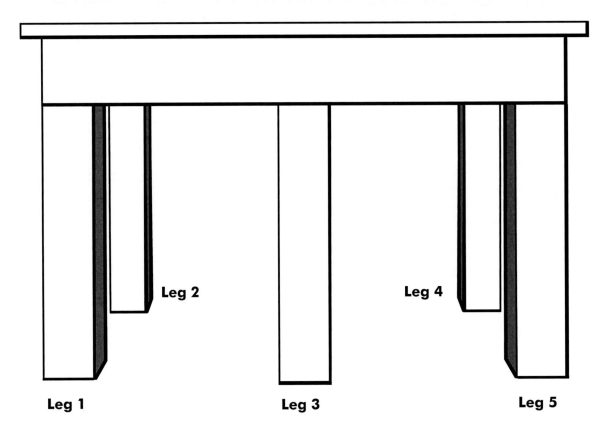

Leg 2

Leg 4

Leg 1

Leg 3

Leg 5

Components of My Healthy Belief:

Leg 1:

Leg 2:

Leg 3:

Leg 4:

Leg 5:

TOOL 5.15: EVIDENCE LOGS

Evidence logs can be helpful in a number of ways, including increasing our awareness as well as strengthening our alternate beliefs. Again, what we log tells us a lot about how we assign meaning.

Now that you have identified your "legs of the table" for the healthy belief you are working on, you know specifically what to look for. Purposefully pay attention to experiences that support the healthy belief you are constructing. This may involve noticing evidence that was always there but you didn't notice before due to your old belief filtering your thinking away from it. You may also work with your clinician on exercises that actually create new evidence that wasn't there before. Purposefully paying attention does not mean making up evidence. If the evidence legitimately isn't there, it doesn't count. Just remember that because of your filter you will be prone to discount things that really do support the belief, so having an open mind is vital.

Consider the example below, and then begin your own evidence log.

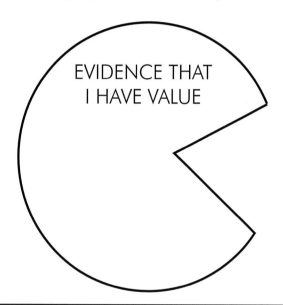

Date	Evidence
11/10	Passed advanced CPR
11/15	Helped my mom
11/19	Donated to Humane Society
11/24	Volunteered at soup kitchen preparing for Thanksgiving

Evidence that I can be _____ (healthy belief) log

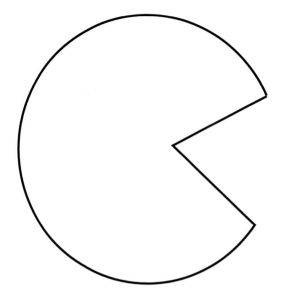

Date	Evidence

Other Tools

One of the toughest things about combatting depression is that the things we need to do to get better are the very things we don't feel like doing. Many people stay depressed for lengthy periods because they say things like, "I'll do more when I feel like it." But depression keeps them from ever feeling like it. So as long as we allow our feelings to dictate our behavior (or lack thereof), we stay stuck.

Thus, one of the tough steps necessary for chipping away at depressed feelings is to *do something even though you don't feel like it*. While it sounds a little cliché, Nike's® old slogan, "Just do it" is applicable here. Research has shown that chemical changes occur in our brain as a result of *doing* things that get us up and moving. A term you may hear in cognitive behavioral therapy to refer to this is *behavioral activation*. While this exact term was used in Beck's early writings in the 1970s, it has, as with most of these "new" approaches, been emphasized lately and is now being seen as its own entity in some circles. Nonetheless, behavioral activation stimulates one physiologically and changes one's environment, even if in subtle ways. Behavioral activation increases the likelihood of modifying factors that could be maintaining depressive symptoms in a number of ways that are often outside our awareness.

Behavioral activation can be facilitated in a number of ways. Two helpful tools are known as *activity monitoring* and *activity scheduling*. *Activity monitoring* involves paying attention, in specific detail, to how we are spending our time. Sometimes we can then draw some conclusions regarding how we could restructure our time to be more helpful when we get to the scheduling stage.

One final rule of thumb to keep in mind: The stronger the depression, the more important the behavioral strategies for combatting it. As depression begins to lift, more cognitive interventions can be employed. Thus, the additional tools in this chapter begin with behavioral activation and other action-orientated skills. Use the following tool to simply pay attention to and write down how you are spending your time. Don't change anything. Just pay attention to and log what you are doing with each hour of your day.

TOOL 5.16: ACTIVITY MONITORING LOG

Example

Time	Activity (Be Specific)
10 am	Got out of bed
11 am	Ate two frozen burritos
12 pm	Watched TV, went on Facebook
3 pm	Went to store
4 pm	Took nap
5 pm	Played video games
8 pm	Ate chips and dip
9 pm	Ran on treadmill for an hour
11 pm	Lay in bed for an hour, couldn't sleep
12 am	Watched TV in bed
1 am	Eventually fell asleep

My Observations:

1. Didn't realize how much time I spent playing video games/on Facebook/watching TV
2. Didn't think about getting on treadmill so late and how might affect my sleep
3. Lay in bed too long when I couldn't sleep
4. Have stopped eating healthy breakfasts
5. Managed to go through whole day without talking to another human being

MY ACTIVITY MONITORING LOG

Time	Activity (Be Specific)
6 am	
7 am	
8 am	
9 am	
10 am	
11 am	
12 pm	
1 pm	
2 pm	
3 pm	
4 pm	
5 pm	
6 pm	
7 pm	
8 pm	
9 pm	
10 pm	
11 pm	
12 am	
1 am	
2 am	
3 am	
4 am	
5 am	

My Observations:

1. _____

2. _____

3. _____

TOOL 5.17: ACTIVITY SCHEDULING

The next step is to use the conclusions you came to regarding how you spend your time to make some changes. Find the blocks of time you were engaging in unproductive (or even counterproductive) behaviors. Be purposeful about what kinds of things you want to be doing during your day. Plan some things that you want to accomplish and write them in during the time frames you intend to do them. Pretend you have an appointment with yourself at each time to do each scheduled event. There are different versions of this tool. This particular version asks you to plan your day in advance and record what you planned. It also has an empty space where you can review your day to see how well you did following through with the plans you intended to keep. Don't use this column as a tool to beat yourself up for what you didn't get done. Rather, use it in a proactive way to help you adjust and plan differently if needed for your next day.

Time	Activity Scheduled	Actual

My Observations:

_____

_____

TOOL 5.18: MASTERY

Research has shown three areas of coping to be especially helpful for people who struggle with depression: *mastery, pleasure*, and *meaning*. *Mastery* skills are especially important for people who value performance or accomplishment. If you are one of these people, you probably feel better about yourself when you get things done, and chances are you have made a to-do list or two in your life! These can be powerful tools for individuals who value performance. If this describes you, try making a list of things to accomplish for the day. Make your list significant enough that it matters to you so that you are able to give yourself credit for having completed it but also realistic enough that you have a good chance of actually accomplishing it. Mastery lists can include basic household chores, errands, or daily business, in addition to steps in pursuit of larger life goals.

Choose from the following list or generate your own tasks you can feel good for having accomplished. And give yourself credit for each thing you accomplish.

Mastery-Related Tasks

1. Thinking I have done a full day's work
2. Cleaning a room in my house
3. Planning for starting a new career
4. Thinking about ways to advance the career I'm already in
5. Running errands
6. Planning a day's activities
7. Doing laundry
8. Putting on makeup
9. Thinking how it will be when I finish school
10. Mowing the lawn
11. Working on my car
12. Pulling weeds
13. Repairing things around the house
14. Taking care of my plants
15. Buying and selling stocks
16. Losing weight
17. Doing embroidery
18. Cross-stitching
19. Joining a club
20. Painting my nails (and noticing when each of the 20 gets done!)
21. Writing poetry
22. Sewing
23. Going to work
24. Gardening
25. Refinishing furniture
26. Making lists of tasks
27. Going bike riding (give yourself credit for each mile!)
28. Completing a task
29. Thinking about past achievements
30. Planning future achievements
31. Making a grocery list
32. Exchanging emails
33. Photography
34. Voting for candidate I support
35. Solving riddles
36. Knitting
37. Crocheting
38. Quilting
39. Doing crossword puzzles
40. Making jigsaw puzzles
41. Doing school assignment
42. Doing therapy homework
43. Paying bills
44. Picking up around the house
45. Volunteering
46. Playing games online
47. Painting the house
48. Saving money
49. Working on a community service project
50. Playing a game on my smart phone

MY MASTERY SKILLS

1. _____

2. _____

3. _____

4. _____

5. _____

6. _____

7. _____

8. _____

9. _____

10. _____

TOOL 5.19: PLEASURE

A clinical term you may hear to describe a type of depressive symptoms is anhedonia, or anhedonic symptoms. These refer to a lack of desire or lack of pleasure. Therefore, pleasurable tasks are vital to incorporate into your regular activity scheduling. Below are a few examples. You may select pleasurable events from this list or come up with your own.

Pleasurable Tasks

1. Soaking in the bathtub
2. Burning incense
3. Kissing
4. Getting a pedicure
5. Thinking about a past vacation
6. Going on a date
7. Nurturing a pet
8. Going for a walk or jog
9. Listening to music
10. Going to a party
11. Flirting
12. Looking at photos from past trips
13. Reading
14. Brushing your hair
15. Giving or receiving a hug
16. Remembering beautiful scenery
17. Playing Frisbee golf
18. Drawing
19. Catching up with old friends on social media
20. Trying a new support group
21. Trying a new church
22. Going to a casino
23. Watching a movie
24. Going to a sporting event
25. Going to the gym
26. Dancing
27. Doing karate
28. Enjoying nature
29. Doing yoga
30. Sleeping
31. Getting a massage
32. Going for a drive
33. Calling a supportive person
34. Flying a kite
35. Praying
36. Buying flowers
37. Getting a manicure
38. Going swimming
39. Watching a sunrise/sunset
40. Riding a bike
41. Relaxing in a hot tub
42. Having a quiet evening at home
43. Drinking a cup of coffee or tea
44. Going to a lake
45. Getting together with old friends
46. Exercising to an aerobics DVD
47. Going to a play
48. Getting on the internet and researching something you enjoy
49. Giving a small gift to someone else

MY PLEASURABLE TASKS

1. _____

2. _____

3. _____

4. _____

5. _____

6. _____

7. _____

8. _____

9. _____

10. _____

TOOL 5.20: MEANING MAKING

A third area associated with depression is *meaning*. This is different for different people. You may be familiar with the story of Victor Frankl, who survived what could be considered among the worst environmental experiences a person could fathom—a concentration camp. Yet he came out with a positive attitude because of his development of, and focus on, the meaning of life. For many people, this involves issues related to religion or faith. For others, it may include close relationships, worthy causes, or other aspects of life. The more consistently we live our lives in accordance with our values, or what we consider to be truly important, the more significance we believe we have, which contributes to our sense of well-being. Use the following meaning-making tool to (1) consider what gives your life meaning—what values are important to you, and (2) identify specific items you can use in your activity scheduling.

Example

To me the most meaningful aspects of life are:

1. Faith

2. Family

3. Education

Specific actions I can take to live in accordance with my values:

1. Attend a church service

2. Help my elderly aunt

3. Study for my test instead of going out

My Meaning-Making Actions

To me the most meaningful areas of life are:

1. _____

2. _____

3. _____

Meaningful actions I will take today include:

1. _____

2. _____

3. _____

MASTERY, PLEASURE, MEANING

Now that you have identified skills in the area of mastery, pleasure, and meaning, pick out several favorites of yours in each area and record them here. Many people find it helpful to write these on a 3x5 card as a reminder of skills they can use throughout their day.

Mastery:

_____

_____

_____

Pleasure:

_____

_____

_____

Meaning:

_____

_____

_____

TOOL 5.21: INTIMACY CIRCLES

Evaluate the relationships you have in your life.

We call these "intimacy circles" and, as a memory device, define intimacy as "into-me-see"—the degree to which we let people see into us.

For instance, as you complete your tool someone you would let "see into" you completely (someone you kept no secrets from) would go in circle #1. Those you would not share anything personal with would go in circle # 5, and so on. The more you trust a person the closer in they go on your circles. The less you trust a person, the further out they go. After listing people where you view them on your circles, answer the questions that follow.

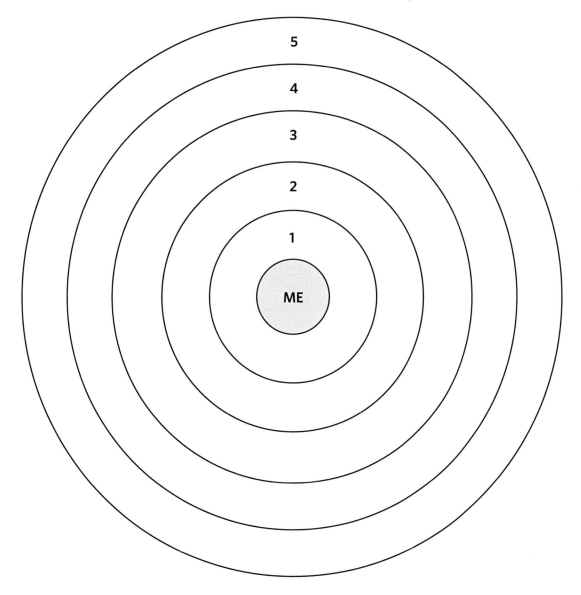

Adapted from *Group Treatment for Substance Abuse*, Velasquez, Maurer, Crouch, and DiClemente, 2001

INTIMACY CIRCLE QUESTIONS

What changes would I like to make to my circles?

_____

Are there people I would like to have closer to me? Further? Who and why?

_____

Some hurtful things I have done that have damaged one or more relationships:

_____

Some helpful things I have done that have helped me in maintaining relationships:

_____

Changes I could make in the way I relate to people may include:

_____

Would I like to add people to my circles who currently aren't there? Why or why not?

_____

What are some qualities of the people I would like to add?

_____

Where might I go to meet people like that?

_____

What are some "red flag" qualities of people I may be drawn to but that I have learned from experience are not good candidates for my circles?

_____

One step I am willing to take today to start working on my circles is:

_____

_____

TOOL 5.22: GRATITUDE

Has anyone ever told you, "Just count your blessings—you have so much to be thankful for"? That advice drives many of us nuts, because the people who are saying those words typically have no idea what you are going through. All human beings need to be validated. Therefore, acknowledging losses, hurts, and needs and having them validated is important. However, the mistake some people struggling with depression make is that they only find people who will validate them, and other times, inadvertently encouraging continuing unhelpful coping. Have you ever heard the phrase "misery loves company"? Some depressed people, usually without meaning to, seek people who will validate their pain without challenging them to try to move forward with more positive thinking and behavior.

It feels good to know that our feelings are valid. However, just because they are valid emotions and it may be completely understandable how we got there, that doesn't mean it's helpful that we stay there. By seeking validation only, many depressed individuals unknowingly develop a "victim mentality," which ultimately fuels their feelings of misery.

However, it is also important to identify positives to focus on. The term silver lining is often used to describe finding a little bit of good in a bad situation. There may be some situations in which we are not able to find a silver lining. If that is the case, it may take looking outside the particular negative situation that is bringing you down and trying to find some positives or blessings in other areas of your life. Perhaps you are not able to find anything positive about being robbed yesterday, but it is still to your advantage that you have a family that can help you, that you still have a place to live, and a dog that brings you much joy. So while it would be dishonest to say, "That robbery was good. I'm glad it happened," it also will not be helpful to your mood if you continue to focus on thoughts such as, "Why do these things always happen to me?"

Thinking about difficult situations in a healthy manner involves both acknowledging painful aspects of situations and also not dwelling on them. Don't let that negative filter creep in and keep you from enjoying other aspects of life even if some of what you are going through is terrible. The following tools will help you do just that: acknowledge legitimate painful situations in your life while also coming up with some positives, or blessings, as well.

Date:

_____

Things I am thankful for and will focus my attention on today are:

1.

_____

2.

_____

3.

_____

TOOL 5.23: MOOD TRACKER

The DSM-5® committee has decided that biologically speaking, bipolar disorder has more in common with schizophrenia than it does with major depression. However, in clinical practice, many still view it as a "mood disorder." This tool is devoted to bipolar disorder. It asks clients to rate their mood on a daily basis using a scale of -5 (extremely depressed) to + 5 (extremely manic). Doing this on a regular basis can help increase awareness of mood, identify patterns, and brainstorm coping skills that can be helpful for each mood state.

	Mon.	Tues.	Wed.	Thurs.	Fri.	Sat.	Sun.	Coping Skills
+5								
+4								
+3								
+2								
+1								
0								
-1								
-2								
-3								
-4								
-5								

My Observations:

_____

_____

TOOL 5.24: BEHAVIORAL COPING CARDS

The final two tools are different types of cards. The first is what is called a *behavioral coping card*. To make use of this tool, it is usually best to identify typical unhealthy coping skills (from Tool 5.4), examine your current circumstances, peruse your healthy new coping skills (Tool 5.8), and pick three of them you could use instead in your current specific situation. Since these are to be used "in the moment," it is best to keep them succinct so as not to overwhelm yourself, as you will often be using them in times of emotional upset. Consult the following example, and then fill out one for yourself. The tools are provided below to show you what they look like and give you practice filling them out, but it works best to get some 3 × 5 index cards that you can strategically place where they will benefit you the most (i.e. if your temptation is to eat emotionally, place the card by your cupboard.)

Example

The next time I feel depressed and am tempted to go to bed, instead I will:

1. Go for a walk around the neighborhood.

2. Call Freddie.

3. Clean house for at least 10 minutes.

My Cue Card

The next time I feel depressed and am tempted to_____, instead I will:

1. _____

2. _____

3. _____

TOOL 5.25: COGNITIVE CUE CARDS

The final tool is a card with a slightly different purpose. Unlike the coping cards, cognitive cue cards do not ask you to write down any behaviors. They are more about your mindset. For these, pick out a rational response you used (in Tool 5.9) that resonated with you. Even better yet, take a swipe at one of those "legs of the table" (Tool 5.14) by trying to reassign meaning at a deeper level. Use the format in the example that is provided and then complete your own cue card. Again, after practicing here, use an actual 3x5 card and place it strategically for your benefit.

Example

"Just because I didn't get anything done today doesn't mean I am a failure. I still have plenty of time to complete this project. And even if it is late, I have contributed in many ways to this company's success, and I will continue to contribute in the future. Today was just one day, and this is just one project."

Your Cue Card

CHAPTER **6**

Anxiety

Common Beliefs
- Helpless
- Vulnerable
- Approval Seeking/Unlovable
- Failure

Common Distortions
- Fortune-telling
- Mind-reading
- Magnifying

Common Automatic Thoughts
- "I can't cope with this."
- "It is unacceptable to not be liked."
- "The world is dangerous."
- "People are untrustworthy."
- "I could get hurt."
- "What if I can't do it?"

Common Feelings
- Anxious
- Worried
- Fearful
- Scared
- Afraid
- Panicked

Common Behaviors
- Avoid
- Isolate
- Shut down

TOOL 6.1: IDENTIFICATION OF TRIGGERS

Anxiety has both biological and environmental components. Some people seem to be "hardwired" to have a higher baseline level of arousal than others. We also know that a number of environmental risk factors combined with a biological predisposition creates varying degrees of anxiety.

Wherever you fall on this spectrum, identifying triggers is an important first step. Even if you seem to be predisposed to a higher baseline of increased arousal, identifying triggers can help you be prepared to cope with anxiety when it comes and, in some cases, decrease the frequency and intensity when it does come. Triggers for anxiety can be environmental or physiological. Answer the following questions to shed light on your anxiety triggers.

To me, anxiety feels like:

_____

_____

I feel anxiety the strongest when:

_____

_____

The last time I remember feeling this way was:

_____

_____

Themes related to my anxiety include:

_____

_____

Some things that I have observed that happen right before I feel this way are:

_____

_____

My Anxiety Triggers

1. _____

2. _____

3. _____

4. _____

5. _____

TOOL 6.2: IDENTIFICATION OF FEELINGS

Emotions have been described by some in terms of being in discrete "feelings families" based on different *types* of emotional states humans experience. Anxious mood states are associated with increased levels of arousal, and a variety of feelings words have been used to describe emotions on that continuum. Pick from the following emotional expressions commonly thought of as being in the anxiety family or come up with your own words. Then list 5 of them on the continuum below with "1" being the least anxious and "5" being the most intense anxiety.

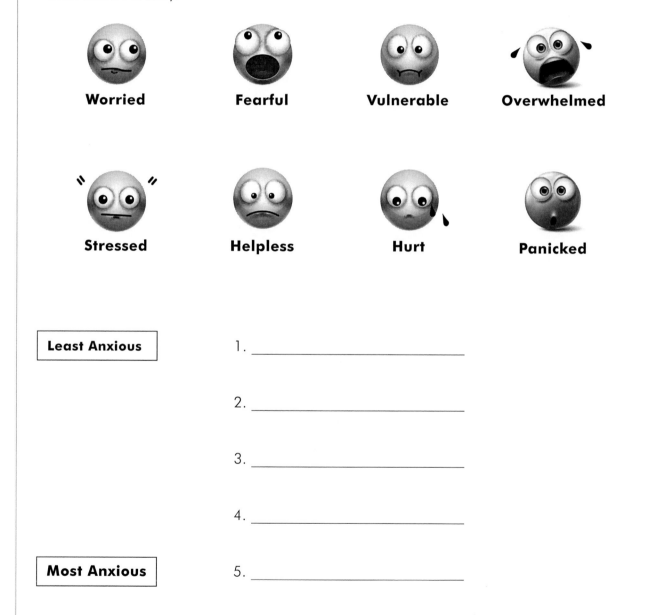

Worried   **Fearful**   **Vulnerable**   **Overwhelmed**

Stressed   **Helpless**   **Hurt**   **Panicked**

Least Anxious	1. _____
	2. _____
	3. _____
	4. _____
Most Anxious	5. _____

■

TOOL 6.3: IDENTIFICATION OF ANXIETY ENHANCING THOUGHTS

The following questions are designed to help you identify your distorted thoughts specifically related to anxiety. Remember, these thoughts will often be related to negative predictions or assumptions.

When _____ happens, and I feel _____,
                  (Trigger)   (Emotion)

what kinds of things am I often telling myself?

If I were in a cartoon, what would the bubble above my head be saying?

_____

_____

If there were a tape recorder in my head recording my every thought, what would it be saying when someone pushed "play"?

_____

_____

Example

I felt...	Because I thought...
Anxious	She will probably say no.
Worried	I'm afraid she may wreck my car. She's never driven a standard shift before.
Panic	The last time I was alone with a man, he abused me. I am in grave danger again.

THOUGHTS/FEELINGS AWARENESS LOG

I Felt ...	Because I Thought...

TOOL 6.4: UNHEALTHY "GO-TO" COPING SKILLS

You may have heard the term "fight or flight." Autopilot coping skills for anxiety often involve "flight" or other avoidant behaviors. But they don't have to. Here is the place to identify what you do when you feel anxious that has not worked for you.

Some "autopilot" behaviors I have engaged in when anxious are:

1. _____

2. _____

3. _____

4. _____

5. _____

6. _____

7. _____

8. _____

9. _____

10. _____

TOOL 6.5: AWARENESS OF CONSEQUENCES

As Tool 6.4 touched on, things that worked in the past don't always work in the present, and things that work in the short term don't always work in the long term. In attempt to increase your awareness, try to identify some of the consequences of your unsuccessful attempts to cope with anxiety.

Example

Autopilot Coping Skill (from Tool 6.4)	Current or Past Negative Consequences
"Chickened out" of interview	I lost out on potentially good job, have trouble paying bills now.
Didn't go out on a date with Jerry	Missed out on a good guy. Now I have to watch Jennifer date him.
Didn't check mail for 2 months	My paycheck is being garnished.

My Awareness of Consequences Log

Autopilot Coping Skill	Current or Past Negative Consequences

TOOL 6.6: CBT CHAIN ANALYSIS

Here is where the rubber meets the road. This is where you get to put it all together. Now that you have mastered the skills covered in the previous tools, identify a specific situation/trigger in your life for your feelings of anxiety. See if you can identify specific thoughts that you had, feelings you experienced, choices you made, and consequences of those choices.

Use the following tool to help you follow the sequence to analyze your response in a particular episode. Also, when you identify your feelings, rate them on a scale of 0–10 with zero being "none" and 10 being "extreme intensity". For instance, if you identify "fear" and it was as scared as you have ever felt, your entry would look like: "Fearful—10."

Once you have done enough of these, you will be able to identify patterns, which can facilitate powerful insights for recovery.

Anxiety Chain Analysis

Event (Trigger)	Anxiety-Producing Thoughts	Anxious Feelings and Intensity	Coping Skills	Results

TOOL 6.7: DESIRED RESULTS

This one is pretty simple. When you look at the undesired consequences of choices in your life in response to anxiety, what are some alternative outcomes you would have liked to have had? What desired results do you have for your future?

Results I would like to create in my future in similar situations:

1. _____

2. _____

3. _____

4. _____

5. _____

TOOL 6.8: NEW ANXIETY COPING SKILLS

Now that you know how you would like situations to end in response to a given trigger, how might you need to change your behavior to create your desired result? This tool offers you an opportunity to brainstorm alternative coping skills you can employ in your battle against anxiety.

When I am experiencing feelings of anxiety, skills that have worked or might work for me include:

1. _____

2. _____

3. _____

4. _____

5. _____

6. _____

7. _____

8. _____

9. _____

10. _____

Challenging anxiety-enhancing thoughts doesn't always make them go away, but it can put up enough of a "fight" that the feelings aren't quite so intense and make it easier for you to confront urges to avoid your fears and use coping skills instead. Use this tool to attempt to challenge or generate some more *rational responses* to your fortune-telling or magnification types of thoughts.

Anxiety Thought Log: Example

Negative Predicting Thought	Rational Response
She will probably say no.	I won't know until I ask. Even though it's been 2 years since I asked a girl out, the last one said yes. If she says no, I'll be right where I am now. I have nothing to lose.
I'm afraid she may wreck my car. She's never driven a standard shift before.	I have to let her try if she's ever going to learn. The car is insured. She's only going six blocks and will be driving slowly, so even if she struggles it is highly likely she'll be fine.
The last time I was alone with a man, he abused me. I am in grave danger again.	Most men aren't abusive. I've been with him often in groups, and he seems gentle. Even though I am alone with him, I am in the theatre, so I'm really not alone. He has been nothing but nice to me. If I'm going to start dating again I have to start somewhere, and he seems like the safest bet I've encountered in a long time.

MY ANXIETY THOUGHT LOG

Negative Predicting Thoughts	Rational Responses

TOOL 6.10: REEXAMINING ANXIOUS FEELINGS

Now that you have attempted to challenge your thoughts, reflect for a few minutes on your feelings. Ask yourself if the feelings have changed? If so, how much has the intensity changed before versus after the new thinking. Are you feeling any completely new feelings? Which new thoughts seem to have the most effect on your feelings? The least? Use this tool to examine the differences and then record your observations.

Automatic Thoughts	Initial Feelings	Intensity

Rational Responses	Current Feelings	Intensity

My Observations:

_____

_____

_____

_____

TOOL 6.11: CHAIN ANALYSIS WITH RATIONAL RESPONSES

Use the chain analysis tool below with your rational responses to see the impact that your new thinking had on your feelings. Be sure to rate the intensity of the new feelings. For instance, you may still be experiencing anxiety, but recognize that if after your initial automatic thoughts your anxiety was a "10," and after your rational responses your anxiety was a "6," that means the new thinking made an impact. Scaling your feelings can help you not make the mistake of black-and-white thinking by saying "I was scared then and I am scared now—this didn't do anything." See how changed thinking, feeling, and behavior affected current results and could affect future results.

Event	Automatic Thoughts	Feelings	Actions	Results
	Rational Responses	**New Feelings**	**New Actions**	**New Results**

TOOL 6.12: DOWNWARD ARROW TO IDENTIFY CORE BELIEFS

As a refresher, *core beliefs* are deeply ingrained beliefs that serve as filters through which we process information. All of our distorted thinking is the product of one or more harmful beliefs. This technique asks us to take a thought and continue to ask, "What would that mean about me if it were true?" until we get at the core belief at the bottom of the distorted thought. If necessary, review the chapter to note beliefs that often contribute to stress. Also, remember that many people need a clinician's help to assist with this for a period of time. Note the example below and then try one on your own using one of your own automatic thoughts.

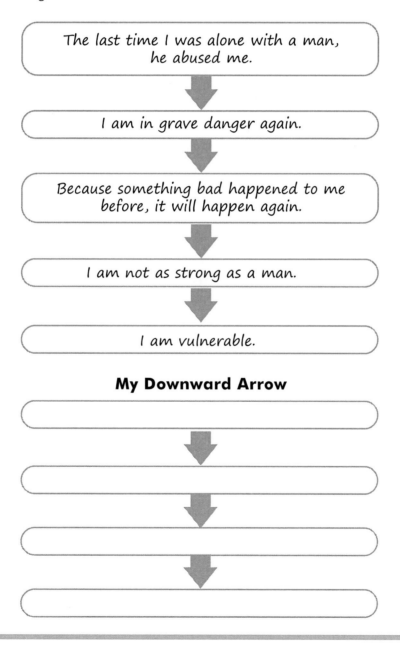

The last time I was alone with a man, he abused me.

I am in grave danger again.

Because something bad happened to me before, it will happen again.

I am not as strong as a man.

I am vulnerable.

My Downward Arrow

TOOL 6.13: IDENTIFYING ALTERNATIVE HEALTHY BELIEFS

Remember, beliefs come in pairs. I teach in my workshops and conferences that it is kind of like a sheet of paper. It inherently has a front and a back side. For each unhealthy belief you identified, you also have an alternate opposite belief. This tool asks you to formulate in your own words what you would want your opposite belief to be. Then use percentages to rate how much you believe your core belief versus how much you believe your alternate belief. These will be used in a later tool to subjectively measure your belief change as you move forward in your recovery.

Example

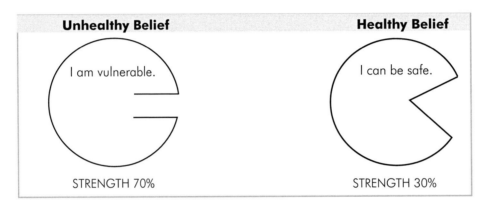

Rating the Strength of My Beliefs

Identifying Components of the Beliefs

Now that you have identified at least one unhealthy belief and an alternate, healthier belief, the next step is to identify what are called the components of the beliefs. To identify the components of the unhealthy belief, it can be a helpful exercise to look back in time to see where these beliefs came from in the first place. To work on changing a belief moving forward, it is necessary to identify how you define the alternate belief *today*.

Beliefs are formulated by the meaning we assign to events or experiences in life. These experiences then become "evidence" to support our beliefs. "Evidence" is in quotation marks because some people count "data" as "evidence" that others do not. It is understandable that those who live through different types of life experiences are more likely to develop different beliefs. Although every person's life experiences are in some ways unique, another phenomenon practitioners encounter is that some clients have strikingly similar backgrounds but develop different types of beliefs. The explanation is that even though the experiences themselves may have been similar, the meaning assigned to them may have been quite different.

Leslie Sokol with the Academy of Cognitive Therapy shares a visual for a belief that compares it to a table. In the same way that a tabletop needs legs to support it, beliefs need similar supporting structures. Experiences in life serve as "evidence" to support these beliefs, based on the meaning that is attributed to them. So in this tool, the "legs of the table" represent evidence one internalizes to support a belief.

This visual can be used in a variety of ways. When working to analyze how you may have acquired an unhealthy belief (such as you identified in your downward arrow) this involves *looking back at past experiences* in life to examine the conclusions you came to in formulating the beliefs you currently hold. Then a different exercise will help you look at the alternate beliefs you are attempting to construct so you know what to look for as you are examining evidence moving *forward* in life.

Because different people can assign different meaning to strikingly similar events, it is not uncommon for two different clients who are looking back at historical evidence that led to the development of a belief that they are "Vulnerable," to identify very different types of experiences or interpretations that led them to the same conclusion about themselves.

Similarly, if the same two people were working to construct alternate beliefs moving forward that they "Can be Safe," they might be "counting" very different types of things as well.

Thus, it is important when doing these exercises to be honest about what your "legs of the table" really are. Not what your parents thought it meant. Not what your faith community or your friends tell you something means. But how you really define meaning. Failing to identify what "counts" *for you* will lead to you logging evidence that makes no difference in your beliefs and ultimately the mood state you are trying to change.

TOOL 6.14(A): ANALYSIS OF COMPONENTS OF UNHEALTHY BELIEF

Start by looking back in time. Use the table visual to identify the components of your beliefs; that is experiences that you went through that were important in contributing to an unhealthy belief you identified when doing the downward arrow. These will help you know specifically what types of experiences will be necessary to create or expose yourself to when modifying your beliefs going forward.

The following questions may be helpful in reflecting on different periods of time in your life to uncover some of the experiences you counted as evidence to support your unhealthy belief as it was being developed. You may need assistance from your clinician to get the most out of this tool.

The first time I ever remember feeling _____ **[belief] was** _____

The people in my life who influenced me to feel that way were:

Family members _____

_____

Friends/Peers _____

_____

Other significant people _____

_____

Experiences during my elementary school years _____

_____

Experiences during my junior high years _____

_____

Experiences during my high school years _____

_____

Experiences during my college/young adult years _____

_____

Significant experiences since then _____

_____

Legs of Table

Fill in the unhealthy belief you are analyzing in the tabletop portion of the structure. Use the exercise in tool 6.14 to insert some of the "evidence" from your past that you have "counted" to support each belief in the legs below. "I am vulnerable" is a common belief with anxiety, so it will be used in this example. Consider the example and then use the blank table provided to identify your components of your own unhealthy belief.

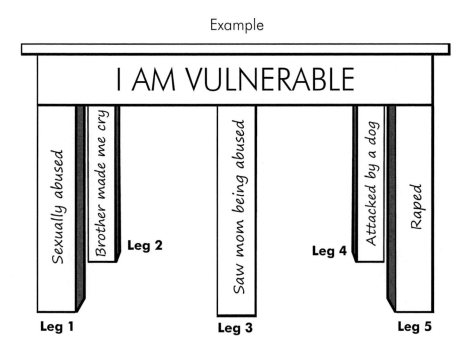

Example

Evidence that I am Vulnerable

Leg 1: Cousin sexually abused me at age 8

Leg 2: Bother would pin me down when I was little and held a frog in my face until I cried

Leg 3: Witnessed my mom being physically abused by boyfriend

Leg 4: Was attacked by a dog as a teenager—was badly hurt and had to be hospitalized

Leg 5: Raped 3 years ago by a man in my support group

MY TABLE WITH COMPONENTS OF BELIEF

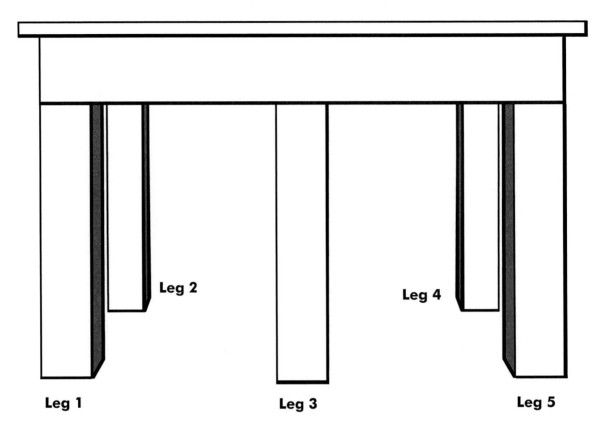

Leg 2

Leg 4

Leg 1　　**Leg 3**　　**Leg 5**

Evidence that supports my unhealthy belief:

Leg 1:

Leg 2:

Leg 3:

Leg 4:

Leg 5:

TOOL 6.14(B): ANALYSIS OF COMPONENTS OF HEALTHY BELIEF

Now that you have identified some of the experiences you assigned meaning to that contributed to formulating your unhealthy belief, take a few moments to consider what evidence might look like to support the alternate healthy belief. For instance, what might you be doing, saying, or being if you "felt safe?" What might others be doing, saying, or being? Consider the following example and then use the blank table provided to identify your own components of your healthy belief.

Example

Evidence That supports healthy belief

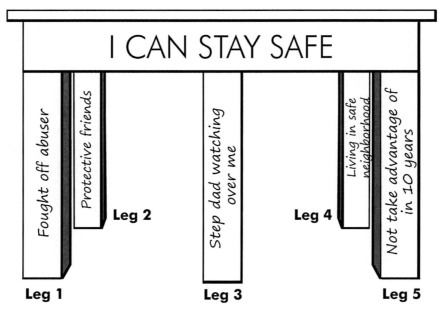

Evidence That I Can be Safe

Leg 1: When I was 14, I fought off a potential abuser

Leg 2: Many friends who helped protect me

Leg 3: My third step dad did watch over me

Leg 4: Now live in a safe neighborhood

Leg 5: I have not been taken advantage of in any way in 10 years

MY TABLE WITH COMPONENTS OF BELIEF

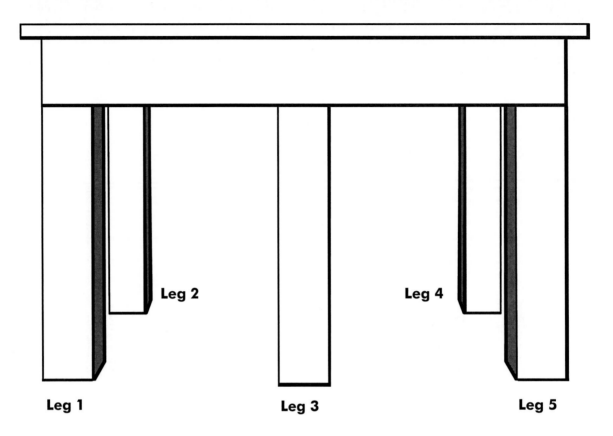

Leg 2

Leg 4

Leg 1

Leg 3

Leg 5

Components of My Healthy Belief:

Leg 1:

Leg 2:

Leg 3:

Leg 4:

Leg 5:

TOOL 6.15: ONGOING EVIDENCE LOGS

Evidence logs can be helpful in a number of ways, including increasing our awareness, as well as strengthening our alternate beliefs. Again, *what* we log tells us a lot about how we assign meaning.

However, now that you have identified your "legs of the table" for the healthy belief you are working on, you know specifically what to look for. Purposefully pay attention to experiences that support the healthy belief you are constructing. This may involve noticing evidence that was always there but you didn't notice before due to your old belief filtering your thinking away from it. You may also work with your clinician on exercises that actually create new evidence that wasn't there before. Purposefully paying attention does not mean making up evidence. If the evidence legitimately isn't there, it doesn't count. Just remember that because of your filter you will be prone to discounting things that really do support the belief, so having an open mind is vital.

Consider the example below, and then begin your own evidence log.

Date	Evidence
9/10	Spend 2 hours in a crowded mall—felt claustrophobic, but nothing happened
9/16	Stayed out past midnight—was with safe people and was fine
9/20	Went to a little bit dangerous part of town. Had people with me and made good choices so I didn't have to miss the theme park like last time
9/23	Went on a date. Fred treated me well

Evidence that I can be _____ (healthy belief) log

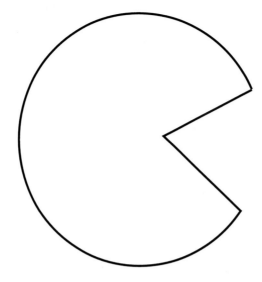

Date	Evidence

Additional Tools

Unhealthy anxiety is developed and perpetuated by believing something is more threatening than it really is and by minimizing our ability to cope with that perceived or actual threat. Many people who struggle with anxiety have experienced actual danger in their lives. Many have been hurt physically or emotionally. But not all people who have been hurt struggle with anxiety. Anxiety persists when we continue to view threats as currently present even when in reality, they may not be present at all or presently exist but to a much lesser degree than we perceive. You may note that I used the term "unhealthy anxiety." At times when we really are in danger and our thoughts start telling us we are at risk and we experience anxiety, it might be considered healthy. Although even in times when fear *is* warranted or completely understandable, it doesn't necessarily mean it is *helpful*.

If we were to put anxiety into a formula, it would look like this:

Anxiety = Risk / Resources

CBT does not try to convince you that you will be fine. CBT helps you evaluate (1) to what degree, if at all, the risks are real and present, and (2) what resources you have that can help you handle the risk. Anxiety often results from a distorted *appraisal of risk*, usually in the form of fortune-telling and magnification, two of the cognitive distortions discussed previously.

Resources come in two forms: *internal resources* and *external resources*. *Internal resources* are qualities you have within yourself that at least in part equip you to deal with the particular fear. Examples include personal strengths, areas of giftedness, personality traits, religious faith or beliefs, and coping skills. *External resources* are entities outside yourself that you can access that may also strengthen your ability to cope with the current real or perceived danger. Examples include family involvement, community resources, and educational information.

Tool 6.16 is devoted to the resources part of the formula.

TOOL 6.16: ANXIETY RESOURCES

Use the following tool to help identify both internal and external resources you have at your disposal that could be harnessed to help with a specific fear. Note that different types of resources may be more relevant and potentially helpful for different fears, it is beneficial to use this tool for each fear you choose to face.

Fear	Internal Resources	External Resources

TOOL 6.17: FEAR HIERARCHY

When dealing with phobias, and really most fears in general, it is important to develop a hierarchy. Usually your practitioner will want to work from your least threatening fear to your most threatening fear. Identify your fears below, rating them from least dreaded to most dreaded.

1. _____

2. _____

3. _____

4. _____

5. _____

TOOL 6.18: ELIMINATE YOUR SAFETY NET!

Avoidant behaviors are the most common type of behaviors used by individuals who struggle with anxiety. It is common for people to cope by using what are called *safety behaviors*.

Safety behaviors are any behaviors that decrease anxiety in the short term, (so the person feels "safe") but in actuality make the anxiety worse in the long term. There is a good chance that some of the "autopilot" coping skills you identified in Tool 6.4 may fit into this category.

One of the most important steps for overcoming anxiety is identifying and eliminating safety behaviors. Many say, "If I give up my safety net, I'll become more anxious." Why would a chapter devoted to helping alleviate anxiety ask you to do stop doing things that make you less anxious? The only way to truly help your anxiety get better in the long run is to retrain your brain to recognize that many of the things you once thought were dangerous are not and that you are generally safer than you previously believed—or that the actual threat isn't nearly as great as you previously thought. The reality is that 90 percent of the things we worry about never happen. Safety behaviors block the brain from learning this crucial lesson.

Most people are not aware that safety behaviors are harmful, and many do not even recognize they are doing them. Therefore, identifying your safety behaviors is an important first step. Take a few minutes and consider behaviors you may be doing that help you feel less anxious initially but that may be keeping you from being able to test and change your fear-based beliefs.

- Having a drink before going to a party to "loosen up"
- Getting multiple "second opinions" to be certain you aren't sick
- Taking the stairs instead of the elevator
- Checking a door multiple times before leaving the house
- Driving instead of flying
- Flying with an "emotional support animal" to keep anxiety down
- Taking the long way home to avoid a certain part of town
- Doing your shopping at 3 a.m. so you will have the store to yourself
- Changing the subject when an uncomfortable subject arises
- Regularly calling your children to make sure they are ok
- Pulse checking or other body scans to ensure you are medically ok
- Carrying extra medications "just in case"
- Changing the channel if a song comes on the radio that reminds you of something unpleasant

Dr. Martin Antony is an Academy of Cognitive Therapy colleague of mine who wrote an excellent book called *The Anti-Anxiety Handbook* (2008) that identifies common safety behaviors present in specific anxiety disorders. This book is certainly worth a consult if you are treating anxiety disorders.

SAFETY BEHAVIORS

Use the chart to identify safety behaviors associated with specific fears you have.

Fear	Safety Behaviors
	1. 2. 3.
	1. 2. 3.
	1. 2. 3.
	1. 2. 3.

TOOL 6.19: FACE YOUR FEARS

Now that you have listed some fears to work on and have identified safety behaviors you engage in, it is time to face your fears! Use this tool to brainstorm some action steps you could take specific to the fear you're working on. This log serves as a map for doing this work and allows for you to identify facing fear behaviors for several areas of anxiety. Fill in your fear and safety behaviors from Tool 6.18 and think of specific ways you could face those fears. The next tool will help facilitate your work as you face one fear at a time.

Fear	Safety Behavior	Facing Fear Action Steps

TOOL 6.20: BECOME A SCIENTIST—CONDUCT AN EXPERIMENT!

Cognitive restructuring refers to changing the content of one's thinking. Challenging thoughts with logic, considering alternative explanations, perspective taking, and examining the evidence are among the techniques used in cognitive restructuring. Behavioral experiments serve as one method for producing evidence to examine and are considered to be a key component of CBT, particularly when working with anxiety. Again, you will rarely hear a true CBT therapist say "just try to stay positive!" CBT is not about being positive. It is about being realistic.

So how do we find out if our fears are realistic or not? We test them. And if we are truly open-minded, we make every attempt to examine the results objectively. Data from the experiment can help us modify our beliefs according to the evidence.

Use the following tool to log the belief you are testing, how much (0–100) you believe it before the experiment, the type of test you do, the evidence gathered, and your belief immediately after the test. Beliefs fluctuate over time. Your "believability" rating may not be the same one hour after the experiment. That is fine. It is important that you record the believability in the moment. With additional time and work, cognitive fortification will eventually help make your beliefs more entrenched, and the ratings will not fluctuate as much. See the following example and then try your own experiment.

Behavioral Experiment Exposure Tool—Example

Date	Belief	Pre-Test (%)	Test	Result	Post-Test (%)
6/13	Bridge will collapse if I go over it	95	Visualize driving over bridge	Made it safely, bridge didn't collapse	90
6/15		90	Watch other cars drive over bridge	55 cars crossed safely in one hour, none fell through	80
6/17		80	Drove over bridge myself first time	Made it safely, bridge didn't collapse	60

MY BEHAVIORAL EXPERIMENT EXPOSURE TOOL

Date	Belief	Pre-Test (%)	Test	Result	Post-Test (%)

TOOL 6.21: TOLERATING UNCERTAINTY

One surefire way to stay anxious is to continue to insist on knowing things *for sure*. The reality is that few things in this life are certain, and when it comes to the future, we can guarantee virtually nothing! Regardless, millions of people drive themselves crazy with thoughts like these:

- *"I must know."*
- *"How could it be?"*
- *"I just can't go on until I know why."*
- *"I have to have an answer."*
- *"I just need to know for sure."*

Many people prone to worry think the same thoughts over and over and over. Some professionals may use a fancy term, "ruminate." I had a patient who said, "I used to be like a cow chewing his cud." Another patient who lived on a farm said, "I'm kind of like that pig who 'wallows' in the mud." Animal comparisons aside, the better we can get at *tolerating uncertainty*, the less anxious we will feel.

My friend and colleague Reid Wilson likes to tell his clients to "want it", as in, wanting what they fear. This sounds counterintuitive. I have had clients say, "Do you know how ridiculous you sound asking me to *want* the very thing that I am in here because I fear?" But an interesting cognitive shift occurs we when change our thinking in that way. When we stop fighting, it often subsides. So, *want* anxiety, welcome trials, and eagerly anticipate time of uncertainty as opportunities for growth. As you face your fears, conduct experiments and eliminate your safety behaviors. Do your best to practice tolerating (and eventually learning to be completely content in) uncertainty.

Peruse the following skills for tolerating uncertainty. Then list some you will try.

- Practice acceptance
- Examine the pros and cons of worry
- List things you have endured in life that were worse than uncertainty
- Pray/meditate
- Improve the moment
- Do perspective exercises
- Do a Google search on "suffer"/" suffering" and then rate your discomfort
- Look for meaning in uncertainty

Rational responses that are helpful for tolerating uncertainty include:

- Asking *"Is there anything I can do?"*—If so, do it! If not, let it go."
- *"Worrying will only hurt."*
- *"Let go and let God."*
- *"Someday I may know, but it's ok not to know now."*
- *"I don't have to know."*
- *"The more uncomfortable I feel, the faster I am growing."*
- *"Uncertainty is uncomfortable, but it's not intolerable"*
- *"It is worth it to beat this."*

MY SKILLS FOR TOLERATING UNCERTAINTY

1. _____

2. _____

3. _____

4. _____

5. _____

TOOL 6.22: OVERCOMING PANIC

Panic attacks and certainly full-blown panic disorder can present challenges above and beyond simple stress. While complete treatment of panic is certainly outside the scope of this book, I wanted to address it briefly and provide one tool for working with it.

A primary difference with the panic symptom set lies with the trigger. Unlike most anxiety, with panic the trigger may or may not be environmental. Anxiety has many physiological symptoms associated with it. People who struggle with panic misinterpret those bodily symptoms, leading to a full-blown panic attack. Thus, treatment of panic requires identifying and challenging the distorted thoughts about the symptoms.

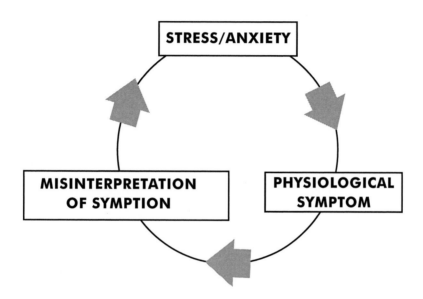

Use the tool below to identify the physiological symptoms you experience when you get-anxious, explore what you interpret them to mean, and generate some alternative explanations. See the example and then try one for yourself.

Physiological Symptom	What I Think It Means	What else It Could Mean
Racing Heart	"I am having a heart attack—I am going to die."	"I am just a little nervous." "I just drank three Red Bulls—I have a lot of caffeine in my system." "A lot of people have a racing pulse. It almost never means they have a heart problem or that they are in danger."

YOUR PANIC TOOL

Physiological Symptom	What I Think It Means	What Else It Could Mean

TOOL 6.23: NIGHTMARE RESCRIPT

Nightmares are essentially stories we tell ourselves during our sleep about past life events, and they can cause significant distress for many people. Sometimes either changing the content of our nightmares or the meaning associated with the nightmare can curb recurring nightmares. This tool can be helpful for many people suffering from recurring nightmares.

Write out your recurring nightmare. If it is too long, write out the most troubling aspect of the nightmare.

_____

_____

How did you feel emotionally?

_____

_____

What bodily sensations did you notice?

_____

_____

How would you like to feel instead?

_____

_____

How would your dream/nightmare have to change for you to feel those feelings? Rewrite your nightmare with this alternative ending.

_____

_____

_____

TOOL 6.24: BEHAVIORAL COPING CARDS

Coping cards can be an invaluable resource to have on hand to use "in the heat of the moment," when you get *emotionally flooded* (with anxiety or other emotions). Since rational thoughts are difficult to access when we're upset, the idea of the coping card is to do the rational thinking ahead of time. That way, when you are emotionally distressed, you will have a ready-made cue card spelling out what to do in that moment. Consult the following example and then fill one out for yourself.

When I feel anxious and am tempted to (safety behavior or other behavior from Tool 6.4)

_____, I can _____

The next time I feel anxious in a meeting and am tempted to make up an excuse to go hide in my office, instead I will:

1. Take a deep breath and count to five.

2. Remind myself I belong there as much as anyone in that room.

3. Accept that I am uncomfortable but that tolerating my feelings is necessary for achieving my goals.

My Coping Card

_____

_____

_____

_____

_____

_____

TOOL 6.25: COGNITIVE CUE CARDS

Unlike coping cards, cue cards do not ask you to write down any behaviors. They are more about your mindset. These should pick out a rational response you used (in Tool 6.9) in a given situation that resonated with you. Even better yet, make an attempt to take a swipe at one of those "legs of the table" (Tool 6.14) by trying to reassign meaning at a deeper level. Use the format in the example that is provided. Then complete your own. Again, after practicing here, use an actual 3x5 card and place it strategically for your benefit.

Just because I felt vulnerable doesn't mean I was in danger. I was in danger when I was with Ron, but Kennon is nothing like him. I now know how to pick healthier guys and am much more equipped to expose myself in small ways. Some vulnerability is necessary for genuine connection, and I do want a meaningful relationship this time.

My Cue Card

CHAPTER **7**

Anger

Common Beliefs
- Powerless (diminished)
- Others are incompetent
- Entitlement
- Punitive

Common Distortions
- Should statements (others)
- Personalization
- Rationalization

Common Automatic Thoughts
- "He should do what I ask!"
- "She shouldn't do that!"
- "It isn't right!"
- "How dare they disrespect me!"
- "It's ok to yell/scream/hit because he deserved it."

Common Feelings
- Mad
- Irritated
- Frustrated
- Annoyed
- Enraged

Common Behaviors
- Yelling
- Screaming
- Using profanity
- Destruction of property
- Verbal, physical abuse

TOOL 7.1: IDENTIFICATION OF TRIGGERS

Anger has both biological and environmental components. Some people seem to be hardwired to have a higher baseline level of arousal than others. We also know that a number of environmental risk factors can predispose people to angry emotions.

Perhaps more than with any other condition, identifying triggers is an important first step when dealing with anger. Even if you seem to be predisposed to a higher baseline of arousal, identifying triggers can help you cope with anger when it does come. Answer the following questions to give you a window into your triggers for anger.

To me, anger feels like (include emotions and physiological/bodily symptoms):

_____

_____

I feel anger the strongest when:

_____

_____

The last time I remember feeling this way was:

_____

_____

Themes related to my anger include:

_____

_____

Some things I have observed that happen right before I feel angry are:

_____

_____

My Anxiety Triggers

1. _____

2. _____

3. _____

4. _____

5. _____

TOOL 7.2: IDENTIFICATION OF ANGER FEELINGS

Emotions have been described by some in terms of being in discrete "feeling families" based on different types of emotional states humans experience. Anger is an emotion that is difficult for some to express. Some people grew up in families where anger was associated with fear. Many people have internalized ideas such as, "anger is always bad" or, "anger always leads to violence." For others, anger is the only emotion they know—or at least the only emotion that is acceptable to express. It is common for people who grew up in families where sharing emotions was a sign of weakness to have developed that "tough guy" or "tough girl" front. For these individuals, expressing other emotions is a sign of vulnerability they aren't willing to reveal. Anger takes many forms and can be felt or experienced to varying degrees. Anger is a normal human emotion. Everyone feels it in some form and to some degree. Pick from the following emotional expressions commonly thought of as being in the anger "family" or come up with your own words. Then list five of them on the continuum below with "1" being the least angry and "5" being the most angry.

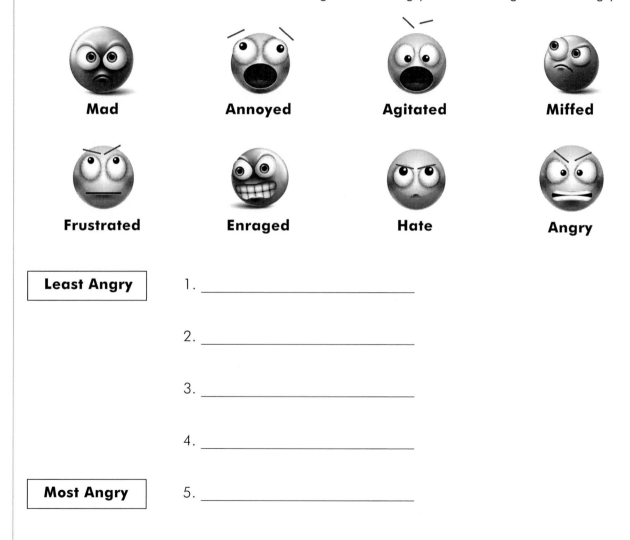

Mad	**Annoyed**	**Agitated**	**Miffed**
Frustrated	**Enraged**	**Hate**	**Angry**

Least Angry	1. _____
	2. _____
	3. _____
	4. _____
Most Angry	5. _____

TOOL 7.3: IDENTIFICATION OF ANGER-RELATED THOUGHTS

The following questions are designed to help you identify your distorted thoughts related to anger. Remember, these thoughts will often contain "shoulds" of some kind.

When _____ happens, and I feel _____.
　　　　　　(Trigger)　　　　　　　　　　　　　　　　　　　　(Emotion)

What kinds of things am I often telling myself?

_____

_____

If I were in a cartoon, what would the bubble above my head be saying?

_____

_____

If there were a recorder in my head recording my every thought, what would it be saying when someone pushed "play?"

_____

_____

Consult the example, and then use the following tool to log the thoughts you identify to be going along with your anger-related feelings.

_____

_____

Thoughts/Feelings Awareness Log - Example

I felt...	Because I thought...
Annoyed	He should turn off his cell phone during the flight like everyone else.
Irritated	She shouldn't have lied to me. They went to the movie and didn't invite me.
Furious	She shouldn't yell at her child.

THOUGHTS/FEELINGS AWARENESS LOG

I Felt ...	Because I Thought...

TOOL 7.4: UNHEALTHY "GO-TO" COPING SKILLS

People typically cope with anger in one of two ways: *internalizing* or *externalizing*. *Internalizing* refers to when people "stuff" their anger, or turn it inward without expressing it. *Externalizing* is when people express anger outwardly, such as lashing out, yelling, destroying property, or harming someone.

Spend a few minutes reflecting on your response style by identifying your "go-to" coping skills for anger.

Some of my "go-to" coping skills when I am angry are:

1. _____

2. _____

3. _____

4. _____

5. _____

6. _____

7. _____

8. _____

9. _____

10. _____

TOOL 7.5: AWARENESS OF CONSEQUENCES

As Tool 7.4 touched on, things that worked in the past don't always work in the present, and things that work in the short term don't always work in the long term. In an attempt to increase your awareness, try to identify some of the consequences of your past unsuccessful attempts to cope with anger. Anger is perhaps the emotion that, when acted on inappropriately, can create the most significant long-term consequences. In an attempt to increase your awareness, consider some of the ways your acting on anger has hurt you in the past. Consult the example and then try your own. Enlisting the help of a support team member is often beneficial in completing this exercise.

Autopilot Coping Skill	Current or Past Negative Consequences
Yelled at girlfriend	Got dumped again
Snapped at boss	Got written up
Kicked hole in wall	Had to pay for repair, didn't have money to go out that Friday

My Awareness of Consequences Log

Autopilot Coping Skill	Current or Past Negative Consequences

TOOL 7.6: CBT CHAIN ANALYSIS

Here is where the rubber meets the road. This is where you get to put it all together. Now that you have mastered the skills covered in the previous tools, identify a specific situation/ trigger in your life for your feelings of anger. See if you can identify specific thoughts that you had, feelings you experienced, choices you made, and consequences of those choices.

Use the following tool to help you analyze your response in a particular episode. When you identify your feelings, rate them on a scale of 0–10 with zero being "none" and 10 being "extreme intensity". For instance, if you identify "irritated" and it was the most irritated you have ever felt, your entry would look like: "Irritated—10."

Once you have done enough of these, you will be able to identify patterns, which can facilitate powerful insight for recovery.

Anger Chain Analysis

Event (Trigger)	Anger-Related Thoughts	Anger Feelings	Coping Skills	Results

TOOL 7.7: DESIRED RESULTS

This one is pretty simple. When you look at the undesired consequences of choices in your life in response to anger, what are some alternative outcomes you would have liked to have had?

Results I would like to create in similar situations:

1. _____

2. _____

3. _____

4. _____

5. _____

TOOL 7.8: NEW ANGER COPING SKILLS

Now that you know how you would like situations to end in response to a given trigger, how might you need to change your behavior to create your desired result? This tool offers you an opportunity to brainstorm alternative coping skills you can employ in your battle against anger.

When I am experiencing feelings of anger, skills that have worked or might work for me include:

1. _____

2. _____

3. _____

4. _____

5. _____

6. _____

7. _____

8. _____

9. _____

10. _____

TOOL 7.9: CHALLENGING ANGER-RELATED THOUGHTS

Challenging anger-related thoughts doesn't make them go away, but it can put up enough of a "fight" that the feelings aren't quite so intense, and it can keep them from boiling over. This can make it easier to use your skills and not act in a way that gets you in trouble. Use this tool to challenge or generate some more rational responses to your "shoulds" and other anger-related thoughts.

Anger Thought Log Example

Should Thought	Rational Response
He should turn off his cell phone during the flight like everyone else.	I wish he would, but I can't make him. The plane isn't going to crash because of it. I can be thankful I have an aisle seat.
She shouldn't have lied to me. They really did go to that movie without me!	She did. She lied to me last month too. I heard her lie to her mother yesterday. It's not reasonable for me to expect her to be honest. I know not to become too close a friend with her because I can't trust her. I can see the movie later with people I trust.
She shouldn't yell at her child.	She is yelling. A lot of parents yell at their children. Just because she snapped doesn't mean she's abusive. If I believe she is, I can turn her in, and there are people who are paid to protect children. I have little say over how that child is raised, but much influence on how my daughter gets raised. Maybe I'll go home and give her a hug.

MY ANGER THOUGHT LOG

"Should" Thoughts	Rational Responses

TOOL 7.10: REEXAMINING ANGRY FEELINGS

Now that you have attempted to challenge your thoughts, reflect for a few minutes on your feelings. Ask yourself if the feelings have changed. If so, how much has the intensity changed before versus after the new thinking. Are you feeling any completely new feelings? Which new thoughts seem to have the most effect on your feelings? The least? Use this tool to examine the differences and then record your observations.

Automatic Thoughts	Initial Feelings	Intensity

Rational Responses	Current Feelings	Intensity

My Observations:

_____

_____

_____

_____

_____

TOOL 7.11: CHAIN ANALYSIS WITH RATIONAL RESPONSES

Use the chain analysis tool below with your rational responses to see the impact that your new thinking had on your feelings. Be sure to rate the intensity of the new feelings. For instance, you may still be experiencing some irritation, but recognize that if after your initial automatic thoughts your irritation was a "10," and after your rational responses your agitation was a "6," that means the new thinking made an impact. Scaling your feelings can help you not make the mistake of black-and-white thinking by saying "I was pissed then and I am still pissed now—this didn't do anything." See how changed thinking, feeling, and behavior affected current results and could affect future results.

Event	Automatic Thoughts	Feelings	Actions	Results
	Rational Responses	**New Feelings**	**New Actions**	**New Results**

TOOL 7.12: DOWNWARD ARROW TO IDENTIFY CORE BELIEFS

As a refresher, *core beliefs* are deeply ingrained beliefs that serve as filters through which we process information. All of our distorted thinking is the product of one or more harmful beliefs. This technique asks us to take a thought and continue to ask, "What would that mean about me if it were true?" until we get at the core belief at the bottom of the distorted thought. If necessary, review the chapter to note beliefs that often contribute to stress. Also, remember that many people need a clinician's help to assist with this for a period of time. Note the example below and then try one on your own using one of your own automatic thoughts.

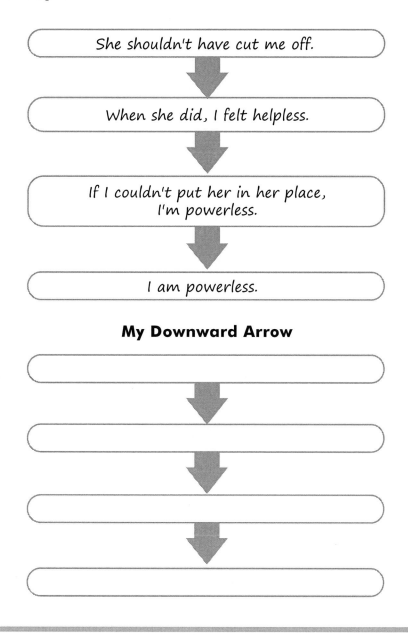

She shouldn't have cut me off.

When she did, I felt helpless.

If I couldn't put her in her place, I'm powerless.

I am powerless.

My Downward Arrow

TOOL 7.13: IDENTIFYING ALTERNATIVE HEALTHY BELIEFS

Remember, beliefs come in pairs. I teach in my workshops and conferences that it is kind of like a sheet of paper. It inherently has a front and a back side. For each unhealthy belief you identified, you also have an alternate opposite belief. This tool asks you to formulate in your own words what you would want your opposite belief to be. Then use percentages to rate how much you believe your core belief versus how much you believe your alternate belief. These will be used in a later tool to subjectively measure your belief change as you move forward in your recovery.

Example

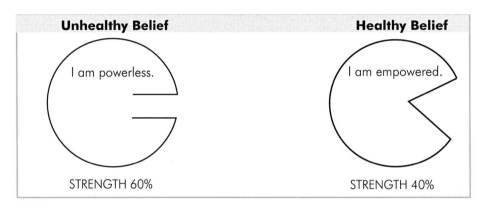

Rating the Strength of My Beliefs

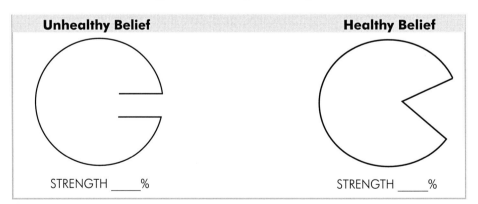

Identifying Components of the Beliefs

Now that you have identified at least one unhealthy belief and an alternate, healthier belief, the next step is to identify what are called the components of the beliefs. To identify the components of the unhealthy belief, it can be a helpful exercise to look back in time to see where these beliefs came from in the first place. To work on changing a belief moving forward, it is necessary to identify how you define the alternate belief *today*.

Beliefs are formulated by the meaning we assign to events or experiences in life. These experiences then become "evidence" to support our beliefs. "Evidence" is in quotation marks because some people count "data" as "evidence" that others do not. It is understandable that those who live through different types of life experiences are more likely to develop different beliefs. Although every person's life experiences are in some ways unique, another phenomenon practitioners encounter is that some clients have strikingly similar backgrounds but develop different types of beliefs. The explanation is that even though the experiences themselves may have been similar, the meaning assigned to them may have been quite different.

Leslie Sokol with the Academy of Cognitive Therapy shares a visual for a belief that compares it to a table. In the same way that a tabletop needs legs to support it, beliefs need similar supporting structures. Experiences in life serve as "evidence" to support these beliefs, based on the meaning that is attributed to them. So in this tool, the "legs of the table" represent evidence one internalizes to support a belief.

This visual can be used in a variety of ways. When working to analyze how you may have acquired an unhealthy belief (such as you identified in your downward arrow) this involves *looking back at past experiences* in life to examine the conclusions you came to in formulating the beliefs you currently hold. Then a different exercise will help you look at the alternate beliefs you are attempting to construct so you know what to look for as you are examining evidence moving *forward* in life.

Because different people can assign different meaning to strikingly similar events, it is not uncommon for two different clients who are looking back to examine historical evidence that led to the development of a belief that they are "powerless," to identify very different types of experiences or interpretations that led them to the same conclusion about themselves.

Similarly, if the same two people were working to construct alternate beliefs moving forward that they are empowered they might be "counting" very different types of things as well.

It is important when doing these exercises to be honest about what your "legs of the table" really are. Not what your parents thought it meant. Not what your faith community or your friends tell you something means. But how you really define meaning. Failing to identify what "counts" *for you* will lead to you logging evidence that makes no difference in your beliefs and ultimately the mood state you are trying to change.

TOOL 7.14(A): ANALYSIS OF COMPONENTS OF UNHEALTHY BELIEF

Start by looking back in time. Use the table visual to identify the components of your beliefs; that is, experiences that you went through that were important in contributing to an unhealthy belief you identified when doing the downward arrow. These will help you know specifically what types of experiences will be necessary to create or expose yourself to when modifying your beliefs going forward.

The following questions may be helpful in reflecting on different periods of time in your life to uncover some of the experiences you counted as evidence to support your unhealthy belief as it was being developed. You may need assistance from your clinician to get the most out of this tool.

The first time I ever remember feeling _____**[belief] was** _____

The people in my life who influenced me to feel that way were:

Family members _____

_____

Friends/Peers _____

_____

Other significant people _____

_____

Experiences during my elementary school years _____

_____

Experiences during my junior high years _____

_____

Experiences during my high school years _____

_____

Experiences during my college/young adult years _____

_____

Significant experiences since then _____

_____

Legs of Table

Use this exercise to insert some of the "evidence" from your past that you have "counted" to support each belief in the legs below. Anger often has to do with an initial experience of feeling diminished or powerless, so it will be used to demonstrate. Consider the example below and then use the blank table on the next page to identify your own components of your own unhealthy belief.

Evidence that I am powerless

I AM POWERLESS

Leg 1: Dad was intimidating
Leg 2: Mom ignored me
Leg 3: Brothers tortured me
Leg 4: Raped at 16
Leg 5: Made fun of at camp

Evidence that I am a powerless:

Leg 1: Dad intimidated everyone in the family and I never had a say

Leg 2: Mom ignored any request I had as a child

Leg 3: When I was young, my brothers would beat me up

Leg 4: Raped at age 16 by someone in juvenile detention

Leg 5: Was humiliated by peers at camp in elementary school

MY TABLE WITH COMPONENTS OF BELIEF

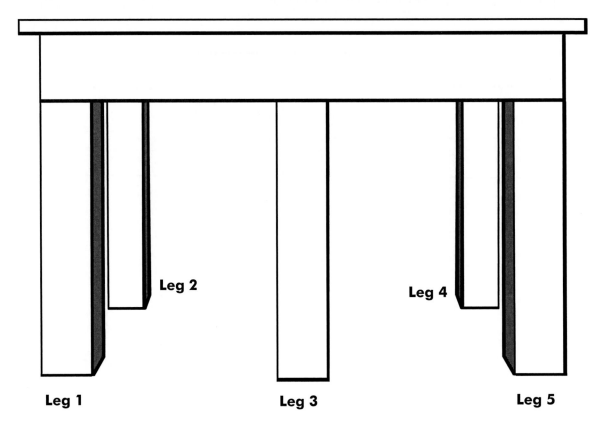

Leg 1   **Leg 2**   **Leg 3**   **Leg 4**   **Leg 5**

Evidence that I am powerless:

Leg 1:

Leg 2:

Leg 3:

Leg 4:

Leg 5:

TOOL 7.14(B): ANALYSIS OF COMPONENTS OF HEALTHY BELIEF

Now that you have identified some of the experiences you assigned meaning to that contributed to formulating your unhealthy belief, take a few moments to consider what evidence might look like to support the alternate healthy belief. For instance, what might you be doing, saying, or being if you felt empowered or did have influence? What might others be doing, saying, or being? Consider the following example and then use the blank table provided to identify your own components of your healthy belief.

Example

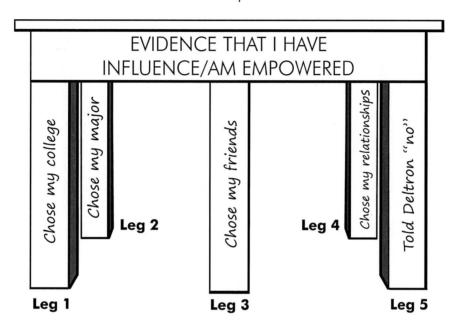

My Table with Components of Belief:

Leg 1: *I chose what college I went to*

Leg 2: *I chose my major*

Leg 3: *I choose my friends*

Leg 4: *I choose who I date*

Leg 5: *I told Deltron "NO" and he is no longer in my life*

MY TABLE WITH COMPONENTS OF BELIEF

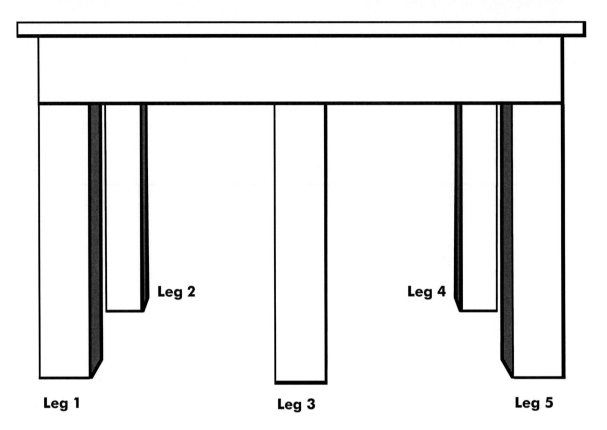

Evidence that supports my healthy belief:

Leg 1:

Leg 2:

Leg 3:

Leg 4:

Leg 5:

TOOL 7.15: ONGOING EVIDENCE LOGS

Evidence logs can be helpful in a number of ways, including increasing our awareness, as well as strengthening our alternate beliefs. Again *what* we log tells us a lot about how we assign meaning.

However, now that you have identified your "legs of the table" for the healthy belief you are working on, you know specifically what to look for. Purposefully pay attention to experiences that support the healthy belief you are constructing. This may involve noticing evidence that was always there but you didn't notice before due to your old belief filtering your thinking away from it. You may also work with your clinician on exercises that actually create new evidence that wasn't there before. Purposefully paying attention to does not mean making up evidence. If the evidence legitimately isn't there, it doesn't count. Just remember that because of your filter you will be prone to discount things that really do support the belief, so having an open mind is vital.

Consider the example below, and then begin your own evidence log.

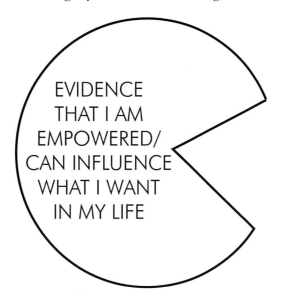

Date	Evidence
6/13	Chose to work out today
6/14	Told friend my preference of movie
6/16	Chose where we ate lunch
6/18	Decided to stay home and not go to the party Jeremy was pressuring me to go to
6/21	Wrote letter protesting animal abuse

Evidence that I can be _____ (healthy belief)

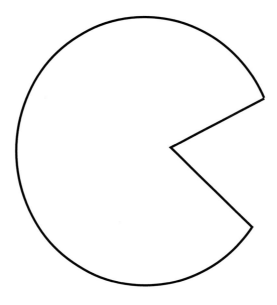

Date	Evidence

TOOL 7.16: VALUES

Anger has everything to do with our values. You may remember that anger is always a product of "should" statements toward others. Whenever we violate our own values, we "should" ourselves and feel guilty. When others violate our values, we "should" them and feel angry. For that reason, it is vital to know what our values are. You may be able to make some connections between your values and your triggers. People value things differently; thus, some triggers that might infuriate one person don't affect others in the slightest. Use the following tool to identify and list your values. Consult the example and then take a few minutes to thoughtfully list your own.

My Values—Example

1. Kindness

2. Honesty

3. Education

4. Caring for the environment

5. Respect for authority

My Values

1. _____

2. _____

3. _____

4. _____

5. _____

Once you have identified your values, you can try to connect your episodes of anger with specific values that have been violated and the "should statement" that resulted from it.

Values Monitor Log-Example

Date	Event	Value Violated	Should Statement
7/13	Kid next to me ignored the flight attendant's instruction to turn off electronic devices	Respect for Authority	"He should turn off his cell phone during the flight like everyone else."
7/10	Friend Joni told me she did not want to go to a movie—then went with my friends without inviting me	Honesty	"She shouldn't have lied to me. They really did go to that movie without me!"
7/13	Saw woman in restaurant yelling at child	Kindness	"She shouldn't yell at her child."

My Values Monitor Log

Date	Event	Value Violated	Should Statement

The final step is to realize that we have zero control over other people's behavior but 100 percent control over our own behavior. Therefore, all we can do is live in ways that support our values. We can then be purposeful about making decisions consistent with those values. Use the following log to monitor your behaviors through the lens of your values.

Example

Date	Value	Behavior
4/21	Kindness	Went out of my way to thank my mother
4/24	Honesty	Said no when a friend offered me test answers so I could cheat with her

Date	Value	Behavior

TOOL 7.17: FORGIVENESS

Many people hear the term *forgiveness* and are immediately turned off. There are probably many reasons for this, but if you have that reaction to it, it is probably a sign that doing some forgiveness work could be beneficial for you. I have often heard people say things like, "Forgiveness—that's spiritual stuff!"

While forgiveness can have spiritual components, it is a vital tool for dealing effectively with anger. *Resentment* (emotional word) and *unforgiveness* (spiritual word) mean essentially the same thing: *anger held onto.* Anger, at any level, that we choose to hold onto fits into this category and contributes to staying unhealthy.

Comprehensively covering this topic is far outside the scope of this tool. However, examining the role of forgiveness in unresolved anger can be a powerful tool in recovery. Most major world religions place an emphasis on forgiveness. Why? Probably because it's good for us! If it is good for us, why do so many people resist it? There are many distorted thoughts associated with an unwillingness to practice forgiveness. Identifying and rationally responding to some of these is the goal of this tool. Consider the example and then try your own.

Forgiveness Thought Log-Example

Distorted Unforgiving Thought	Rational Response
I will not give him the satisfaction of my forgiveness.	Forgiveness is not for them—it is for me. The old adage says, "Unforgiveness is like swallowing a drop of poison every day waiting for the other person to die." I will not continue to give him control over my life now that I have a choice.
Forgiveness is like saying what she did to me is ok.	Forgiveness is not saying that at all. Forgiveness is saying what she did is still as unacceptable as it was the day it happened, but that I am choosing not to hold it against her any longer—for my sake.
Forgive and forget—and since I don't think I can forget, then I must not be able to forgive.	There are some things in life I will never forget. Actually, if I forget, I may not learn from past situations. Just because I will never forget has nothing to do with my ability to forgive.

If I forgive him that means I have to trust him again, and there's no way that's happening.	Forgiveness is about the past. Trust is about the future. I can forgive him but never trust him again. Forgiveness is always healthy for me, regardless of his behavior, but trust is earned. I can forgive and still set whatever boundaries I want with him.
I'm just not ready to forgive—I'll forgive when I feel like it.	Anger comes from shoulds. Forgiving means working to give up my shoulds. So, until I start working on it, I'll never get around to feeling like it. Forgiveness is first granted, then felt.
I'll forgive her when she apologizes to me.	It may be easier if she apologizes, but what if she never does? If I tell myself I will not take steps to better myself until she does—and perhaps she never will—then I'm continuing to give her the power to keep me miserable. I will no longer give her that.
Time heals all wounds. I don't have to do anything—it will just get better with time.	Time can help me think about a situation more objectively, but the reality is I can hold a grudge as long as I want to. If time is all it took, no one would go to their grave angry. If I don't want to be one of those people, I have to actually initiate and participate in the forgiveness process. It takes work, but it will be worth it.

Identify and rationally respond to your own distorted thoughts preventing you from beginning your process of forgiveness.

FORGIVENESS THOUGHT LOG

Distorted Unforgiving Thought	Rational Response

Once you have identified your thoughts that may have kept you from beginning the process of forgiveness, you are ready to start. People practice forgiveness in many ways. Some steps you may want to consider to get you started are as follows.

Possible Forgiveness Steps-Example

1. Journal

2. Meditate

3. Pray

4. Talk to a therapist or trusted friend

5. Talk to clergy

6. Challenge "shoulds" toward person who wronged you

7. Practice acceptance

8. Make an attempt to empathize

9. Participate in religious services

10. Get involved in support group or cause

My Forgiveness Steps

1. _____

2. _____

3. _____

4. _____

5. _____

6. _____

7. _____

8. _____

9. _____

10. _____

TOOL 7.18: ASSERTIVE LETTER WRITING

One tool helpful for venting feelings involves writing an assertive letter. This tool can take several different forms and can be used in a variety of ways. One helpful way of approaching this is to write two letters with different purposes. The first is simply to *vent angry feelings*. This is never intended for the person you are angry at to see. In this letter, be as honest as you can. Use whatever language you need to use. These letters often aren't pretty! Then review the letter with a therapist or friend. Decide if there is value in the other person receiving a version of the letter. If you decide there is, modify the letter with a new intent: *saying what you believe you need to say in a way that you think the person can hear it*. Consult with your therapist regarding which is the best way to proceed in your particular situation. The following is a format that many have found helpful for this type of letter. This is just a guideline. You may omit emotions that do not apply or add emotions or descriptions that are not included. Use language with which you are comfortable.

Dear _____,

Feeling	Assertive Expression
Anger	*"I don't like it when..."* *"I hate it when ..."* *"It frustrates me when ..."* *"It infuriates me when you ...."*
Depression	*"I feel sad when ..."* *"It hurts when ..."* *"I feel lonely because ..."*
Anxiety	*"It scares me when you ..."* *"I am afraid of ..."* *"I worry the most about ..."*
Guilt	*"I'm sorry that ..."* *"I feel like I should have ..."* *"I do regret ..."*
Love	*"I love you because ..."* *"I appreciate that you ..."* *"I understand that ..."* *"I respect you because ..."* *"I need you in my life for ..."*

Sincerely, _____

P.S. What I need from you is _____

TOOL 7.19: SELF-MONITORING

Self-monitoring is an important tool to use in managing anger. Some people go from "0 to 60 in 2 seconds," and others feel anger building gradually. Many people aren't aware of when their anger intensifies, or of behaviors they turn to as a result of feeling angry. The tool of self-monitoring will help you learn to observe your own feelings and behavior more accurately. Observing and recording feelings and behavior helps immediately, as you become more aware of when anger is present and its impact on your actions. Self-monitoring does not come easily, and most people believe they are better at it than they really are.

Self-monitoring takes practice. Perhaps the easiest way to get started is with behaviors you have no desire to change. Some people start with going to the bathroom, brushing their teeth, or getting in their car. Start by observing *frequency* and *duration*; that is, how *often* you do the behavior, and once you do it, how *long* the behavior continues. Some people are painfully aware of behaviors that need modifying, while others have less insight. Also, because anger is experienced on a continuum, some people may often not "count" anger because "it wasn't that bad." Just as when someone trying to lose weight may say, "That bite of cake didn't count because it was just one bite," people dealing with anger may often deny "smaller" manifestations of anger. In doing so, they lose objectivity with regard to observing their anger. One helpful strategy involves enlisting a person whom you trust and frequently spend time with to assist you. Ask him or her to monitor your behavior independent of your monitoring efforts, and at the end of the week, compare the friend's log with yours. If there is a large discrepancy between his or her log and yours, this is a sign you may not be observing your behaviors accurately.

A final tip is to find a way of recording behaviors as they occur. Many people carry a golf counter or use their smartphone or other electronic device that they always carry, so as not to forget to record incidents. Once you get better at observing your behavior, then you can begin observing your anger itself. Review the examples below and try your own on the next page.

Self-Monitoring Log-Example

Date	Behavior	Frequency	Duration
7/2	Temper tantrum	2x	5 min, 2 min

Angry Feelings Monitoring-Example

Date	Event/Trigger	Intensity	Duration
12/3	Boss yelled at me	8	20 min

Self-Monitoring Log

Date	Behavior	Frequency	Duration

Angry Feelings Monitoring

Date	Event/Trigger	Intensity	Duration

TOOL 7.20: SOOTHING STRATEGIES

When an infant is screaming, what most frequently calms him or her down? A warm bottle, a mother's arms, or a cozy blanket. All are attempts to *soothe*. When we are children, it is our parents' job to meet our needs and come up with ways to soothe us. As adults, it is our job to figure out ways to soothe ourselves. And when anger is at its highest, this is often a difficult chore, but this is when it is also most necessary.

Soothing strategies decrease our physiological arousal; they calm us down. Examples might include taking a warm bath, getting a massage, drinking a cup of hot tea, listening to calming music, or burning incense, to name just a few. Many clients who struggle with angry emotions give into the feelings and act out in ways that hurt them or others in their situations because they have not adequately learned to self-soothe when getting "worked up." Spend a few minutes considering behaviors from your coping skills list that might have a soothing or calming effect on you and list your top five favorites. Get help from friends, family, or professionals if needed. Having brainstormed these ahead of time will give you options to use in the heat of the moment and could save you massive consequences down the road.

My Soothing Strategies

1. _____

2. _____

3. _____

4. _____

5. _____

TOOL 7.21: IMPROVE THE MOMENT

For individuals who experience intense and seemingly unbearable angry emotions, an important part of coping effectively at times simply involves "weathering the storm." Some days, the goal is not self-growth but simply survival—and to survive without acting on your anger in ways that hurt yourself or your situation. Marsha Linehan, the founder of Dialectical Behavior Therapy (DBT), wrote on the importance of one's ability to just "get by" and created an acronym to describe several ways to "**IMPROVE** the moment." The acronym (Linehan, 1993) is as follows:

Imagery
Meaning
Prayer
Relaxation
One thing in the moment
Vacation
Encourage

There are obviously many possible applications of each of these. One such relaxation exercise I was taught specifically for anger (that is a little more mindfulness-based) goes like this:

- Pay attention to where in your body you feel your anger.
- Breathe in and out from your diaphragm three times.
- Every time you exhale, visualize your breath exhaling the anger out of your body (some clients visualize the movie *The Green Mile*).
- With every exhale recite:
  - "May I be free from anger."
  - "May I be free from suffering."
  - "May I be at peace."

This type of exercise is not for everyone. Identify strategies you think might be helpful for you in each area, using the **IMPROVE** acronym as a guide.

Imagery _____

_____

Meaning _____

_____

Prayer _____

_____

Relaxation _____

_____

One Thing in the Moment _____

_____

Vacation _____

_____

Encourage Others _____

_____

TOOL 7.22: DISTRACTION

A coping skill can be defined as *any solution one uses in an attempt to solve a problem.* Coping skills fall on a continuum from healthy to unhealthy. Some coping skills are helpful for certain problems but not helpful for other problems. One specific type of coping skill is called a *distraction technique.*

A distraction technique might be defined as any coping skill that requires you to *think.* Examples include counting to 10, calling a friend, reciting the alphabet, listening to music, and watching TV (if you are actually following the lyrics or plot). These skills are based on the principle that you can only think one thought at a time. Your thoughts may be racing or going back and forth between two or more thoughts or swirling through your head like a tornado, but you can only think one thought at a time.

Sometimes people have thoughts that are racing or "swarming" to the point that they *feel* like they are not able to change them. When this is the case, rather than attempt to evaluate them, it can be helpful to simply distract yourself. While this doesn't help restructure or change the content of your thought about the bothersome trigger it can give your mind a break from moments of intensity. Some people view thoughts as the tape that is playing over and over in their heads. Distracting oneself can be similar to "changing the channel" in your mind to help lower the intensity of what you are feeling.

When used on a regular basis, distraction is really just an unhealthy form of avoidance. But when used selectively and strategically, distraction techniques can be a powerful way to help you weather the storm until you can calm yourself down and come back to face the problem more effectively. Consider some coping skills that inherently require thought and assemble a list of distraction techniques.

My Distraction Techniques

1. _____

2. _____

3. _____

4. _____

5. _____

TOOL 7.23: TIME OUT

There is nothing new or original about this tool. In fact, people have probably been using the time-out technique for centuries. It is most commonly associated with modifying children's behavior, but it may be one of the most important strategies for managing anger for adults as well. Failure to use this technique in moments when it would be useful has resulted in hurt feelings, wounded relationships, destruction of property, and prison sentences.

Many people can recognize how this may be helpful in times when they are not "in the moment" but are incapable of using it in times when they really need to. Using this tool requires some degree of mastery of previous tools, including self-monitoring. If we do not realize how angry we are getting or what behaviors our dysfunctional thoughts are tempting us to do, we often don't realize until it's too late that it's time to take a time-out. For this reason, awareness of one's anger style is important.

For instance, if you are a person whose anger builds slowly over time, you probably can afford to postpone taking a time-out longer than others. Conversely, if you are an impulsive person who can go "from 0 to 60" in a matter of seconds, it is probably more important for you to take a time-out, even as early as when you recognize that your anger is a level 1 or 2.

Below are some tips for taking time outs.

Do's

Do remove yourself from the upsetting situation before you act in a way that could create unwanted consequences.

Do stay gone long enough to cool down. In some cases, this may mean an hour. Other circumstances may require staying away for a day or more.

Do use distraction initially. Force yourself to think about something else to help decrease your level of physical arousal so that you can think more clearly. It is important not to tell yourself "Don't think about this," or it is likely you will continue to. Rather, identify other things to think about to consume your thoughts. Examples could include planning a vacation, surfing the internet, counting to 100, or immersing yourself in a movie, football game, or other visual activity that requires your attention.

If you aren't able to concentrate, **do** something physical: Go for a walk, run, bike ride, or garden—anything physical can be helpful.

Once you calm down, **do** try to think rationally how to resolve the situation.

If necessary, **do** consult a friend or person you trust.

Do get validated. Find someone who can validate your feelings and understand where you are coming from and constructively encourage you how to respond.

Don'ts

Don't use alcohol or drugs while in your time-out.

Don't find "yes men" (or "yes women") who will fuel your "shoulds." These people seem to be validating initially but only serve to "add fuel to the fire" and make us angrier at the person we are already angry at—which is not helpful in the long run if we want or need to maintain an ongoing relationship with that person.

Don't use the time-out as an excuse to completely avoid situations that need to be dealt with. The purpose of the time-out is to *temporarily* remove yourself so you can go back and deal with the situation, not to *permanently* avoid it, many people try to avoid dealing with such situations, but this keeps conflict unresolved and allows anger to continue to simmer.

My Takeaways: _____

_____

_____

TOOL 7.24: BEHAVIORAL COPING CARDS

This tool is called a *behavioral coping card*. To use this tool, it is best to identify typical unhealthy coping skills (from Tool 7.4), examine your current circumstances, peruse your healthy new coping skills (Tool 7.8), and pick three of them you could use instead in your current situation. These could come from you time-out skills, soothing strategies, distraction techniques, or anything else you have identified that could be helpful for you. Since these cards are to be used "in the moment," it is best to keep them succinct so as not to overwhelm yourself in a time of emotional upset. Consult the following example, and then fill out one for yourself. The cards below are provided to show you what they look like and give you practice filling them out, but it is best to get some 3x5 cards that you can strategically place where they will benefit you the most (i.e., if your temptation is road rage, put it on the dashboard of your car).

The next time I feel enraged I will:

1. *Get on the treadmill.*

2. *Take a time-out/scream into a pillow.*

3. *Write an angry letter—don't send but take it to my therapist.*

My Coping Card

The next time I feel enraged I will:

1. _____

2. _____

3. _____

TOOL 7.25: COGNITIVE CUE CARDS

This tool is a card with a slightly different purpose. Unlike the coping cards, the cue cards do not ask you to write down any behaviors. They are more about your mindset. For these, pick out a rational response you used in Tool 7.9 in a given situation that resonated with you. Better yet, try to take a swipe at one of those "legs of the table" Tool 7.14 by trying to reassign meaning at a deeper level. Use the format in the example that is provided to then complete your own. Again, after practicing here, use an actual 3x5 card and place it strategically for your benefit.

Just because I got yelled at by my boss doesn't mean I am completely powerless. I have control over many areas of my life. If I take my anger out on someone who doesn't deserve it, I am letting them win. Not retaliating is not a sign of weakness, it is a sign of strength and self-control. That person no longer has the power to piss me off to the point I do stupid things.

My Cue Card

CHAPTER 8

Addictive Behaviors and Bad Habits

Common Beliefs
- Insufficient self-control
- Defectiveness
- Failure

Common Distortions
- Rationalization

Common Automatic Thoughts
- "I have to have it now."
- "I can't wait."
- "I have no self-control."
- "I can't delay gratification."

Common Feelings
- Increased sense of urgency
- Physiological adrenaline rush
- Decreased conviction

Common Behaviors
- Impulsive (unplanned) substance use
- Sexual promiscuity
- Binge or other "emotional eating"
- Reckless driving, spending/shopping sprees
- Other self-harming behaviors

TOOL 8.1: IDENTIFICATION OF TRIGGERS

People engage in "impulsive" and "addictive" behaviors for different reasons. The term "addictive" is in quotation marks because there is still some debate regarding its use. Brain scans differ in some significant ways from people who are addicted to substances, for instance, versus people who suffer from a "gambling addiction." Treatment approaches however are fairly similar. Some motives for engaging in addictive or other impulsive behaviors include: a quick "feel good" response, the need to stay in control, and an attempt to regulate shame-based emotions. Understanding these can sometimes provide insight into triggers. Use the following tool to answer questions that may guide you in identifying some of your triggers.

The last time I acted in an impulsive manner was:

_____

_____

I did it in response to:

_____

_____

Themes of times I have acted impulsively include:

_____

_____

Emotions I feel before engaging in my addictive behaviors or bad habits include:

_____

_____

People I notice I am around when or just before engaging in my addictive behaviors or bad habits include:

_____

_____

My Triggers for Addictive Behaviors/Bad Habits

1. _____

2. _____

3. _____

4. _____

5. _____

TOOL 8.2: IDENTIFICATION OF FEELINGS

Emotions have been described by some in terms of being in discrete "feeling families" based on different types of emotional state humans experience. Unlike previous tools, impulsive or addictive behaviors can be influenced by a number of different feelings families. Pick from the following emotions that commonly precipitate addictive behaviors or bad habits or come up with your own words. Then list five of them on the continuum below with "1" being the least agitated and "5" being the most intense agitation for you.

Unsettled

Urge

Agitated

Powerless

Craving

Stressed

Discouraged

Shame

| **Least Intense Feeling** | 1. _____ |

2. _____

3. _____

4. _____

| **Most Intense Feeling** | 5. _____ |

The following questions are designed to help you identify your distorted thoughts specifically related to addiction. Remember, these thoughts will often be related to impulse control, intolerance of strong emotions, or urges to engage in some form of addictive behavior.

When _____ happens, and I feel _____,
        (Trigger)   (Emotion)

What kinds of things am I often telling myself?

_____

_____

If I were in a cartoon, what would the bubble above my head be saying?

_____

_____

If there were a tape recorder in my head recording my every thought, what would it be saying when someone pushed "play?"

_____

_____

Log the thoughts you identify that go along with your impulsive feelings.

_____

_____

Thoughts/Feelings Awareness Log-Example

I felt...	Because I thought...
Vengeful	It's ok to act spiteful because she made me mad.
Sense of urgency	I have to have that item now.
Unmotivated	It's ok to binge, because I felt upset—food will soothe me, and nothing else will help. I can't stand feeling this way.

MY THOUGHTS/FEELINGS AWARENESS LOG

I Felt ...	Because I Thought...

TOOL 8.4: UNHEALTHY "GO-TO" COPING SKILLS

Most people develop a set of standard "go-to" coping skills when they want to feel good quickly. Perhaps you have heard the term *autopilot*, referring to just falling back on the same old skills that in some way feel comfortable but often don't help. Usually these behaviors "worked" in the past but no longer work. Also, some may continue to work in the short term, but may be making problems worse in the long term. A few such examples that people turn to include alcohol, drugs, promiscuous sex, spending, or shopping. Before figuring out healthy skills to use when these urges creep up, generate a list of what you have been trying that has *not* been working. This simply means evaluating and identifying behaviors that could be addictive, impulsive, or constitute bad habits for you.

Identifying My Addictions

The last time I engaged in an addictive, impulsive or habitual behavior was:

_____

_____

I believe the behavior has become an addiction or bad habit because:

_____

_____

The behavior, bad habit, or addiction I will be targeting is:

_____

_____

I believe the habit or addiction first started:

_____

_____

I engage in the behavior: _____
(how often)

The place I usually do it is:

_____

The emotions I feel frequently prior to engaging in the behavior are:

_____

The people in my life that have the power to trigger me to an emotional state where I may be tempted to engage in these behaviors are:

_____

_____

Other circumstances often present when I engage in the behavior include:

_____

_____

TOOL 8.5: AWARENESS OF CONSEQUENCES

All unhealthy coping skills, including bad habits and addictions, "work" in the short term. We get something out of them, or we would not continue to do them. However, that is the main criteria used in this book for determining to what extent a behavior is "healthy" versus "unhealthy"—the degree to which it causes long-term consequences, or what the DSM calls functional impairment. As you complete this tool, ask yourself how the habit has hurt you physically, emotionally, relationally, spiritually, financially, and occupationally. Glance at the example, then list all the habits or addictions you can think of that you struggle with as well as the present or future consequences of those.

Autopilot Coping Skill (habit)	Current or Past Negative Consequences
Alcohol	$100 per month I could put toward rent or education Angers/hurts my partner Parents threaten to cut me off
Marijuana	Suspended from football team Costs a lot of money Grades dropped four straight years Lost my job

My Awareness of Consequences Log

Autopilot Coping Skill (habit)	Current or Past Negative Consequences

TOOL 8.6: CBT CHAIN ANALYSIS

Here is where the rubber meets the road. This is where you get to put it all together. Now that you have mastered the skills covered in the previous tools, identify a specific situation/trigger in your life that precipitated your urge to act impulsively. See if you can identify specific thoughts that you had, feelings you experienced, choices you made, and consequences of those choices.

Use the following tool to help you follow the sequence to analyze your response in a particular episode. Also, when you identify your feelings, rate them on a scale of 0–10 with zero being "none" and 10 being "extreme intensity". For instance, if you identify "restless" and it was the most restless you have ever felt, your entry would look like: "restless—10."

Once you have done enough of these, you will be able to identify patterns, which can facilitate powerful insights for recovery.

Chain Analysis

Event (Trigger)	Rationalizing Thought	Feelings	Habit Behavior	Results

TOOL 8.7: DESIRED RESULTS

This one in pretty simple. When you look at the undesired consequences of your substance use or other habit behavior, what are some alternative outcomes you would have liked to have had? What desired results do you have for your future?

Results I would like to create in my future in similar situations:

1. _____

2. _____

3. _____

4. _____

5. _____

TOOL 8.8: NEW COPING SKILLS

Now that you know that you would like to prevent many of these outcomes, how might you need to change your behavior in response to that trigger to create your desired result? This tool offers you an opportunity to brainstorm a list of general options you can choose from to manage future cravings and urges. Write as many coping skills as you can think of here. The cards in a later tool will be situation specific.

Some coping skills I could try next time I am tempted to engage in one of my habit behaviors:

1. _____

2. _____

3. _____

4. _____

5. _____

TOOL 8.9: CHALLENGING ADDICTION/HABIT-RELATED THOUGHTS

In the same way that recognizing but continuing to engage in unhealthy behaviors rarely gets us far in recovery, recognizing distorted thoughts but not changing them also keeps us stuck. Here is your opportunity to identify specific permission-giving thoughts (the excuses you tell yourself) and generate a list of challenges. This often consists of reminding yourself why the behavior is not ok. Review the example and try your own.

Thought Log-Example

Permission-Giving Thoughts	Rational Response
It's ok to fire off a hateful email because she made me mad.	It's not ok. I am working toward building healthy relationships. I am angry but acting this way will only hurt me and sabotage my goals.
I have to have that new game system now.	I want it, but I don't need it. We need money for prescriptions. We can't afford it. I can walk away.
It's ok to binge eat because I feel upset. Food will soothe me, and nothing else will help. I can't stand to feel this way.	It's not ok to binge for any reason. I can now tolerate intense emotions better than before. I'll hate myself afterward. I'll feel fat. I'll feel depressed. I have other coping skills I can use.

Permission-Giving Thoughts	Rational Responses

TOOL 8.10: REEXAMINING URGES

Now that you have attempted to challenge your thoughts, reflect for a few minutes on your feelings. Ask yourself if the urges or cravings have diminished in any way. If so, how much has the intensity changed before versus after the new thinking? Are you feeling any completely new feelings? Which rational responses seemed to have the most effect on your feelings? The least? Use the tool provided to examine the differences and then record your observations.

Automatic Thoughts	Initial Feelings	Intensity

Rational Responses	Current Feelings	Intensity

My Observations:

_____

_____

_____

_____

_____

_____

TOOL 8.11: CHAIN ANALYSIS WITH RATIONAL RESPONSES

Use the chain analysis tool below with your rational responses to see the impact that your new thinking had on your feelings. Be sure to rate the intensity of the new feelings. For instance, you may still be experiencing cravings, but recognize that if after your initial automatic thoughts your urge level was a "10," and after your rational responses they were a "6," that means the new thinking made an impact. Try not to make the mistake of black-and-white thinking by saying "I wanted to use then and I still want to use now, this didn't do anything." See how changed thinking, feeling, and behavior affected current results and could affect future results.

Event	Automatic Thoughts	Feelings	Actions	Results
	Rational Responses	**New Feelings**	**New Actions**	**New Results**

TOOL 8.12: DOWNWARD ARROW TO IDENTIFY CORE BELIEFS

As a refresher, *core beliefs* are deeply ingrained beliefs that serve as filters through which we process information. All of our distorted thinking is the product of one or more harmful beliefs. This technique asks us to take a thought and continue to ask, "What would that mean about me if it were true?" until we get at the core belief at the bottom of the distorted thought. Many people need a clinician's help to assist with this for a period of time. Note the example below and then try one on your own using one of your own automatic thoughts.

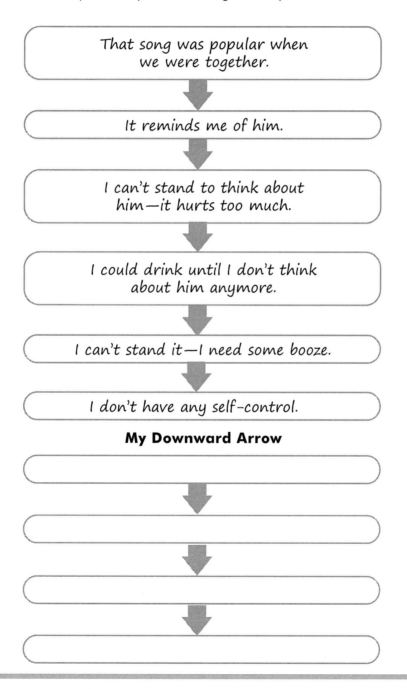

That song was popular when we were together.

It reminds me of him.

I can't stand to think about him—it hurts too much.

I could drink until I don't think about him anymore.

I can't stand it—I need some booze.

I don't have any self-control.

My Downward Arrow

TOOL 8.13: IDENTIFYING ALTERNATIVE HEALTHY BELIEFS

Remember, beliefs come in pairs. I teach in my workshops and conferences that it is kind of like a sheet of paper. It inherently has a front and a back side. For each unhealthy belief you identified, you also have an opposite belief. This tool asks you to formulate in your own words what you would want your opposite belief to be. Then use percentages to rate how much you believe your core belief versus how much you believe your alternate belief. These will be used in a later tool to subjectively measure your belief change as you move forward in your recovery.

Believability Ratings
Example

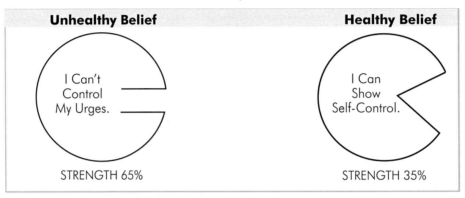

Rating the Strength of My Beliefs

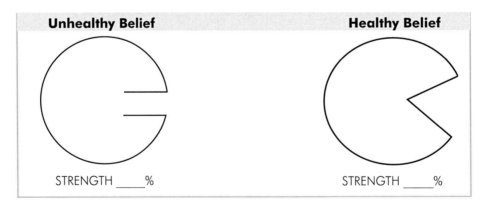

Identifying Components of the Beliefs

Now that you have identified at least one unhealthy belief and an alternate, healthier belief, the next step is to identify what are called the components of the beliefs. To identify the components of the unhealthy belief, it can be a helpful exercise to look back in time to see where these beliefs came from in the first place. To work on changing a belief moving forward, it is necessary to identify how you define the alternate belief *today*.

Beliefs are formulated by the meaning we assign to events or experiences in life. These experiences then become "evidence" to support our beliefs. "Evidence" is in quotation marks because some people count "data" as "evidence" that others do not. It is understandable that those who live through different types of life experiences are more likely to develop different beliefs. Although every person's life experiences are in some ways unique, another phenomenon practitioners encounter is that some clients have strikingly similar backgrounds but develop different types of beliefs. The explanation is that even though the experiences themselves may have been similar, the meaning assigned to them may have been quite different.

Leslie Sokol with the Academy of Cognitive Therapy shares a visual for a belief that compares it to a table. In the same way that a tabletop needs legs to support it, beliefs need similar supporting structures. Experiences in life serve as "evidence" to support these beliefs, based on the meaning that is attributed to them. So in this tool, the "legs of the table" represent evidence one internalizes to support a belief.

This visual can be used in a variety of ways. When working to analyze how you may have acquired an unhealthy belief (such as you identified in your downward arrow) this involves *looking back at past experiences* in life to examine the conclusions you came to in formulating the beliefs you currently hold. Then a different exercise will help you look at the alternate beliefs you are attempting to construct so you know what to look for as you are examining evidence moving *forward* in life.

Because different people can assign different meaning to strikingly similar events, it is not uncommon for two different clients who are looking back to examine historical evidence that led to the development of a belief that they "have no self-control" to identify very different types of experiences or interpretations that led them to the same conclusion about themselves.

Similarly, if the same two people were working to construct an alternate belief moving forward that they "can control urges," they might be "counting" very different types of things as well.

Thus, it is important when doing these exercises to be honest about what your "legs of the table" really are. Not what your parents thought it meant. Not what your faith community or your friends tells you something means. But how you really define meaning. Failing to identify what "counts" *for you* will lead to you logging evidence that makes no difference in your beliefs and ultimately the mood state you are trying to change.

TOOL 8.14(A): ANALYSIS OF COMPONENTS OF UNHEALTHY BELIEF

Start by looking back in time. Use the table visual to identify the components of your beliefs; that is experiences that you went through that were important in contributing to an unhealthy belief you identified when doing the downward arrow. These will help you know specifically what types of experiences will be necessary to create or expose yourself to when modifying your beliefs going forward.

The following questions may be helpful in reflecting on different periods of time in your life to uncover some of the experiences you counted as evidence to support your unhealthy belief as it was being developed. You may need assistance from your clinician to get the most out of this tool.

The first time I ever remember feeling _____[belief] **was** _____

The people in my life who influenced me to feel that way were:

Family members _____

_____

Friends/Peers _____

_____

Other significant people _____

_____

Experiences during my elementary school years _____

_____

Experiences during my junior high years _____

_____

Experiences during my high school years _____

_____

Experiences during my college/young adult years _____

_____

Significant experiences since then _____

_____

Legs of Table

Fill in the unhealthy belief you are analyzing in the tabletop portion of the structure. Use the exercise above to insert some of the "evidence" from your past that you have "counted" to support each belief in the legs below. "Insufficient self-control" is a typical belief involved with addictions and bad habits, so it will be used to demonstrate. Consider the example and then use the blank table provided to identify your components of your own unhealthy belief.

Example

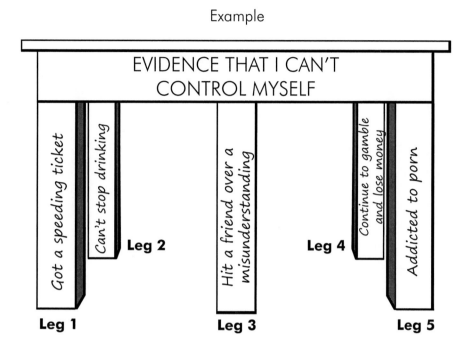

Evidence that supports my unhealthy belief:

Leg 1: *Got pissed and got in car and floored it and got ticket from cop who was in the neighborhood*

Leg 2: *Couldn't stop my urge to drink*

Leg 3: *Hit friend I thought was hitting on my girlfriend*

Leg 4: *Lost $1000 in casino*

Leg 5: *Was addicted to porn for six months*

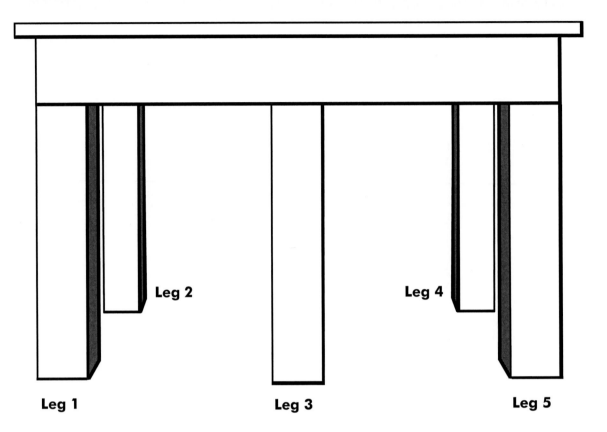

EVIDENCE THAT SUPPORTS MY UNHEALTHY BELIEF

Leg 2

Leg 4

Leg 1

Leg 3

Leg 5

Evidence that supports my unhealthy belief:

Leg 1:

Leg 2:

Leg 3:

Leg 4:

Leg 5:

TOOL 8.14(B): ANALYSIS OF COMPONENTS OF HEALTHY BELIEF

Now that you have identified some of the experiences you assigned meaning to that contributed to formulating your unhealthy belief, take a few moments to consider what evidence might look like to support the alternate healthy belief. For instance, what might you be saying or doing if you had self-control?" Consider the following example and then use the blank table to identify your own components of your healthy belief.

I Can show Self-Control

SELF-CONTROL

Leg 1: Didn't yell at Dad
Leg 2: Didn't drink myself numb
Leg 3: Didn't engage in reckless sex
Leg 4: Didn't over spend at Christmas
Leg 5: Limited my drinks

Evidence that I can show self-control:

Leg 1: Wanted to yell at my dad and didn't

Leg 2: Wanted to drink until numb when I got dumped, but stopped at two

Leg 3: Turned down sexual advance I previously would have said yes to

Leg 4: Wanted really badly to buy extra Christmas presents at mall but fought off urge

Leg 5: Only had one margarita with my Mexican food

MY TABLE WITH COMPONENTS OF BELIEF

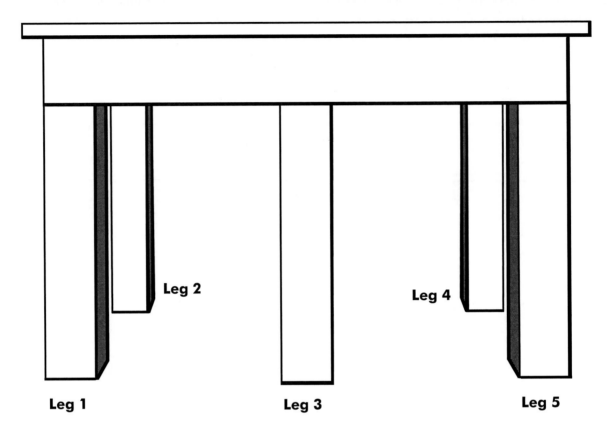

Leg 2

Leg 4

Leg 1

Leg 3

Leg 5

Evidence that I can show self-control:

Leg 1:

Leg 2:

Leg 3:

Leg 4:

Leg 5:

TOOL 8.15: ONGOING EVIDENCE LOGS

Evidence logs can be helpful in a number of ways, including increasing our awareness, as well as strengthening our alternate beliefs. Again, *what* we log tells us a lot about how we assign meaning.

Now that you have identified your "legs of the table" for the healthy belief you are working on, you know specifically what to look for. Purposefully pay attention to experiences that support the healthy belief you are constructing. This may involve noticing evidence that was always there but you didn't notice before due to your old belief filtering your thinking away from it. You may also work with your clinician on exercises that actually create new evidence that wasn't there before. Purposefully paying attention to does not mean making up evidence. If the evidence legitimately isn't there, it doesn't count. Just remember that because of your filter you will be prone to discount things that really do support the belief, so having an open mind is vital.

Consider the example below, and then begin your own evidence log.

Date	Evidence
12/12	Drank no alcohol at Christmas party
12/13	Only had one margarita with Mexican food
12/16	Stayed within budget at mall
12/20	Tempted to buy extra presents but didn't
12/24	Chose not to eat pie at Christmas dinner

Evidence that I can control my urges/impulses

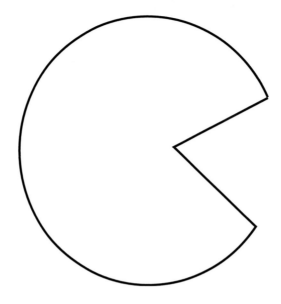

Date	Evidence

TOOL 8.16: PROS AND CONS

Many versions of pros and cons exercises are available. This one was prepared by Jonathan von Breton, who is a professional advisor to **SMART** Recovery and is reprinted with permission, specifically to help people work through and grow out of addictive behaviors. Complete the following exercise and answer the questions that follow.

Four Questions About My Addiction

What do I enjoy about my addiction? What does it do for me? (Be specific.)	What do I think I will like about giving up my addiction? What good things might happen when I stop my addiction?
What do I hate about my addiction? What bad things does it do to me and to others? (Give specific examples.)	**What do I think I won't like about giving up my addiction? What am I going to hate, dread, or dislike about living without my addiction?**

Four Questions About My Addiction: A Cost-Benefit Exercise

These four questions can provide you with a lot of useful information with which to grow out of your addiction(s). The more honest and complete your answers, the more this exercise will help you.

1. **What do I enjoy about my addiction? What does it do for me (be specific)?**
   List as many things as you can that you liked about whatever you are/were addicting yourself to.

- Where possible, find alternative ways of achieving the same goals.
- Recognize positive thinking about the addiction as a potential relapse warning sign.
- Realize that there are some things you liked about the addiction you will have to learn to live without.
- List what you enjoy about your addiction so you can ask yourself if it is really worth the price.
- Realize that you aren't stupid; you did get something from your addiction. It just may not be working on your behalf anymore.

2. **What do I hate about my addiction? What bad things does it do to me and to others (give specific examples)?**
List as many of the bad, undesirable results of your addiction as you can. Here it is extremely important that you use specific examples. Specific examples have much greater emotional impact and motivational force!
- Ask yourself honestly "If my addiction was a used car, would I pay this much for it?" If you wouldn't pay this much for it, why not?
- Review this list often, especially if you are having a lot of positive, happy thoughts about all the great things your addiction did for you and how much fun you had in pursuing it.

3. **What do I think I will like about giving up my addictive behaviors?**
List the good things you think/fantasize will happen when you stop your addiction.
- This provides you with a list of goals to achieve and things to look forward to as a result of your new addiction-free lifestyle.
- This list also helps you to reality-test your expectations. If they are unrealistic, they can contribute to relapse based on disappointment, depression, or self-pity.

4. **What do I think I won't like about giving up my addiction?**
List what you think you are going to hate, dread, or merely dislike about living without your addiction.
- This list tells you what kinds of new coping skills, behaviors, and lifestyle changes you need to develop in order to stay addiction free.
- It also serves as another relapse warning list. If all you think about is how much life sucks now that you are not feeding your addiction, you are engaging in a relapse thought pattern that is just as dangerous as only focusing on what you liked about your addiction.

This is not a do once and forget about it exercise. It is an ongoing project. Most people simply can't remember all of the positive and negative aspects of addiction and recovery at any one time. Furthermore, seeing all the negative consequences of addiction listed in one place is very powerful. Most people do not absolutely know what they will like or not like about living free of their addictions until they have done so for some time. I know of people who continued to add items to all four questions for a full six months.

TOOL 8.17: IDENTIFYING MY HABITS AND ADDICTIONS

The habit or addiction I will be targeting is:

_____

_____

This habit or addiction first started:

_____

_____

I typically engage in the behavior: _____

(How often?)

The place I usually do the behavior is:

_____

_____

The time of day I usually do the behavior is:

_____

_____

The emotions I usually feel before I do the behavior are:

_____

_____

The people in my life that have the power to trigger those emotions in me include:

_____

_____

Other circumstances that often present when I engage in the behavior include:

_____

_____

My habit or addiction has hurt me in the following ways:

My physical body:

_____

_____

My sleep habits:

_____

_____

My relationships:

_____

_____

My emotions:

_____

_____

My spiritual life:

_____

_____

Medically:

_____

_____

Financially:

_____

_____

TOOL 8.18: WHAT'S MY WHY?

One of the keys to overcoming addictions and bad habits is to identify the function of the behavior. People often do bad things for good reasons. Identifying the reasons is essential for finding replacement behaviors that can fill a similar function with less damaging consequences. Use the example below to help you complete your own tool on what *your* why is.

What's My Why? Example

What? (Habit or Addiction)	Why? (What I Get out of It)
Taking Adderall recreationally	Gives me energy
Smoke pot	Helps me relax Helps me "numb out"
Bite fingernails	Gives me something to do when I'm stressed

What's My Why?

What? (Habit or Addiction)	Why? (What I Get out of It)

TOOL 8.19: SSS TOOL (SUBSTANCE-SPECIFIC STRATEGIES)

Identifying the function of unhealthy behaviors can shed light on what replacement behaviors may be the most effective. Certain behaviors may be helpful coping skills in general, but if they don't help us meet the need that is behind the problem behaviors, they likely won't work in our effort to reverse that particular habit. Use the example below to brainstorm some replacement behaviors you could use instead of your habit behaviors to meet your specific need with less damaging consequences.

Need (My "Why")	SSS (Healthier Strategies That Could Meet That Need)
1. "I need energy to do my job."	- Get adequate sleep - Change my diet - Increase my exercise - Get blood tests to see if I need vitamins, minerals, or other supplement or medicine - Start my work project even though my energy level is lower than I'd like it to be
2. "I want to feel numb and not think about something bad."	- Learn distress tolerance techniques - Deal with my problems so intrusive thoughts don't keep coming back - Take a hot bath - Read a moving story - Talk about how proud I am of my child - Listen to a funny podcast - Listen to one of my go-to songs - Call my friend and go to a movie
3. "I need something to do when I get anxious."	- Use a distraction technique - Count to 100 in my head - Get on a treadmill - Clench my stress ball - Remind myself all the reasons I will be ok

MY SSS TOOL (SUBSTANCE SPECIFIC STRATEGIES)

Need (My "Why")	SSS (Healthier Strategies That Could Meet That Need)
1.	
2.	
3.	

TOOL 8.20: SELF-MONITORING

Self-monitoring is an important tool to have whether striving to break a bad habit or addiction, managing a full-blown mental illness, or working toward achieving any type of personal goal. First, monitoring is a way of increasing our awareness to our triggers, thoughts, moods, and habit behaviors. It is only after we gain awareness to the presence of these that we can intentionally work to change them. Especially early in the process, many people say things like, "That's just the way I am" or "That's just me." Viewing it in this way makes it *seem* unchangeable (like our eye color). As we get better at developing awareness as to when these things come and go, and to our environment and thought processes as they do, we can change who we thought we "just were" for the better.

Secondly, monitoring is a way for us to tell if we are growing. As we get better at paying attention to certain thoughts, moods, and habit behaviors, we can get better at noticing if they are improving over time.

Perhaps the easiest way to get started is to start with behaviors you have no desire to change. Some people start with going to the bathroom, brushing their teeth, or doing the dishes. Start by observing *frequency and duration*; that is, how *often* and how *long* you do the behavior.

Self-monitoring does not come easily, and most people believe they are better at it than they really are. But the more you practice, the more self-aware you become. The more self-aware you become, the better insight you have into habit behaviors that you might want to change that could have a profound positive impact on your recovery and personal growth.

The following tool can help you get better at paying attention to a behavior that you choose to start with, even if you have no desire to change it. You will then use this skill in completing your Habit Tracker targeting actual bad habits.

Behavior(s) of focus:

_____

_____

I will pay attention to this more in the following way:

_____

_____

One morning practice I can implement into my daily routine that can help me shift my focus to paying attention to the behavior I am trying to catch myself in is:

_____

_____

How often do I notice myself doing this behavior?

_____

_____

Do I observe specific emotions when I catch myself doing the behavior?

_____

_____

What can I use to help bring my attention to this behavior when I start to do it (a reminder on the toilet, a sticky note on the pantry door, a flavor I don't like on my hands so I notice every time I start to put my fingers in my mouth)?

_____

_____

A person who lives or works with me that could be a support in this by pointing out to me when they observe me engage in the behavior is:

_____

_____

A practical way I will keep track of how many times I do the behavior a day is (e.g., little notepad in pocket, "notes" in smartphone, step counter or clicker):

_____

_____

Other factors that might be important for me in improving my monitoring and increasing my awareness are:

_____

_____

TOOL 8.21: RELATIONSHIP CIRCLES AND ACCOUNTABILITY

Evaluate the relationships you have in your life.

We call these "intimacy circles" and, as a memory device, define intimacy as "into-me-see"—the degree to which we let people see into us.

For instance, as you complete your tool someone you would let "see into" you completely (someone you kept no secrets from) would go in circle #1. Those you would not share anything personal with would go in circle # 5, and so on. The more you trust a person the closer in they go on your circles. The less you trust a person, the further out they go. After listing people where you view them on your circles, answer the questions that follow.

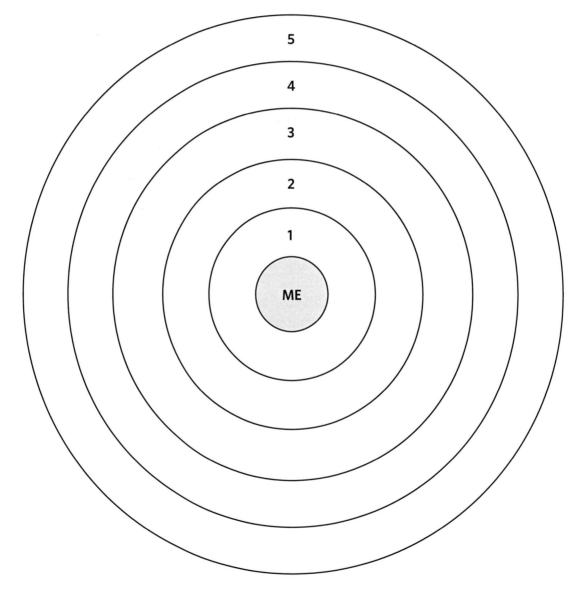

Adapted from *Group Treatment for Substance Abuse*, Velasquez, Maurer, Crouch, and DiClemente, 2001

INTIMACY AND RELATIONSHIP CIRCLES QUESTIONS

Some of the people in my circles I can count on to help me with my addictions or bad habits are?

_____

_____

People in my circles that tempt me or influence me to continue my bad habits or addictions are:

_____

_____

Some relationships I have damaged/lost as a result of an addiction or bad habit include:

_____

_____

Some helpful things I have done that have helped me in maintaining supportive relationships are:

_____

_____

Changes I could make in the way I relate to people may include:

_____

_____

Would I like to add people to my circles who currently aren't there? Why or why not?

_____

_____

What are some qualities of the people I would like to add?

_____

_____

What are some "red flag" qualities of people I may be drawn to but that I have learned from experience are not good candidates for my circles?

_____

_____

I commit to talk to the following three people from my circles to be part of my accountability team that I can call for support in times I am having a hard time managing my urges. I will put their names and numbers somewhere that is readily accessible and that I can find easily in times of need.

Name   **Way to Contact**

_____   _____

_____   _____

_____   _____

TOOL 8.22: HABIT TRACKER

Here is where it gets difficult. Use your awareness skills *to pay attention to every time you have an urge to do the behavior, whether you did it or not.* You will not catch every time—that is fine. Do the best you can. Log the date, time, what your urge was to do, what emotion you were experiencing and how strongly you felt it, if you did the habit behavior or not, and if not, on a scale of 0–10, how close you came to giving in to the urge and acting. This is a royal pain to begin with. But the more consistent you become with this over time, the better you will get at reversing unwanted habits. If you quit completing these, you are unlikely to succeed. Use the example to start completing your own.

Example

Date	Time	Urge	Emotion/ Strength	Did I do? Y/N	If no, how close? 0–10
4/13	7:00	Drink alcohol	Agitation (7)	N	9

My Habit Tracker

Date	Time	Urge	Emotion/ Strength	Did I do? Y/N	If no, how close? 0–10

TOOL 8.23: BEHAVIOR OVER BELIEF (BOB)

As you master the use of your habit tracker, closely monitoring your behaviors and urges, an additional step to integrate involves thoughts and beliefs. You may recall the term rationalization from the cognitive distortions section at the beginning of this book. A cognitive term for this specific use of rationalizing is *permission-giving beliefs*. Every time anyone consciously engages in a behavior that is against their moral values or is not in their best interest, they do so only after giving themselves permission to first. A general template for identifying permission-giving beliefs could be:

It's ok to _____, because _____.
                            (behavior)   (excuse)

One example I hear working with clients in the area of addictions is *"It's ok to use drugs, because I think they should be legal."*

They may believe this, but the reality is that the substance in question is *not* legal at this time and place. So in helping the client examine potential pros and cons, it is important to consider potential sociological, legal, and family-related consequences. Use the BOB (Behavior over Belief) Tool to identify some of your permission-giving beliefs that could be facilitating your bad habit or addictive behavior, as well as to consider how you might increase your effectiveness by behaving differently in spite of what you believe.

BOB Tool

Date	Permission-Giving Belief	Habit Behavior Tempted to Do	SSS (Alternative Behavior)
8/11	"It's ok to take a drink because what she said made me depressed."	Drink vodka	Call a friend. Have a nice meal. Sit in the hot tub.

TOOL 8.24: BURNING THE BRIDGE

Once you have identified your triggers and your addictive or bad-habit behaviors, and you have increased your awareness regarding your temptations to engage in them, the next step is getting more effective "in the moment" at not acting on your urges. The cards in Tool 8.25 can be helpful with this.

However, a crucial first step is to *safeguard your environment*. This "bridge burning," as Dr. Lane Pederson calls it, is a term that is often associated with clients with suicidality. Whether it refers to killing oneself, going to the casino, or using heroin, the reality is that adults can choose to do just about whatever they want to. People with addictions often have urges to do things that the rational part of them knows is not in their best interest. So if part of you wants to indulge while the other part of you knows it's best to restrain, you are not alone. Bridge burning is simply doing anything you can that will make it less likely for you to engage in the behavior in the moment and give more time for intervention.

Some safeguarding can be done preemptively. For instance, if you are in your first month without alcohol and are trying to break a habit, you can "burn a bridge" by not keeping any alcohol in the house. Other safeguarding must be done "in the moment," which is much harder. For people who have urges to self-harm, it means making sure all objects that could be used to do so are removed. For people who are having suicidal thoughts, it might mean having high-lethality medications locked up under someone else's supervision. If you are having an urge to binge eat and you have the food you like to binge on at the house (for some necessary reason), it may mean you need to leave the house. If your urge is to spend, you could limit your own access to funds or allow an accountability person to do so. Depending on the area your unhealthy urge involves, your steps will be different.

One client of mine made sure he was with other people when his urges increased because he knew he would not engage in the behavior if someone else was there. After connecting with them and participating in some form of joint activity, he noticed the urge, no matter how strong, eventually passed.

Spend some time considering specific areas you may need to safeguard and what that might look like for you.

Specific steps I could take ahead of time that would make my environment safer and less tempting are:

_____

_____

_____

Things I could do "in the moment" to burn the bridge when an urge comes:

_____

_____

_____

For me, bridge burning might include:

_____

_____

_____

Use the following tool to list the specific habit behaviors you have identified and think of some specific ways you could "burn the bridge" that will buy you a little more time to change your mind about engaging in the behavior you are desiring to change.

Habit behavior	Steps I will take to safeguard

TOOL 8.25: COPING CARDS AND CUE CARDS

This tool is a *behavioral coping card*. To make use of the coping card, simply copy a habit behavior you are targeting and identify three of your SSS (alternative coping skills) behaviors that you think would work in a specific situation.

Since these are to be used "in the moment," it is best to keep them succinct so as not to overwhelm yourself as you will often be using them in a time of emotional upset.

Consult the following example using the client from the previous tool, and then try one yourself!

The next time I feel hurt and am tempted to drink vodka, instead I will:

1. *Call a friend.*

2. *Have a nice meal.*

3. *Sit in the hot tub.*

My Coping Card

The next time I am tempted to _____ I will:
(habit or addiction)

1. _____

2. _____

3. _____

The final card has a slightly different purpose. Unlike the coping cards, the cue cards don't deal with any behaviors. They are more about your mindset. These should pick out a rational response you used (in Tool 8.9) related to why it is *not* in your best interest to engage in the habit behavior.

Even more powerful would be to deal with your thoughts about your setback. Relapse is a part of recovery. Whether trying to stick to a certain diet or kick a drug habit, almost everyone has setbacks of some kind along the way. But the way one thinks about their failures (in this case relapsing into habit behaviors) is crucial for overcoming the obstacle you are battling.

Consider the following example, then try a cue card of your own. With both types of cards, use the template provided to practice, but then transfer your answers onto actual 3x5 cards you can strategically move to places you will see them most.

Just because I gave in and drank the vodka doesn't mean I am a horrible person who will not achieve my goal. I went 11 straight days and now I had one slip. I am a valuable person that is loved by God and a few people in my support system. I am going to meet with my sponsor, tweak my relapse plan, and get back on the horse and start riding again. I will beat this thing!

My Cue Card

CHAPTER 9

Resilience and Relapse Prevention

Resiliency is a topic that is gaining increasing attention in the psychotherapy literature as well as having been a popular topic in coaching circles for years. Webster's dictionary defines resilience as "the ability to recover from or adjust easily to misfortune or change." Resilience is composed of many factors. Various authors describe it differently. However, the bottom line is that resilient people know how to bounce back when things don't go their way, regardless of what life throws at them. And I would add, this is the primary trait needed for dealing with life's setbacks or, in the clinical setting, what we call "relapses."

Windy Dryden (2012) identifies four factors associated with resilience.

High frustration tolerance: The ability to endure periods of strong emotional distress is perhaps one of the most overlooked aspects to navigating life successfully. Resilient mindsets propel one to be able to withstand these onslaughts of life without constant complaining, self-pity, or even worse, acting in some impulsive or destructive manner to alleviate the distress.

Keeping things in perspective: Extreme thinking has been addressed earlier in this book. Cognitive distortions of black-and-white thinking and magnification/catastrophic thinking cause people to jump to extreme conclusions when troubles arise. So the ability to maintain perspective—that is, acknowledge setbacks but be able to scale them appropriately in the grand scheme of things—plays an important role in maintaining the hope to carry on.

Self-acceptance: Many people "beat themselves up" in the face of failure or setbacks. Forgiveness, self-compassion, and an acceptance that all human beings make mistakes are vital components of a mindset that facilitates resilience. Self-critical thoughts are often not deserved, and even when placing the responsibility on oneself is to some degree "fair," continuing to dwell on the mistake over time is never helpful for moving forward. I believe humor can prove helpful in this area. In the hypersensitive world we live in where people are constantly offended, the art of laughing at oneself has been lost. Laughing at one's self (or others) with the right heart behind it can provide much-needed levity and also facilitate not magnifying the significance of one's mistakes. Avoiding self-critical internal dialogue is a vital feature of a mindset that can quickly regain the disciplined action required to move forward boldly toward one's goal.

Adaptability: Adaptability has been addressed earlier as well. Flexibility in thinking and behavior is especially crucial in the area of resilience. Flexibility in thinking facilitates better problem solving. Rigid thinkers often are not even capable of generating a sufficient range of possibilities to have the most effective choice at their disposal. The ability to adapt to typical ways of going about life can be helpful in (1) avoiding unnecessary setbacks, and (2) bouncing back quickly when one does have a relapse or setback of any kind. The set of tools in this chapter is devoted to helping clients with both of these.

Prochaska and DiClemente's stages of change model (2006) spawned the popular **motivational interviewing** technique and posits that any time people make a change of any kind in their lives, they do so in a series of changes. I describe their original five stages in the following way:

Pre-Contemplation   **Preparation**   **Maintenance**
I------------------------I------------------------I------------------------I------------------------I
                 Contemplation   **Action**

Pre-Contemplation: This is the stage before someone thinks about making a change. The thought has not occurred to them that a situation they are currently in is hurtful in some way or that it could be improved.

Contemplation: This is the stage in which it has been brought to someone's attention that a change may be called for in a certain situation. Sometimes a person reaches this stage as a result of a family "intervention" that is often quite direct, however many times this comes about in more subtle ways, such as someone realizing while on the golf course that they have gained a little more weight than they realized and may want to consider becoming more active or being more cognizant of their diet.

Preparation: In this stage, a person has considered the situation, decided to make a change, and started taking initial preparatory steps. This could include starting to update a resume, intentionally planning finances differently, or purchasing healthier food.

Action: Action is pretty straightforward. One starts putting those preparatory steps into action: making phone calls, sending out resumes, getting on the treadmill, actually taking food to work for lunch rather than going out every day, etc.

Maintenance: This final stage focuses on maintaining the initial action steps. Many people have good intentions and hit the gym for the first week, only to fall back into old habits. This stage emphasizes maintaining discipline, contingency planning, and staying the course. In doing so, positive habits then become new ways of life.

These stages apply whether a person is working to overcome an addiction or mental illness or trying to make an everyday lifestyle change such as becoming more physically fit, pursuing career advancement, or seeking healthier relationships. Thus, relapses, or setbacks, will look different, depending on what someone is working on in life. (A future tool helps identify what that looks like specifically for you).

Also, it should be noted that one can be in different stages with different problems or pursuits. For instance, one might be in the pre-contemplation stage when it comes to quitting smoking, but in the action stage when it comes to making a relationship change. The goal, then, is to develop the awareness to realize what stage you are in with each life area that is relevant to you, decide what your next step will be, and move towards positive growth. Use the following tool to identify areas of life you wish to make a change in, what stage you are in, and what your next step will be in each area. If you are unsure of what area(s) to change, ask the three people closest to you to give you honest feedback regarding areas they think you may benefit from changing.

TOOL 9.1: STAGES OF CHANGE

Friend Consulted	Areas of My Life Where My Friend Would Like to See Me Consider a Change
	1. 2. 3.

Area of Life Considering Change	Stage of Change I Am Currently In	Action Steps I Will Take to Progress Toward Next Stage
		1. 2. 3.
		1. 2. 3.
		1. 2. 3.

TOOL 9.2: DEFINING RELAPSE

John Ludgate (2009) defines relapse as a "recurrence of symptoms after a period of improvement." As mentioned in Tool 9.1, this is sometimes related to a mental health concern or an addiction, and sometimes it is merely a setback in terms of achieving one's goal. Thus, a relapse or setback behavior is different depending on what you are working on. If you are trying to be more assertive, perhaps "shutting down" and not asking for what you want when a situation presents itself may constitute a setback. If you are working to lose weight and find yourself eating an entire bag of potato chips, for you, that is a setback. If you are trying to maintain sobriety and give in to an urge to drink alcohol one evening, that is a relapse or setback for you.

Using the area of life you identified in the previous tool to work on, list what a setback or relapse would look like for you. Remember, you get to define what are successes and failures relative to your goals.

For me, relapse or setback behaviors would include:

_____

_____

_____

_____

_____

TOOL 9.3: DECREASE VULNERABILITY TO NEGATIVE EMOTIONS

The term "coping skill" is common if not overused in behavioral health vernacular. I got to the point that if I saw the word "coping skill" in another treatment plan or heard it used in another group I was going to have a nervous breakdown myself! Coping skills are obviously important. The term is just used in such a generic way that it often lacks meaning. And coping skills are inherently defensive in nature. To use a sports analogy, it is important to be able to play defense, however, to win the game a person or team must usually also be able to generate some offense. For the less athletically inclined, it is a good idea to own a fire extinguisher, but wouldn't it also be nice to know something about fire prevention? Yes, coping skills are necessary to have when life has thrown a challenge at us. It is also empowering to be able to proactively do what we can to prepare ourselves ahead of time to decrease our vulnerability to these challenges.

Likely everyone can relate to the concept that the more stressed out or tired we are, the more vulnerable we are to engage in negative behaviors that come naturally to us. For example, if you have a tendency to be "short" with people in the first place, this impatient trait is probably magnified when you are stressed out or if you didn't get enough sleep the previous night. The same is true of any less-than-desirable trait any of us have. Consider what you can do in each of the following areas to build up your resistance.

Exercise: Research has demonstrated again and again the many physical and psychological benefits of exercise.

Do you have a current exercise regimen?

_____

_____

_____

What changes, if any, would benefit you to implement in this area?

_____

_____

_____

Sleep: Likewise, sleep is an area that has been the focus of research for many years. We used to think depression, anxiety, and other stressful emotional states *caused* sleep problems. Some now argue that it is the other way around, and that lack of sleep causes physical and emotional problems. We are also discovering that there are many things not related to medication that we can do to improve our sleep. There are things we all can do to improve our sleep. The following questions may help you discover them:

Do you have a current bedtime routine?

_____

_____

_____

What activities can be part of a "wind down routine" you can do before you go to bed to calm down your mind and body in preparation for sleep?

_____

_____

_____

What obstacles to sleep do you deal with on a regular basis? Electronic devices? Temperature? Noise? Media content, conversations, physical activity, caffeine intake too close to bedtime? Other?

_____

_____

_____

What changes, if any, would benefit your bedtime routine?

_____

_____

_____

Emotional Strength: Increasing positive emotions can also make us less vulnerable to negative ones. Hobbies, things that make us laugh, activities that we find soothing or pleasurable can be helpful, just to name a few. These are often everyday things. Common responses here include watching sports, listening to music, painting nails, getting a massage, spending time on social media, or watching movies.

This one is pretty simple. List some things you enjoy doing that help you feel good:

_____

_____

_____

Relational Support: Perhaps you have heard the expression *we are only as sick as our secrets*. Everyone has secrets. And bad habits and addictions thrive within an environment of secrecy. Support, accountability, and transparency are crucial for living life in "recovery" from anything that ails us and keep us moving forward in the direction of the growth we desire.

Refer to Tool 5.21 for a more in-depth dive into your relationships and consider the following questions.

Who in my life do I allow to see the "real me" with no secrets?

_____

_____

_____

Who in my life do I have the most fun with?

_____

_____

_____

Who do I spend time with that challenges me intellectually?

_____

_____

_____

Who in my life do I spend time with that challenges me to grow spiritually?

_____

_____

_____

Who in my life do I spend time with that challenges me to grow emotionally?

_____

_____

_____

When my back is against the wall and I need support, I can contact:

Name   Way to Contact

1._____

2._____

3._____

Spiritual Strength—Many people draw strength to overcome obstacles in life from their faith or spiritual practices. How might you incorporate this aspect into your recovery and growth plan?

Spiritual practices or disciplines I can incorporate into my recovery and growth plan include:

_____

_____

_____

TOOL 9.4: RESILIENCE MINDSET

The previous tool discussed behaviors—some things you can *do* to decrease your vulnerability to negative emotions. The next tool addresses your thought life, which is at least equally important to prepare you to deal with the storms of life. Peruse the chart below and consider which of the unhealthy mindsets many people struggle with from time to time. Use the thought log that follows to list your unhealthy thoughts on the left side and challenge them with some alternative ideas you want to work to come to believe. Get help from friends or your practitioner as you continue to find or create evidence to support your truth in life.

Unhealthy Mindsets	Healthy Mindsets
• "Since I haven't accomplished my goal yet, I never will (so I might as well quit)." • "This life event is crushing—I will never get over it." • "I don't have any options." • "Life should be fair. Since life isn't fair, I might as well not try again." • "I can't do anything. I am a victim—life happens to me." • "I must feel comfortable."	• "Just because I haven't accomplished my goal yet, doesn't mean I am not heading in the right direction." • "This was a big blow, but I can bounce back." • "There are always options—sometimes there are no great options, but I always have choices. I could ask someone to see if they see options I don't." • "Life is not fair. Everyone has positive and negative things that aren't fair. Wrong things happen in life. My future is still up to me." • "I have had some bad luck experiences in my past, but I can still influence my future." • "I expect to have some discomfort as I am learning and growing."

Thought Log

Give Up Thought	Resilient Challenge

TOOL 9.5: ANALYZING MY SETBACK

The first part of this discussion has revolved around cultivating a resilience mindset and putting proactive strategies in place to decrease the likelihood of a setback or relapse in the first place. The second part involves what to do *when you do* slip. Remember that "relapse is a part of recovery." Not one of us is perfect and we will all have setbacks when attempting to achieve our goals. Analyzing the circumstances around which we slip is vital for moving forward in a positive direction. A chain analysis is a powerful tool for accomplishing this. This is where you start by identifying the trigger for the relapse or setback, and then try to figure out the thoughts and feelings that led you from that point to the relapse/setback behavior. Working with a practitioner is often helpful for learning how to do these and discovering places in the chain where you can intervene to do something differently. Note the example and then try one for yourself with the guidance of the questions below.

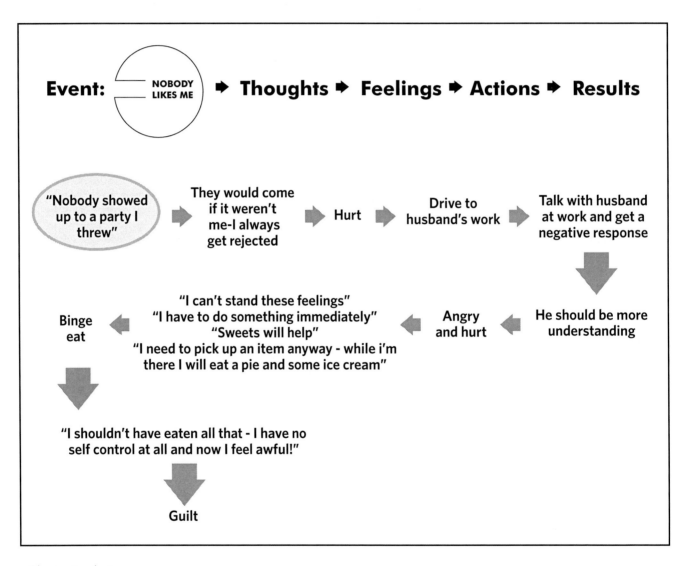

Chain Analysis

- What could this person have thought or done differently to get a different outcome?
- What could her coping card look like?
- What kinds of things would you like to see on her relapse prevention plan?

Coping Card

The next time I feel depressed and am tempted to binge eat, instead I will:

1. *Go for a run*

2. *Drink water*

3. *Distract myself by removing myself from where food is*

Now analyze your situation.

Identify and record you trigger: _____

What thoughts, feelings, or behaviors led to your relapse behavior?

_____

_____

What was your setback behavior?

_____

_____

What did you tell yourself or do after the behavior?

_____

_____

What could you have done or thought differently to get a more positive outcome?

_____

_____

What changes would you like to include on your own relapse prevention plan as a result of this incident?

_____

_____

What might your coping card look like?

_____

_____

Coping Card

The next time I am tempted to _____, I can...

_____

_____

_____

TOOL 9.6: FAILING FORWARD

"Fail faster" is a common phrase in the coaching world. *Forbes* magazine published an article by the exact title of "How to fail faster and why you should" in 2018. And don't forget the infamous Michael Jordan commercials where he chronicles his shots missed (over 9000), games lost (nearly 300), and game-winning shots not executed (26), and ends with the powerful line, "I have failed over and over and over in my life–and that is why I succeed." This point is well taken that most people fall short of what they want in life because they are too afraid of failing to take their "shot."

However, let's not forget the flip side of this. Now we see too many people heeding the coaching advice of "experts" that have had them jump into endeavors irresponsibly, make a mess of a situation so badly that it damages their confidence, and they give up the pursuit of their dreams. As with most things, the best approach is likely somewhere in between. The key is not necessarily the willingness to fail, but the *manner in which one thinks about the failure.* For people that have taken irresponsible, careless plunges that hurt their confidence, their chances at success, their reputation, or worse yet, other people, this can be a tougher pill to swallow. But how we think about our setbacks is the key. Remember the stages of change from Tool 9.1? Every time any of us is working on making a change and has a setback, we go right back to the contemplation stage and get to think about how we will view our setback. The motivational speaker Les Brown has become associated with the famous Willie Jolley quote "a setback is a setup for a comeback." And it can be with the right mindset.

The following thought logs list some common unhelpful thoughts in response to setbacks/relapses. If we are going to do what best-selling author John C. Maxwell calls "fail forward" in life, we need to be able to challenge thoughts like this. While it is impossible to identify every self-defeating thought you could have in response to failures in life, this tool gives you a little practice. These are the types of thoughts you will need to get good at combatting to "fail forward" toward your goals in life.

Unhealthy Thought	Rational Response
"Because I have been doing this so long, I cannot change—this is just the way I am."	

Unhealthy Thought	Rational Response
"Since I screwed up once, I might as well keep doing it—I can go all out!"	

Unhealthy Thought	Rational Response
"Because I can't keep from slipping, I am just a failure."	

Unhealthy Thought	Rational Response
"Since I screwed up, I am right back where I started, and all my progress is for nothing."	

Unhealthy Thought	Rational Response
"Since I am not as good as so and so, I will never measure up."	

Other Unhealthy Thoughts	Rational Response

TOOL 9.7: THINGS I'M DOING RIGHT

Just because you had a relapse doesn't mean you aren't also doing some things right that need to remain in place as you move forward. While it was necessary to examine the circumstances surrounding your setback, it is also important to keep a balanced perspective. Black-and-white thinking (cognitive distortion covered in Chapter 1) makes it difficult to realize that it is possible to be doing some things right and at the same time have made a mistake. In an attempt to maintain this perspective, make a list of all the things you have been doing right in pursuit of your goal that you will want to continue in addition to making the changes you identified above.

1. _____

2. _____

3. _____

4. _____

5. _____

6. _____

7. _____

8. _____

9. _____

10. _____

TOOL 9.8: THE ROAD TO RECOVERY

As you move toward your goals, keep "success" in perspective. No two people's journeys look the same, and, as mentioned, for most, it does not mean mistakes will not be made. It usually doesn't mean life will be smooth sailing up the mountain. Life will continue to change, and you will continue to need to adapt to meet your goals and continue to move forward. Many people believe the road to recovery is a smooth, gradual, continuous upward climb—represented by the line on the top. They are then taken aback when the road throws them some curves—as represented by the line on the bottom. Life always has ups and downs. So it is important to have the proper mindset to be ready to deal with life's challenges head-on and to be able to accurately view where you are.

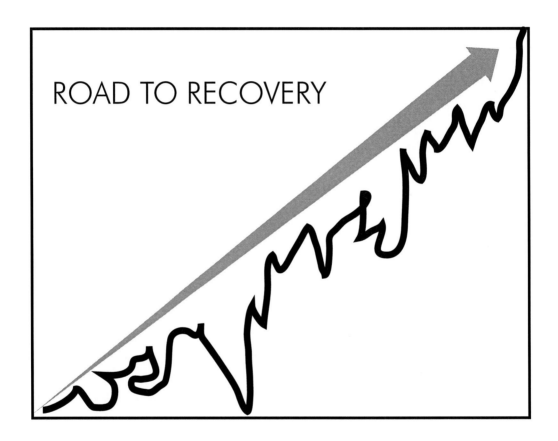

When life is going smoothly, enjoy the ride. But don't be complacent. While we cannot predict every twist and turn life may throw at us, we can remain diligent about staying focused and remaining disciplined with regard to our personal missions.

On the flip side, just because you have some setbacks, keep in perspective where you started and where you are currently in relation to that. Many people have a tendency to compare themselves with where they want to be, reinforcing where they are *not*, rather than comparing themselves with where they started, reinforcing *how far they have come*. The following tool aims to prepare you for both the peaks and the valleys.

MONITORING MY PROGRESS

Think about an area of your life where you are working to make changes. Reflect on where you were in that area before you started taking any steps toward growth. Write about what it felt like, who you were with, what you were doing, how much money you were making, how often you were engaging in certain behaviors, or any other markers that could be a helpful barometer to measure where you have come from.

When things are going well, I need to be diligent about doing these behaviors that I believe contribute to my ongoing success:

_____

_____

As things continue to go well, I need to be aware that I still have the following vulnerabilities and be sure to have safeguards in place:

_____

_____

When I have a setback, I need to remember where I started, and realize that even though I took a step back from where I was, I have still made the following progress that wasn't negated by my mistake:

_____

_____

I will remain focused on the future rather than the past by:

_____

_____

When I view this recent setback realistically and put it in perspective, I can see both good and bad. The downside was:

_____

_____

The most helpful mindset for me to approach this with moving forward is:

_____

_____

TOOL 9.9: RELAPSE PREVENTION SESSION

If you are a coach or therapist starting to work with individuals in recovery of some kind, the following can serve as a loose guideline for how you might approach a session from a cognitive behavioral perspective.

1. Did you relapse this week?

2. If yes, tell me what happened (conduct chain analysis)

3. On a scale of 0-10 how close did you get?

4. At what point during the week were you most tempted to use/engage in "setback" behavior? What were you doing?

5. On a scale of 0-10 how strong was the craving at that time?

6. "What was going through your mind at the time?

7. What kept you from relapsing? Anything else?

8. How many times this week were you tempted to use but didn't?

9. What skills did you use to resist the urges?
   a. Behavioral skills (what did you do?)
   b. Cognitive skills (what did you think?)

10. What did you do right this week?

11. What changes do you need to implement this week?

TOOL 9.10: RELAPSE PREVENTION PLAN

Now that you have done everything you can to prepare *not* to have a relapse, looked at the best mindset to approach relapses when they do occur, and tried to put your area of focus into perspective by looking at strengths and vulnerabilities in a balanced way, it is time to tweak your relapse prevention plan. Keep what you are doing well. Make necessary changes. And keep this plan at the top of your priorities. This may serve you the rest of your life. Or you may revamp it tomorrow. Remember these are working documents. But this is your relapse prevention plan for now.

Things I am doing well and I would like to continue to include:

_____

Changes I am making based on my most recent setback include:

_____

I know I will be most tempted when:

_____

I will be prepared to deal with temptation this time because:

_____

Skills (if any) I need to learn or improve:

_____

My support people in place are:

_____

My daily routine consists of:

_____

Personal strengths I have that will help me succeed in this endeavor include:

_____

Other details of my plan:

_____

3

Adapting CBT for Different Settings

A final frontier of this text is coaching. I realize even including this in a book of this nature will immediately alienate a few people. And I have to admit, I was among those until recent years. We can "should" (see Chapter 1) it all we want. The reality is coaching is here to stay. It is a billion-dollar industry. As of this writing, 1.1 million coaches are registered on LinkedIn. Life coaching has transformed the lives of millions of people who rightly or wrongly have bought in to the stigmas associated with psychotherapy and have sought assistance in their life journey from other sources. Business coaching has helped companies with employee retention, staff morale, and overall effectiveness in serving their clientele. I have even learned recently that companies can have personality disorders! So my conclusion is that since millions of people worldwide will seek coaching services every year, rather than pretend it is not real, why not offer the most effective method of change as an option for people in this space? Thousands of less qualified practitioners are working with folks using less proven methods of change.

Also, there are people in different parts of the world that either don't have access to traditional treatment or are on waiting lists that are years long. Many of these folks are seeking coaching services and programs as well. My belief is that CBT can be truly life changing and that the more we can disseminate it to groups who previously did not have access to it, the better.

Among the several differences between treatment and coaching is that psychotherapy treats psychological disorders, whereas coaching promotes personal growth and goal achievement. For instance, a psychotherapist would offer empirically supported treatment for someone presenting with PTSD, OCD, schizophrenia, or other recognized diagnosis. A dating coach, to the contrary, would help facilitate awareness regarding client thoughts and behaviors as they attempt to improve their social skills and help them change their interactional patterns with their partner. A fitness coach might help clients identify and achieve their personal goals related to health and wellness. A business coach would help a company identify and change culture problems in mindset, use of time, interactional styles with staff and clients, and so on.

Although coaching is generally sought by higher-functioning individuals, the two don't have to be mutually exclusive. Someone with diagnosable panic disorder may seek a coach to help them leave an abusive relationship or find future relationships that are more compatible. The coach may need to assist with anxiety that arises that prevents the client from choosing a type of relationship that is healthy for them, but the coach is not directly treating panic disorder.

Many coaches simply rely on their own personal experience in the given area the client is desiring growth in. However, in more recent years, there has been a thirst in this community to incorporate approaches that are adaptations of proven psychological models. Cognitive behavioral coaching (CBC) is one such example. CBC is supported by research. It retains the collaborative and goal-directed, growth-oriented elements of other coaching approaches, but it also incorporates specific cognitive strategies designed at identifying and restructuring thought processes that have been blocking individuals' and companies' goal achievement.

Since coaching is much less formal than psychotherapy, the format of section 3 will reflect those differences and be presented in a parallel manner. Although the theoretical constructs will be discussed in a more conversational way, the concepts remain the same. All behaviors, whether they cross the "threshold" of clinical concern, are driven by beliefs. Tools used may be less technical but will retain the goal of identifying and changing belief-driven behaviors presenting obstacles to goal achievement.

Although the focus is goal achievement versus symptom management, obstacle behaviors will be dealt with similarly: by making them overt, facilitating increased client awareness to such behaviors, identifying thought processes contributing to them, and assisting to promote new mindsets and action steps.

This section addresses a few common areas relevant to coaching clients; time management, performance, stress management, dealing with difficult people, and belief-based communication.

CHAPTER **10**

Time Management

A friend of mine once rushed into a meeting 10 minutes late and joked, "Has anyone seen my time? I think I've lost it!"

Many people operate on overdrive. Overbooked. Overscheduled. Productivity requirements. Quotas. Deadlines. Always rushed. Burned out. The demands of modern life have made it increasingly difficult to live with any margin. This sense of urgency can often rob us of our peace and keep us from enjoying the moment. "I don't have the time" is probably the most common excuse heard in variety of professional and personal settings. "My life is crazy," or "I don't have the time other people have" are also commonplace.

The reality is that we all have 168 hours in our week, and we get to spend it how we choose. Put bluntly, nobody uses their time in a manner that they did not choose. That's right; you did not do anything today or yesterday that you did not choose to do! This is not always as simple as it may sound. It may require making some hard choices related to relationships, jobs, feelings, and priorities.

And we may suffer consequences if we don't devote time to completing a certain task or seeing through a certain commitment. But just about every situation we are currently in has come about as a result of a decision we have chosen to make.

Many who are initially offended by having it put this way are eventually relieved to hear that they actually have inadvertently been contributing to their stress by *not* making time management a priority. It is easy to "go through the motions" not being intentional about how we spend our time. So the good news is if choices contributed to having "no time," new, more intentional choices can also empower us to create "additional time" in our lives. This chapter is designed to help you develop insight to some of the time-related choices you may have been making outside your awareness and to be more consciously purposeful about your choices with regard to how you are spending your time.

Most, if not all, problems with time management fall into one of three categories. Lack of motivation, lack of awareness, or interfering beliefs. Lets' start with number 1.

Lack of Motivation
While awareness is the primary beginning problem for most people struggling to manage their time, some people actually have some insight into how their 168 hours are "getting away from them" but lack the motivation to do anything about it. An adapted version of the expressions of concern tool used in the addictive behaviors chapter can be helpful here as well. This exercise asks to you ponder whether anyone in your life has voiced any concern in this area, what their concern is, and what the reason is. Review the example given and then complete your own tool.

TOOL 10.1: EXPRESSIONS OF CONCERN

Example

Person	Concern	Reason
1. Boss	1. Working overtime	1. Unauthorized pay
2. Wife	2. Coming home late	2. Damaging relationship with wife and children
3. Accountant	3. Consistently late submitting tax information	3. Late fees and penalties

Observation: *"I need to care about this more than I do—my family and my livelihood are at stake."*

My Expressions of Concern

Person	Concern	Reason
1.		
2.		
3.		

Observations:

_____

_____

TOOL 10.2: TIME AWARENESS

This tool can be helpful for clarifying exactly how you spend your time. It asks you simply to pay attention to and record how you spend your time. Change nothing. (Some people's people-pleasing beliefs motivate them to make changes, so they have something more "acceptable" to write down for their therapist or coach to see!). Simply record, in 30-minute increments, how you are spending your time. Review the example given and then complete your own.

Awareness Tool-Example

Time	Activity
7 a.m.	Get up
8 a.m.	Go to work
9 a.m.	Check work email, Facebook, surf the net
10 a.m.	Work on project
12–2 p.m.	Have lunch
2 p.m.	Talk with coworker in cubicle next to me
3 p.m.	Work on Penske file
4 p.m.	Run into a question—boss has just left office—have to wait an hour on him to call me back
5 p.m.	When I get my question answered, worked another hour until hit good stopping place
6 p.m.	Went to gym
9 p.m.	Get home

My Awareness Tool	
Time	**Activity (Be Specific)**
6 a.m.	
7 a.m.	
8 a.m.	
9 a.m.	
10 a.m.	
11 a.m.	
12 p.m.	
1 p.m.	
2 p.m.	
3 p.m.	
4 p.m.	
5 p.m.	
6 p.m.	
7 p.m.	
8 p.m.	
9 p.m.	
10 p.m.	
11 p.m.	
12 a.m.	
1 a.m.	
2 a.m.	
3 a.m.	
4 a.m.	
5 a.m.	

My Observations:

1. _____

2. _____

3. _____

4. _____

5. _____

TOOL 10.3: ELIMINATE THE WASTE

This tool builds on the last one. Analyze your observations. Now that you have noticed some elements related to how you spend your time that you previously "missed," what changes could you implement that correspond with each "opportunity" you identified. Consider the example, and then work to eliminate your own waste.

Example

Observation	Proposed Change
Get up late and rush out the door—didn't even see wife and kids in morning.	If I got up earlier, I could see kids and wife more. I could even work out in the morning.
Spent more time in morning on internet than I realized.	After I check my work email, turn my internet off so I won't be tempted to get back on it so I can get right to work.
Did not realize how long we stayed at lunch—probably do that pretty frequently.	Make concentrated effort to be aware of time—cut lunch to one hour—leave margin for traffic to get back if we go across town.
Talked to coworkers more than I thought in P.M.—running late caused me to miss my boss which caused me to be there even later.	I can be friendly, but then tell Dara I need to get back to my project so I can get out of here sooner—she values family time, so she will "get it." I don't even think she realizes how chatty she gets.
Got home as kids were going to bed, wife gave me cold shoulder again.	If I worked out in the morning, I could get home a lot sooner—even if I don't stay focused during the day, I could get home sooner. I can plan a family evening one time a week that will give me a time I have to be done and home by.

MY ELIMINATE THE WASTE TOOL

Observation	Proposed Change

TOOL 10.4: IDENTIFY YOUR PRIORITIES

I once heard it said that if we want to know what we really value the most, we need look no further than two places: our credit-card statements and our calendars. We espouse many other values to take top priority in our lives. But the reality is we spend our money and our time on the things that are most important to us. In a chapter devoted to time management, this begs the obvious question: What is really most important to us? And what implications does that have in terms of how we may choose to alter how we spend our time? Use this tool to guide your process of increasing your awareness in this area and making the changes you desire.

Step 1 in this process involves completing the following priorities inventory tool.

Priorities Inventory Tool

Stated Priority	On a Scale of 1–10, How Important Is It
Education	
Service	
Spouse/Dating	
Relationship with children	
Financial success	
Work achievement	
Personal growth	
Physical beauty or attractiveness	
Physical health	
Travel	
Kindness	
Entertainment	
Comfort	
Religion/Faith/Culture	
Quality/Orderliness	
Other	

Now that you have identified priorities and rated their importance to you, step 2 in this process involves reviewing your credit-card statements, and your calendar for the past 3 months. What themes do you see in your spending and how you spend your time? Any common threads? What takeaways did you glean from this tool that you can incorporate into your time management changes?

_____

_____

_____

TOOL 10.5: INTENTIONAL LIVING LOG

You have likely heard the phrase "prioritize your schedule." A popular approach in the coaching world suggests that this might actually be a backward way to think about it. Rather than *prioritizing our schedules*, how might our calendars look different if we *scheduled our priorities?* Now that you have identified what priorities are most important to you, this task is more easily accomplished. Use a modified version of the monitoring log you completed earlier to be intentional about scheduling more of the things that are important to you.

Many people respond to this type of mindset as "pie in the sky." I have had people at live seminars say things like, "I don't know what kind of world you live in, but most of us can't just do what we want! We have obligations!" We all have obligations. But this kind of closed-minded thinking is what keeps people from growing regardless of the area of life. Even the smallest changes in how we go about our days can carve out at least *some* time we can shift to include more of our priorities. It has been beneficial to think of these as *"want to's"* versus *"have to's."* Even if your schedule still consists of 95 percent "have to's," intentionally incorporating just one, even if small, "want to" into each day is at least a start, and in and of itself can make a big difference in life satisfaction.

New York Times' best-selling author John C. Maxwell has authored a book titled *Intentional Living*. This is an idea I have found to be quite helpful, and this mindset and language is reflected in these tools. Complete the following checklist. Before each week, identify some "have to's" and some "want to's" that you can choose from when completing your intentional living log.

To-Do Checklist Tool

"Have To's"	"Want To's"
1. _____	1. _____
2. _____	2. _____
3. _____	3. _____
4. _____	4. _____
5. _____	5. _____
6. _____	6. _____
7. _____	7. _____
8. _____	8. _____
9. _____	9. _____
10. _____	10. _____

TOOL 10.6: STRATEGIC SCHEDULING

One final tip: Being strategic about *how* you go about scheduling your day is important. For instance, after making similar lists to the ones above for each day, I ask myself: Where do I *have* to be when?

- Are there tasks I can only accomplish at certain times of the day?
- At what point in the day is my thinking the clearest?
- If so, what do I need to *save* until that part of the day versus what do I need to put on my calendar earlier in the day because it cannot be done elsewhere?
- Are there times that I could multitask?
- Are there times that it is *not* in my best interest to multitask?
- What, if anything, can I delegate?
- How can I make the best use of my time today?

A glimpse into my personal mindset around how I approach this:

For starters, when I was originally approached about writing the first edition of this book, I said "No." I did not see myself as an author (I still don't). I didn't have a desire to write it. I didn't know *why* I would write it, and I didn't know *when* I would write it.

The short story as to why I changed my mind? YouTube cat videos. I walked onto a plane one day flying home from Los Angeles where I had just done a 3-day conference, and the guy next to me on the plane was watching cats do these ridiculous tricks off a sofa on YouTube. I could not believe how amused he was as an adult. This guy proceeded to watch similar videos the entire 3-hour flight.

I then made a point to be nosy. That is, rather than zoning out and going through the motions as was my practice at the time, I made it a point just to be more aware of my surroundings. I particularly paid more attention to what people were doing on the plane. It BLEW ME AWAY the number of people who were watching mindless videos or playing pointless games. It is only then that the thought occurred to me to do some math. I quickly estimated in my head, *"I speak in almost 100 cities per year. I have average flight/layover time of 10 hours per trip. I have 8 nights per month alone in hotel rooms I am usually watching sporting events."*

Filling in the numerical blanks is outside the scope of where we are going. But the conclusion I came to is that I had MANY hours being used unproductively during my travel. The result of my changes? I wrote my entire first book in planes, airports, and hotel rooms. I did not use one minute of my "free time." And before I realized it, I had a best seller that benefitted many people (my *why* for future books became clearer through that process), simply by making more intentional use of the time I was already spending doing essentially nothing.

Other examples from my daily life would include that I spend 4 hours a week with my girls at their gymnastics practice. (2 hours per day, twice a week). One of those hours each day they are practicing across the gym where they are out of my view. I have learned to make use of this time. During the time I *can* see them, I put my laptop away and make my best effort to focus my attention solely on them. However, during those 2 hours a week I cannot see them anyway, I block in my schedule to accomplish a task I can do on my laptop. Also, I take into consideration that this facility has Wi-Fi, so if need be, I can schedule a project that requires online activity.

If I am going to visit my parents for the weekend, I know there will be time there that I will want to focus on family and put my devices away, but I also know there will be some idle time people will be doing their own thing that I can be productive. I also know the internet is spotty out there in the "boonies."

Thus, when planning my week, I strategically schedule the two hours I will have at gymnastics for work that requires internet, while planning to block the free hours at my parents for a project that does not require internet. I have a client who makes use of the time she is taking a bath (but doesn't use anything that could not get wet—she does tasks that requires those items earlier in the day), a client who makes use of the time in the carpool line while waiting to pick up her son from school, and a coworker who works on her phone while sitting her usual 20 minutes in the Sam's Club outside pick-up line.

None of this is rocket science. It doesn't take an Ivy league education. It simply requires developing the mindset to be intentional, the willingness to take a moment to think ahead, and proactively scheduling strategically and accordingly. By doing so, you will eliminate most if not all of those times you end up "wasting" time because "I didn't have internet when I needed it" or "I just didn't think to have that list with me or I could have gotten something done."

By strategically planning out your daily schedule in a way that you can use your "have to" hours to your benefit, you can make the most of your 168 hours. Oh, and you will likely watch fewer cat videos.

With these tips in mind, complete another log purposefully scheduling your upcoming week. Use your prior work to consider how you can accomplish your "have to's" yet eliminate waste and schedule your priorities. Some people enjoy using a different color or highlighting "want to's" in a way that they stick out in the calendar and one can make sure to have a certain amount of "yellow" every day or at least every week.

MY STRATEGIC SCHEDULING TOOL

Time	Activity (Be specific)
6 a.m.	
7 a.m.	
8 a.m.	
9 a.m.	
10 a.m.	
11 a.m.	
12 p.m.	
1 p.m.	
2 p.m.	
3 p.m.	
4 p.m.	
5 p.m.	
6 p.m.	
7 p.m.	
8 p.m.	
9 p.m.	
10 p.m.	
11 p.m.	
12 a.m.	
1 a.m.	
2 a.m.	
3 a.m.	
4 a.m.	
5 a.m.	

How did you do? After your first week of purposeful scheduling, it is vital to examine how you did. My experience is that the majority of people complete one or two of these logs and then quit. I don't know that I have worked with anyone who has lived their first intentional week exactly like they planned to. These take work. Regularly paying attention to the choices we make with regard to our time and becoming skillful at making tweaks to our personal scheduling along the way is hard. Consistency is the key to success.

The purpose of this next tool is to list what you *planned* to do and then what you *actually* did during given time frames. This exercise actually requires you to combine your intentional living log skills (priority-based scheduling ahead of time) with your mindfulness "in the moment" monitoring skills you first used when simply recording how you currently spent your time.

Use the tool to see how you did. Work with your therapist or coach to make changes you desire moving forward.

TOOL 10.7: EVALUATING MY FOLLOW-THROUGH

Time	Activity Scheduled	Actual
6 a.m.		
7 a.m.		
8 a.m.		
9 a.m.		
10 a.m.		
11 a.m.		
12 p.m.		
1 p.m.		
2 p.m.		
3 p.m.		
4 p.m.		
5 p.m.		
6 p.m.		
7 p.m.		
8 p.m.		
9 p.m.		
10 p.m.		
11 p.m.		
12 a.m.		
1 a.m.		
2 a.m.		
3 a.m.		
4 a.m.		
5 a.m.		

My Observations:

Interfering Beliefs

It is well established that beliefs drive behavior. This principle has been emphasized in earlier chapters addressing issues of clinical concern, but this tenet is just as relevant whether the behavior is making a suicidal act or deciding to talk to a coworker instead of focus on a project. If you have a clinical background, you are familiar with the term *target behavior*. When working with coaching clients, I often use the term *obstacle behavior*. In the case of the previous tool the client completed, these will be behaviors that show up in their "actual" column. They are the behaviors the client actually chose to do instead of the behaviors they committed to do as part of their revamped intentional time management scheduling.

Since beliefs drive behavior, one advantage cognitive behavioral coaching has over other approaches is that it is uniquely qualified to identify beliefs behind obstacle behaviors and work on them. While someone may have chosen to engage in an obstacle behavior rather than their desired/planned behavior for a number of reasons, this section focuses on three common beliefs that interfere with well-intentioned schedules and undercut efforts to more effectively manage time: beliefs related to perfectionism, procrastination, and people-pleasing.

Perfectionism

Webster's dictionary defines perfectionism *as a disposition to regard anything short of perfect as unacceptable.* Perfectionism affects every area of life: work performance, romantic relationships, friendships, parenting, just to name a few. Perfectionism is associated with increased stress levels. Elevated stress levels have been associated with higher occurrences of a number of medical conditions. Perfectionism really has become a cancer in the lives of millions of people and is the most common obstacle that keeps millions of people from managing their time effectively.

Cognitive Features of Perfectionism

In terms of Jeff Young's schemas described in Chapter 1, perfectionists have, among others, a version of the unrelenting standards belief in combination with a failure belief. Thus, as even Webster's generic definition alludes to, people who have these high standards and don't meet them often feel like a failure. Some perfectionists hold these beliefs related to unrelenting standards only toward themselves, whereas many expect perfection from others as well.

Two of the more prominent cognitive distortions in the perfectionist are "should" statements and black-and-white thinking (rigid thinking). Examples include:

- *"*This project *has to* be done perfectly."
- "If we don't have a perfect solution, we *have to* keep looking."
- "Since others will slack off, I *must* do everything myself."
- "Since I didn't do my routine perfectly, I *need to* keep practicing"
- "I/We *have to* know for sure—if we don't get this right, we will regret it, and regret is unacceptable!"
- "If I rehearse my lines just one more time, I'll have a flawless performance."
- "Your proposal should be more precise. Since it isn't, we *have to* keep talking about the specifics."
- "If I don't do this absolutely *perfect*, I am a complete failure."

Do you notice the demanding, extreme, and rigid features of this mindset? These are the types of thoughts that are likely to be addressed in your perfectionism thought logs. Thinking in these ways routinely leads to some common problem behaviors that often become obstacle behaviors to target in coaching or therapy.

Behavioral Features of Perfectionism

Perhaps the most common obstacle to time management seen with perfectionists has to do with taking significantly longer that others to complete the same task. Perfectionists working with cognitive behavioral coaches or therapists often underestimate the amount of time it may take them to complete a task. Not only will they underestimate it ahead of time when completing their intentional living logs, they also won't recognize it "in the moment" as they are exceeding their allotted time for a given task. The phrase "he couldn't see the forest for the trees" doesn't ring truer with anyone than the perfectionist. This over focus on the minute details (the trees) limits their awareness to recognize the bigger-picture consequences (the forest) related to task completion, maintaining relationships, and staying employed. Overpreparing, over-rehearsing, overthinking, over-discussing, and overanalyzing (including the inability to know when to quit) are all common obstacles seen in perfectionists.

Change Strategies and Action Plans

Due to the perfectionist mindset, real change often proves to be long, tedious, and hard work. Many coaches frankly are unprepared to help people with these struggles make meaningful changes that last. I had a client one time who, prior to seeking my services, sought help from a coach who told him to sing a song every morning when he woke up in which he vocalized the words "do it" one hundred times in different tunes. While creative, this type of cute and surface level "coaching strategy" illustrates the all-too-common phenomenon of coaches underestimating the power rigid beliefs often hold in clients' lives. Anyone who claims to "cure you of your self-limiting beliefs" in thirty minutes on stage (or in a few coaching sessions) does not have enough of an understanding of the dynamics involved to be truly helpful when these compelling beliefs are present. Whoever you are seeking coaching or therapy from needs to understand that when deeply held beliefs and rigid thinking are involved in the mindset, a *process will need to be worked through over time.*

Even within the limited scope of this book, addressing perfectionistic beliefs that impact effective time management, the importance of validation should be stressed. I have heard it said that validation is the WD-40 of change. We as people seem to need to be "loosened up" a little before we are ready to move forward. Validation is always important, but it is especially so with this group of people who have a behavior style that is considered more *ego-syntonic* than others. That is, perfectionists typically have less insight into the harmful effects of their behavior than others. It is only after validating perfectionists that coaches will be most effective in challenging problematic mindsets and obstacle behaviors.

I made the following statement to one of my perfectionistic clients:

"I know that there are a lot of slobs (using his language) out there Boyd, and the world really would be a lot better off if more people paid attention to detail. I mean, just the other day I had to take something back to the store due to low-quality work. While this is true, it is also true that your wife is threatening to divorce you and you are mandated to see me by your employer. I know how important your marriage and your job are to you. Have you heard the expression that sometimes our greatest strengths can become our biggest weaknesses?..."

At that point, he was still hesitant, but at least open to what I had to say next. So once my foot was in the door, I was able to point out in more depth how his attention to detail was *helpful* for his specific job on his specific team, but then also help him see how it kept him from keeping within the parameters of the intentional living log we had completed the week before. I was then able to amplify what my academy of cognitive therapy colleague, Marty Antony (2009), calls distinguishing between functional versus dysfunctional perfection.

Some helpful questions he poses to facilitate these discussions include:

- Are my standards higher than others?
- How often am I able to meet them?
- Do I expect others to meet those?
- How do those standards affect me in important areas of my life?
- Ultimately, do my standards help me meet my goals or present obstacles to meeting my goal?

Elaborating on the implementation of all of these tools for perfectionists is beyond the scope of this chapter on time management, but other helpful strategies and action steps useful for helping this population keep obstacle behaviors at bay and actually doing what they planned include:

- Challenging rigid thinking
- Learning to see shades of gray
- Learning to compromise
- Examining the pros and cons of striving for perfection
- Tolerating uncertainty
- Using cognitive cue cards to reinforce mindset shifts
- Using coping cards to increase compliance with action steps

Procrastination

Procrastination is another major obstacle to effective time management. One definition of procrastination is *putting off until later what would be in one's best interest to do now, thereby creating undesirable consequences.* More simply put, I have heard procrastination described as a thief of time.

Most of us procrastinate to one degree or another. Small amounts of procrastination usually produce few if any consequences. The more procrastination becomes an ingrained way of responding and is used to cope with major events in life, the higher the stakes get. Also, some people may procrastinate in just one area; they may put off doing work and miss deadlines but demonstrate no significant procrastination in their interpersonal relationships or other non-work life. In clinical terms, this would be a more discrete manifestation. For other people this is their modus operandi—they procrastinate across the board. In clinical terms, this would be evidence of more pervasive procrastination-related beliefs contributing to the putting off (a form of behavioral avoidance).

Regardless of contexts of life affected, Surveys show 20 percent of adults report regularly being significantly affected negatively as a result of procrastination (Persaud, 2005).

The idea of "self-leadership" is now a popular topic at breakout sessions in leadership conferences. Procrastination might be thought of as a failure of self-leadership.

Procrastination is really a form of avoidance. And like the previous section on perfectionism, could be expanded to an entire chapter of its own. But for the purpose of this book, the scope of this topic will be limited to procrastination-related beliefs interfering with time management.

Cognitive Features of Procrastination

Procrastination has a less-precise cognitive makeup than perfectionism. That is, all perfectionists have one if not both beliefs identified by Young of unrelenting standards and failure. While the cognitive specificity at the belief level is more varied in the procrastinator, common themes still emerge that are worthy to be addressed, particularly at the automatic thought level.

The primary distortion to be addressed with this group is *rationalization*, or permission-giving beliefs. Remember that any time that any of us procrastinate, we give ourselves permission to put something off for one reason or another.

The basic form most rationalizations take is:

"It's ok to put off _____, because _____."

Common examples include:

- "It's ok to put off studying because I don't like it and something else would be more fun."
- "It's ok to skip class because I can just make up the work later."
- "It's ok not to have that confrontation with her because I'm not sure what she's going to say, and if I don't ask, I can put off rejection a little longer."
- "It's ok not to do an internship this semester because I can do two next year."

These are just a few of many possible examples. But the theme here is giving self-permission to put something off for some reason. Sometimes the "reason" given is superficial and avoidant in and of itself. Sometimes the reason may provide a window to an underlying core belief. Either way, the task of the coach or therapist is to identify (1) the task being avoided, and (2) the reason being given. These will be targets for change strategies and action plans.

Again, unlike perfectionists who all have unrelenting standards and failure beliefs, procrastinators can have a variety of underlying beliefs. A client of mine who is a procrastinator at work identified the rationalization "It's ok to put off working on my project because Sue needs help with hers." Although when we used the downward arrow technique (described in Chapter 1), we identified something a little deeper.

Client: I think I told myself that it was ok to put it off because Sue was really struggling and needed my help.

> **Dr. R:** You always have been considerate. But remember we said that procrastination almost always involves avoidance? I'm wondering was there anything about the specific project that you were avoiding?

Client: Ummmmm...

> **Dr. R:** Do you feel confident about your ability to complete the project?

Client: I guess I didn't feel the most confident about it.

> **Dr. R:** What would be the worst thing that could happen if you didn't have it mastered?

Client: I guess, if I'm honest, I might not really know how to do it.

> **Dr. R:** And what might happen if you didn't know how to do it?

Client: I'd do it wrong.

> **Dr. R:** And what would happen if you did it wrong?

Client: My boss would criticize me.

> **Dr. R:** And what would be the worst part about your boss criticizing you?

Client: (voice raising, becoming visibly upset) I could get fired from this job just like I did my last two!

> **Dr. R:** (in quieting, sympathetic voice) "And that would mean that...?

Client: (sinking quietly) I am such a loser.

In this case, there was a failure belief driving his procrastination. However, other clients might have put off their task and helped a co-worker due to self-sacrifice, people-pleasing, or a number of other schemas at the "root" of the problem. Thus, identifying the motive is paramount.

Behavioral Features of Procrastination

These are pretty straightforward. Identify the avoided activities that accompany the permission-giving statements. Then move to changing them.

Change Strategies and Action Plans

Dryden (2000) has articulated four stages to overcoming procrastination: Awareness, goal-directed behavior, committing to short-term discomfort in exchange for long-term gain, and persistence. Review the following summary and incorporate these into your time management tools.

1. **Awareness.** We can't change what we don't recognize we are or aren't doing. While some procrastination may be less conscious, most of the time there is some specific dread involved. Some people set timers on their smartphones; other use reminders on their computers. Many people increase their awareness by simply putting a visual of their intentional living log somewhere that will be in front of them the majority of the day. This serves as a constant reminder of the time frames they have committed to and helps keep focus "top of mind."

2. **Goal directed behavior.** Here is where the coach's suggestion of singing "do it now" in the shower could have a place! Creative tactics could play a role here, but the bottom line is developing collaboratively with the client a specific plan to attack the behavior, making adjustments along the way, as necessary.

3. **A commitment to tolerate short-term discomfort in exchange for long-term gain.** As with perfectionists, toleration of discomfort is a vital component to having breakthroughs in this area. Where the perfectionist has to learn to tolerate the uncomfortableness of uncertainty, the procrastinator's charge is to improve their ability to tolerate the unpleasant emotions that will arise as they confront the event they had previously been putting off. Helping clients recognize that intense emotions need not be anything to fear is an important part of this work.

4. **Persistence.** Remember, there is no magic cure. Work the process. Develop the plan. Work the plan. When clients put off the action, help increase their awareness to the mindset driving the choices. On the flip side, revisit the **What's My Why Tool** from chapter 10. Provide a reminder of why they are working toward what they are working toward in the first place. Identify the rationalizations/ permission-giving ideas facilitating procrastination. Challenge the thoughts, rework the plan. Do it again. Rinse and repeat.

People Pleasing

When was the last time you said yes to someone when you really wanted to say no? In an age where brashness grabs the headlines, the overwhelming silent minority actually suffer from problems on the *other* end of the spectrum. People pleasing contributes to employees being taken advantage of in work settings, members getting burned out in churches and nonprofits, and people getting stuck in unhealthy and even abusive relationships. And, as it relates to this chapter, people pleasing drives behaviors that interfere with one's ability to manage time.

Another one of the most common behaviors that keeps people from following through with intentional living logs is people pleasing. It seems innocent enough. In fact, it even seems "noble," "good," and "compassionate"—all values our society lauds. So how could these traits possibly present obstacles?

Cognitive Features of People Pleasing

In terms of Jeff Young's schemas, these behaviors come out of what is technically called an *approval-seeking schema*. This is the belief in people who must have the approval of others. People with strong beliefs have the rigid (black-and-white) thinking discussed earlier.

Common thoughts include:

- "If I don't help, he might not like me."
- "If I say no, she will be upset."
- "The most important thing is not to rock the boat."
- "If somebody is upset with me, it would be unbearable."
- "I should do whatever it takes to keep her on my good side."

The theme in this thinking is pretty clear as well. The mindset shift necessary here is to get clients to realize what Terry Cole-Whittaker famously put it in her best-selling self-help book, that "what you think of me is none of my business (1988)."

Behavioral Features of People Pleasing

Obstacle behaviors here involve saying 'yes' when it is in one's best interest to say 'no.' It is not that saying yes is *never* a good idea. When law enforcement instructs you to do something, your boss gives you a nonnegotiable directive, or your doctor gives you medical advice about a serious condition are likely times when a "yes, sir" is indicated. People pleasing gives way to obstacle behaviors, however, when a person is saying yes often enough that it interferes with their ability to live consistent with their stated priorities.

Change Strategies and Action Plans

1. Awareness and self-monitoring

2. Criteria for saying yes

3. Continuum of people who care what they think

4. Seeing the relational benefits of time management—that is, spouse/boss pleased with you rather than stranger you barely know

5. Being ok with others not being ok with your response—tolerating emotions

TOOL 10.8: PROCRASTINATION ACTION PLAN

My Procrastination Obstacle Behaviors

What am I putting off?

_____

_____

Procrastination Thoughts That Need to Be Challenged

What reasons am I telling myself it is ok to put it off?

_____

_____

What's my why?

What do I have to lose if I continue to make excuses and avoid?

_____

_____

What will I gain that I desire if I do what needs to be done?

_____

_____

My action plan for confronting what I dread and spending my time the way I really want to is:

_____

_____

TOOL 10.9: PEOPLE PLEASING AND PERFECTIONISM ACTION PLAN

My People Pleasing Perfectionistic Obstacle Behaviors

People in my life I am likely to say yes to this week that have the most potential to distract me:

_____

_____

People Pleasing Thoughts That Need Challenge

Why will I tell myself it is ok to invest time in them rather than stick to my plans?

_____

_____

What's my why?

What do I have to lose if I remain rigid?

_____

_____

What will I *gain* that I desire if I become more flexible?

_____

_____

My action plan for spending my time the way I really want to is:

_____

_____

Summary Tips for Retaking Control of your Time

- Examine how you are currently spending your time. Pay attention to detail. Note what really sticks out to you about what you are currently doing.

- Be honest about your priorities. How we choose to spend our time reflects what is really most important to us, regardless of what we tell ourselves.

- Clarify what excuses you are telling yourself that is making it easy for you to put off things that you say you'd like to prioritize.

- Give up your need to be perfect. Focus on the big picture. Don't allow unnecessary details to bog you down.

- Say no to things that are lower on your priority list—it is possible to be involved in too many noble causes. Only commit to things you have time for at that point in your life, and work to get better at telling people no.

- Develop a plan based on those priorities—devote time only to those things that you deem the most valuable.

- As you develop your plan, create *margin*—leave time for unforeseen events, traffic, things out of your control.

CHAPTER 11

Performance and Self-Esteem

Performance is an area of concern for clients as well as many employers. Clients are often referred to therapy or coaching by employee assistance programs, work-related third parties, or at times employers themselves. Employers undoubtedly have an external motivation related to improved performance or productivity.

A majority of people, however, are more *internally* motivated to work on these obstacles. Concerns related to performance not only affect people in their roles as employees of organizations or businesses but also can be a source of anxiety and insecurity for athletes, musicians, actors, and many others where success is determined based on their ability to perform when it is their time to step into the spotlight. Although this is obviously crucial when one's livelihood is dependent on ability to deliver, many people experience problems in the area of performance even when it relates to a hobby or something they do for "fun."

Susy was a pianist. She loved having the ability to play a variety of songs. She played for large groups of people at concert halls and for small family get-togethers at Christmas. Certain types of music, in her words, "restored her soul." However, even at age 32 after many years' playing at various competitive levels, she still suffered tremendous performance anxiety before she played. This anxiety was triggered whether her audience was two people or two thousand people. It didn't matter. At the most recent family get-together when her uncle complimented her, she responded by saying, "There really should have been more contrast in the last song."

Jane also was a pianist. She actually was less talented than Susy. She played less frequently and had a more diverse range of interests. When she played, however, even in front of her largest audiences (which were usually much smaller than Susy's), it felt "liberating" to her, and she enjoyed every minute of it...even when she made noticeable mistakes.

Some people see this chapter title and ask "How is performance related to self-esteem? For some people it is not. For people like Jane, their ability to perform has no impact on their self-esteem. For others, such as Susy, a subpar performance can be absolutely crippling. So what is the difference? Some people's self-esteem is tied directly to their performance, whereas others is not. This chapter is devoted to coaching those individuals who struggle with performance related to low self-esteem.

How Do I Tell if Self-Esteem is Tied to Performance?

So what is the difference between Susy and Jane? Two factors need to be assessed to determine if a performance-related issue can be attributed to self-esteem.

1. The Type of Beliefs

I recall hearing early on in my training through the Beck Institute a couple of fancy terms referred to as "performance-oriented schemas" versus "sociotropic schemas." The non-psycho-babble explanation for this is simply that people with performance-oriented beliefs (or schemas) get triggered in *response to stimulus related to performance, achievement, or accomplishment*, whereas people with sociotropic schemas get triggered more frequently in response to *relational interactions*. So this really can be boiled down to the questions: What is most important to them? Performance or people?

Readers familiar with the DISC personality profiles (Dominant - D; Inspiring - I; Supportive - S; and Cautious - C) might recognize that D's and C's in that model of human behavior will fall in the "performance" category, whereas S's and I's will fall in the "people" category. In terms of beliefs driving behavior (covered in Chapter 1), D's and C's will almost always have stronger "failure" beliefs, versus S's and I's who will likely have more beliefs related to approval seeking and self-sacrifice. So what does this mean in terms of this topic? Most people who struggle with performance-related self-esteem are D's and C's on the DISC! It should also be noted that S's and I's can have a similar presentation, however with them, performance is usually linked to *letting another person down* (i.e., disappointing a parent or teacher) versus just not being "good enough."

2. The Components of the Belief

This brings us to the second factor involved in determining if performance is linked to self-esteem. Once you have identified the belief, the therapist or coach must determine, if there is in fact a failure belief present, if that is what is driving the behavior. In clinical terms, one must assess the *components of the belief* (Tool 5.14).

The easiest way for a coach to do this is to observe carefully the types of things that trigger the person's feelings of anxiety or insecurity. Let's consider Susy and Jane again briefly. It became clear to me very quickly that Susy had a failure belief that was triggered every time she played the piano. She experienced anxiety every time she predicted she might not perform perfectly and was extremely critical of herself every time a performance fell short of perfect. So piano performing was clearly an important component of her failure belief and thus linked directly to her self-esteem.

Jane actually had a failure belief as well. The difference was that piano performance was not a component of that belief. She was not triggered in that area of life. Now if she was criticized at work by her supervisor, she **would** experience strong emotions at times. If work performance was a problem for her, then coaching in this area could be relevant.

When clients present with performance-related issues, I first want to see what else is going on in the person's life. Medical challenges, problems at home, and a whole host of other factors could be involved in poor performance in a given area that don't have to do with self-esteem. If the client and I collaboratively determine that the problem is related to one of these ancillary areas, coaching obviously takes a different course.

If the issues do appear to be related to self-esteem, the same general protocol for any CBT/CBC is followed: targeting behaviors and beliefs. A general rule of thumb: to the extent that the belief is true, the behaviors need to be the primary area of focus. To the degree that the belief is false, the beliefs themselves need to be addressed.

Assessing the Validity of the Belief

As with concerns in any other area, cognitive behavioral coaches must start by exploring collaboratively with the client to what extent the belief is true. For instance, James identified having a belief "I am so bad at what I do I am certain to lose my job." How could James and I determine the extent to which the belief was true? For starters, we went on a fact-finding mission. We collected information from:

- his teachers at school
- the person overseeing his practicum
- his coworkers
- his current supervisor

- a previous supervisor
- data/reports from previous work-related projects
- previous performance evaluations

To the degree we determined the part of his belief about being "bad at what I do" was true, we would focus on ways of improving his skills to make him better at what he does. CBC, like CBT, is not just about positive thinking. We would not simply try to build him up saying daily affirmations about how good he is and then send him back to the workplace to create more evidence to the contrary. We would equip him to be able to create authentic evidence to support a belief that he was skillful at his craft. We would then work to help him focus on, recognize, accept, and internalize this evidence so his beliefs about himself (self-esteem) would genuinely change over time. If it was determined he needed no skills training, we would jump straight to this belief-level work.

A quick note: You may note the language "to the degree the belief is true" being used above. This may be an area that requires attention for some clients with black-and-white thinking. Most beliefs are not just either true or false (although some are). Rather, usually they are truer or less true. For instance, as we sought data about James, we were able to draw some conclusions about *how* "good" or "bad" he was at his job. But it would have been impossible to verify that he was 100 percent good or 100 percent bad. We all fall on a spectrum of performance in any given area.

Self-Worth versus Self-Acceptance

Before we go any further, a quick clarification on terminology nuances. It is common in popular culture to hear terms like "self-esteem," "self-acceptance," "self-love," "self-image," "self-worth," and many others used synonymously. It is my belief that often in this field people make up new terminology to describe old ideas so they can gain recognition for "coining a term." While this phenomenon only muddies the waters, I do believe that it is important to differentiate between "self-worth" and "self-acceptance."

According to the Cambridge Dictionary, *self-worth* is "the belief and confidence in your own abilities and value." Thus, doing "self-worth" work would consist of identifying those components of the client's belief about what is worthwhile or valuable. While this will vary significantly from person to person, common ideas in clients I have worked with include the following:

- being physically attractive
- having material wealth
- practicing religious faith
- being highly educated
- having social status
- performing/accomplishing at work or hobbies
- being a "good" parent/grandparent

- being a "good" spouse
- being a "good" friend
- feeling approved of by others
- caretaking
- living a "moral" life
- living one's life consistent with a cause

Self-Acceptance

Alternatively, *self-acceptance* might be defined as "achieving a state where the individual fully and conditionally accepts him or herself whether he or she accomplishes tasks competently and whether other people approve or not." (Ellis, 1975). This work would require little if any identification of the components of the belief; rather, the emphasis is on complete acceptance of all facets of his whole person. When one accepts that he is separate from his personal qualities and choices, this task becomes a little clearer. Some clients find self-acceptance by developing affirmations or mantras that may say something as simple as this:

- I am inherently valuable because I am a human being.
- All human beings are fallible and have imperfections. I have mine, but these don't change who I really am.

TOOL 11.1: AFFIRMATIONS

Lets start with self-acceptance. Write a list of affirmations or statements that you believe may move you toward a more global sense of self-acceptance.

_____

_____

_____

_____

_____

_____

_____

_____

TOOL 11.2: WHAT ARE THE "LEGS" TO YOUR TABLE?

As mentioned in Tool 5.14, Leslie Sokol uses a visual of a table to represent a belief. As we develop beliefs during our lives, the meaning we attribute to events becomes the supporting "evidence" that a belief is true. These evidences are represented by "legs" supporting the table.

It is helpful to identify the "evidence" in our mind as to why a belief is true. It is only then that we know how to go about deconstructing it. This is again where much coaching that focuses only on generic "positive thinking" falls short. If we aren't attacking the specific types of thoughts responsible for emotional distress, we will continue to feel poorly about ourselves. To follow the visual metaphor, if the goal of belief change is to kick all the legs out from under the table (false belief), the coach (or therapist) is often kicking at legs that aren't there, and not going after the legs that are. Thus, the "table" continues to stand. This is why many people's self-esteem never improves in a meaningful and sustaining way over time.

The following tool uses the table visual metaphor to help you identify the components of your self-limiting, failure-related beliefs at the root of your low "self-esteem." Consider the example, and then identify your own "legs."

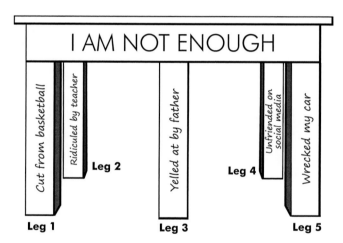

Evidence that I am a failure:

Leg 1: *Cut from 8th grade basketball team*

Leg 2: *Ridiculed for science project by teacher*

Leg 3: *Father yelled at me in garage for mistake on construction project*

Leg 4: *Unfriended on social media by classmate*

Leg 5: *Wrecked my car*

Building a New Table (Belief)

Now that you have identified some of the legs supporting your self-limiting failure "table," it is time to identify the components of your new belief: a belief that you can succeed! Use the following tools to prepare you for developing the framework for your new table.

TOOL 11.3: PICTURE SUCCESS

Think about what success means to you. Think specifically about your particular area of concern. If your performance-related obstacles were completely eliminated, what would that look like? Draw a picture to represent what complete success would look like in this area.

TOOL 11.4: PERFORMANCE FROM A-Z

Self-esteem doesn't come from out of thin air. We can't just repeat positive affirmations that deep down we don't believe and expect self-esteem to appear overnight. Maybe you remember the line from *What About Bob?* in which Bill Murray's character, Bob Wiley, starts reciting, "I feel good, I feel great, I feel wonderful" over and over and over. Yet no matter how many times he repeated those words, it was obvious that repetition alone didn't help him believe them. There are many myths surrounding self-esteem. Self-esteem can't be gained by any magic-wand waving or mysterious tapping done in a therapy session. It has to come from somewhere. As discussed above, we have to do things that we consider worthwhile or possess qualities that we consider valuable and then *give ourselves credit* for possessing a particular skill or having a specific attribute.

Now that you have pictured what success looks like for you, think specifically about the attributes, qualities, and skills you have (even if you believe they need to be further developed) that will help you succeed. Using the following A to Z tool to guide you, list one word that starts with each letter of the alphabet that describes a positive quality you possess. Enlist friends, family, coworkers, supervisors, coaches, teammates, peers, or others who know you well enough to provide input. In response to positive feedback, it is likely that critical voice inside your head will want to argue from time to time, discounting something that is said. Resist the urge to argue with them and write the word down anyway. This will be "grist for the mill" for your work down the road.

A _____

B _____

C _____

D _____

E _____

F _____

G _____

H _____

I _____

J _____

K _____

L _____

M _____

N _____

O _____

P _____

Q _____

R _____

S _____

T _____

U _____

V _____

W _____

X _____

Y _____

Z _____

A TO Z QUESTIONS

Of all 26 attributes shared, which are most relevant to the area of performance you are working on?

1. _____

2. _____

3. _____

4. _____

5. _____

6. _____

7. _____

8. _____

9. _____

10. _____

Of the ones you listed, which three are the easiest for you to believe?

1. _____

2. _____

3. _____

Which three are the most difficult to believe?

1. _____

2. _____

3. _____

Of the three qualities that are easiest to believe, describe how you use each of them effectively to enhance your performance.

_____

_____

_____

Now that you have drawn your picture, enlisted support people to clarify your specific strengths, and identified which mean the most to you, it is time for you to use those to formulate specific legs to your new table—or as the components of your new belief: a belief that you can be a success. Record the attributes you have identified as the "legs" of your table.

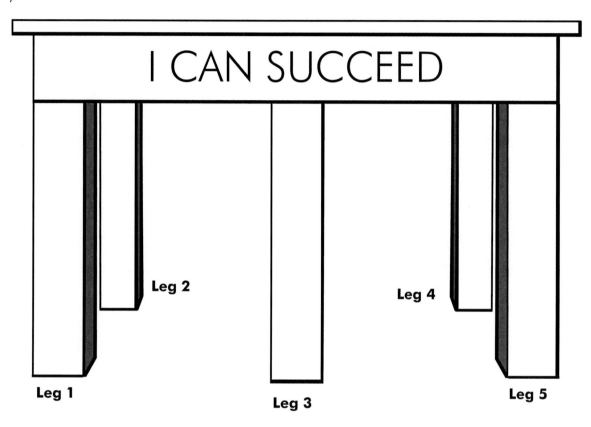

I CAN SUCCEED

Leg 1

Leg 2

Leg 3

Leg 4

Leg 5

Evidence supporting my new belief:

Leg 1:

Leg 2:

Leg 3:

Leg 4:

Leg 5:

TOOL 11.6: FEED YOUR BELIEF

This tool has been around for so long, I am not even sure who to attribute it to. It simply involves making a "to do" list. Many people make and operate from these without realizing their complete value. Likely, it is mostly people with performance-oriented beliefs (D's and I's) who are doing them, because people-oriented persons (S's and I') don't care! But since people with performance-oriented beliefs *do care*, recording, paying attention to, and then checking off completed tasks can actually give people a feeling of accomplishment and provide a boost to self-esteem. Note that it is important to start small. It is better to have fewer items on a list that you are able to complete than to have a more ambitious list you are not able to get to. This can be the difference between encouragement and triggering feelings of inadequacy for D's and I's.

To Do List

_____

_____

_____

_____

_____

_____

_____

_____

_____

TOOL 11.7: REDEFINE SUCCESS

When I was growing up, we always went to my Grammy and Grandad's for Christmas, Thanksgiving, and a few other special occasions. Those rare occurrences were the only time I ever saw my grandad expand the dinner table. His homemade wooden table pulled out and his handcrafted leaves could be inserted to make the table larger. It also required additional legs to support the expanded surface area.

For people whose beliefs are tied to accomplishment, "to do" lists can initially feed those performance-oriented beliefs and provide feelings of satisfaction and fulfillment. Days in which you "get a lot done" are likely "good" days. So "to do" lists can be helpful for creating these days on a more regular basis. But wouldn't it also be nice to feel good about one's self whether you accomplished anything or not? I come from a family of farmers where a rainy day was a "wasted day." If there is only one thing in life that is meaningful to you and you can't do it that day, or even worse, ever again, your self-esteem is in some trouble. Most people know someone who fits the mold of the seemingly independent businessman whose entire identity was tied up in his career that withers after retirement as he has no idea who he is outside that role. Similarly, a woman who has gained much self-esteem throughout her entire life from appearance—based compliments moves into her 50s and 60s and becomes depressed as she gets less recognition for outward appearances.

By adding "legs" to our success/value-related "tables"—that is, expanding the ways we define ourselves and what we view as important in life—we can dramatically improve our performance and limit our sense of devastation when we fall short.

Reexamine your A–Z Tool as well your picture of success, and answer the following questions:

What roles do I play in life that I have considered less important that I could make more of a priority?

_____

What gifts or talents or strengths do I have, not in the performance area, that I could I could start to use on a more regular basis?

_____

What hobbies or causes could I make more of a priority in my life?

_____

If I had to pick just one new leg to my table, what would it be?

_____

TOOL 11.8: PRODUCTIVITY PLANNER

Many people doing performance-related coaching are high achievers and are often task-oriented individuals. If this is you, this may very well be reflected in what you wrote as you filled in your legs of the table above. While you likely gain a sense of fulfillment by *accomplishing* projects and mastering tasks, it is also likely that when you fall short, you get triggered, since a good day likely entails "getting a lot done." This tool challenges you to rethink how you approach your "to do" lists and schedule your day accordingly.

Being intentional about how we spend our time is one of the most important keys to success. And what is success anyway? We each define that differently. Thus, it is important to prioritize our time each day according to *our* values—whatever it is that is most important to us. This might involve faith, family, friends, income, education, or whatever you believe to be important in life. We all have things we "have to" accomplish in life as well. The following tool is a way to help you be intentional about how you spend each day. Many of the world's most successful people plan weeks, months, and even years in advance. This doesn't mean not leaving room for flexibility or spontaneity, but it does mean that you can probably take a bigger picture look at how you are prioritizing your time. So plan ahead for how you will spend your week. When your week is over, you can revisit this exercise and see how your plans compare with what you actually did.

Devise a plan to get your "have to's" done, but also put plans in place to accomplish your dreams and live your life in the most fulfilling way possible. And remember not to prioritize your schedule—*schedule your priorities*. There is a *big* difference! Best wishes in taking charge of your life.

Priorities	**Have To's**
☐ _____	☐ _____
☐ _____	☐ _____
☐ _____	☐ _____
☐ _____	☐ _____
☐ _____	☐ _____

| | Monday | | Tuesday | | Wednesday | | Thursday | | Friday | | Saturday | | Sunday | |
	Planned	Actual	Planned	Actual	Planned	Actual	Planned	Actual	Planned	Actual	Planned	Actual	Planned	Actual
7 am														
8 am														
9 am														
10 am														
11 am														
12 pm														
1 pm														
2 pm														
3 pm														
4 pm														
5 pm														
6 pm														

TOOL 11.9: SUCCESS JOURNALING

Now that you have identified some of those tasks that naturally feel "worthwhile" to you as well as some newer activities intended to expand your sense of value/success, it's time to start paying attention to when you actually make choices consistent with those components of your belief. More clinical versions of this tool are called evidence logs. Pay particular attention to how you feel after completing the task or doing the activity. Be sure to link your feeling with the specific task you accomplished; make sure to give yourself a pat on the back and accept credit for doing what you did. Think about how you just made a difference in your workplace or in your relationships or in your world. Have conversations about this with your therapist, coach, or another important person in your life to help you internalize these as part of your expanded identity.

This tool requires discipline. It is probably both the most helpful tool you could have and also the most difficult one to follow through with regularly.

Pay attention to how your self-esteem changes gradually over time as you make more intentional choices around what is important. Some people even find it useful to rate to their self-esteem subjectively on a scale of 1 to 100, re-rating after each journal entry.

Date	Priority Choice	Self-Esteem Rating

TOOL 11.10: MONITORING NEGATIVE SELF-TALK

Self-talk is a term often used to describe the dialogues we have in our minds, or what we tell ourselves. We are quite aware of some self-talk, but much of it is less conscious. Self-talk can be negative or positive. The negative self-talk of the individual with self-esteem and performance-related problems typically involves 1) a voice predicting the performance will fall short before it is even attempted, and 2) a critical voice condemning her for not getting enough done or not doing something "good enough" while it is being done or after it is over. Common examples include:

- "It's unacceptable to make a mistake."
- "Criticism is terrible."
- "If I screw up, I'll lose my job."
- "You messed up again. You are so dumb."

Few people are as aware as they perceive themselves to be. Even before mindfulness had burst into the consciousness of the therapeutic community, a basic ability to detach and observe one's thoughts was vital. Without that ability, it was, and still is, impossible to know what thoughts to try to change!

A segment of the mindfulness and acceptance community (see Chapter 4) would argue it is not even necessary to deal with the content of thoughts. However, Martin Luther's words still ring true: "You cannot keep birds from flying over your head but you can keep them from building a nest in your hair."

If we don't want our negative thoughts coming from our low self-esteem to get the best of us, we have to fight back!

How do I know what to fight my self-talk with?

We have several weapons at our disposal when we notice a negative thought creeping in:

1. **Accept:** Accept that a thought is just a thought, notice it, allow it to pass in and out of your mind and move on.

2. **Distract yourself:** As mentioned earlier in the book, this is not a recommended long-term strategy. But if dwelling on a certain thought is affecting your performance in the moment, there is nothing wrong with shifting your focus to something else even if you haven't come to terms with it at a deeper level at that time.

3. **Challenge the thought**: We can challenge a thought in a number of ways.

   - *Use good old-fashioned logic.* Does it make sense? Ask a trusted person if it makes sense. Although none of us are completely objective, make your best attempt to be fair.
   - *Fact check.* When they are indeed facts (and not opinions put forth as facts), facts don't lie. Look at research studies. Consider probability. Poll others. Gather information all the information you can, and then be intellectually honest.
   - *Use imagery.* Close your eyes, Picture a scene where you were competing. Imagine yourself moving forward in a competent moment. Pick a time of success in your past and go there in your mind. Recreate helpful aspects of that past scene in the present.
   - *Use inspirational passages.* Use Bible verses, other religious text, or affirmations. Harness motivational quotes or poems. Remember, these are not just your favorite passages. Anything that inspires your thinking that is related to the legs of your table can be powerful.

- Jury duty. Examine the evidence. Look to see if there is empirical evidence to support what you are saying. Historical evidence can be examined, or ongoing evidence can be monitored.
- "How's it workin' for ya?" This saying made famous by Dr. Phil really addresses the issue of pragmatism. Even if there is valid evidence supporting some of your critical thoughts about self in events in the past, the question, How helpful is it for me to focus on this moving forward? almost always facilitates the shift to forward thinking that is essential for overcoming your obstacle.

CHAPTER **12**

Stress Management

Stress means different things to different people. It is interesting that the Oxford English Dictionary provides the following definition:

"A state of mental or emotional strain or tension resulting from adverse or demanding circumstances."

This is interesting to me in that this definition inherently gives what you may have heard referred to as *an external attribution*. One of the problems is that "adverse circumstances" is subjective. I remember years ago a study in the *New York Times* that said 90 percent of people polled believed their job was in the top 10 percent of most stressful jobs. This always resonated with me because I remember vividly a day in my psychotherapy practice where I had five people come in one particular day—and in consecutive hours I hear this (almost verbatim):

- "I am a fireman, so I have the most stressful job."
- "I am a teacher, so you know I have the most stressful job."
- "I am a nurse on a hospital unit, so I have the most stressful job there is."
- "I work in corporate, so, you know, environments really don't get much more stressful than that."
- "I am a stay-at-home mom and we have three kids—what I do all day is just as stressful as any paid job someone could have!"

Granted, if we developed a continuum of stressful situations and ask five hundred people's opinion, most if not all of the above scenarios would likely be rated toward the top. But I have also seen ER physicians respond in much calmer manners than office secretaries.

The point here is that stress is a subjective experience, and if we attribute it only to "adverse (external) circumstances," we forfeit much of the power we as humans have to use our mindset and choices to impact our states of being as we deal with external circumstances.

Thus, it is of vital importance to do what Bill O'Hanlon referred to as "de-packaging it"—that is to break it down to operationalize it and define exactly what it means to the person or organization you are working with.

Workplace stress has been getting increasing attention. As coaching gains acceptance, many people prefer it to therapy to avoid a stigma. As this continues to happen, life coaches find themselves dealing with stress-related issues more often as well.

Let's begin at the organizational level. Even after devoting almost two decades of my career to developing significant expertise in working with personality disorders in the clinical setting, I recently had an "a-ha" moment of sorts when it hit me that companies can have personality disorders as well! People with personality disorders are thought to (1) experience more stress than most, and also (2) create stressful environments and conversations for others. As I spoke with two particular clients coincidentally on back-to-back days, this parallel hit me, as I was able to see the same dynamics playing out within organizations that

I saw so frequently in individual people. Certain organizations are known for having more than their fair share of high conflict people. It stands to reason, the more "difficult" people an organization has, the more stressful the work environment will be for all involved.

Stress is among the most common work-related health problems. It has been estimated to be responsible for 11.4 million working days lost. The average person takes 27.5 days off per year. This obviously has significant financial implications. It affects organizational productivity, job satisfaction, staff retention, workplace morale, company reputation, and overall results.

Research on working conditions has identified a number of risk factors within the workplace that have been associated with higher levels of stress among employees (McKay Park. 2004).

Risk factors include:

▪ Demands
▪ Issues related to control
▪ Support
▪ Relationships
▪ Role change

In terms of personal stress, manifestations often include:

▪ Irritability
▪ Less time for stated priorities
▪ Weight gain
▪ Increased blood pressure
▪ Sleep disturbances
▪ Increased substance use
▪ Back and neck tension

While differences do exist from environment to environment, the general principles related to what contributes to "stress-related emotions" as well as the strategies for managing stress cut across contexts. So make modifications you find useful and enjoy the following tools for managing stress.

TOOL 12.1: THE STRESS ASSESS TEST

Stress is a subjective experience. Different things are stressful to different people. Research has identified some common life events experienced as stressful to most people. A deep dive into these is beyond the scope of this chapter, but an initial personalized assessment can be helpful.

Peruse the following common stressors, and rate, on a scale of 0–10 (0 being "not stressful at all" and 10 being "the most stress I have ever experienced") how stressful you experience each to be for you. If you have not experienced a given event, simply put N/A. This will give you an idea of your triggers for stress and specific areas to be cognizant of.

_____ Conflict with a Spouse

_____ Conflict with a Coworker

_____ A Minor Run-in with the Law

_____ Problems Sleeping

_____ Parenting Difficulties

_____ Having a Poor Date

_____ Death of a Spouse

_____ Major Illness

_____ Tension with Supervisor

_____ Change in Routine

_____ Child Behavior Issues

_____ Getting Fired

_____ New Job

_____ Somebody Upset with You

_____ Difficulty Paying Bills

_____ Divorce/Relationship Ending

_____ Decreased Contact with Kids

_____ Problem with Hobbies

_____ Church Adjustment

_____ Legal Problems

_____ New Relationship

_____ Retirement

_____ Change in Income

_____ Sickness of Loved One

_____ Sexual Difficulties

_____ Change in Family Dynamics

Other: _____

TOOL 12.2: THE CONSEQUENCES OF STRESS

Stress can have many adverse effects on us. Research has shown physiological, behavioral, and emotional consequences of stress, just to name a few. Often these manifest in quite subtle ways and "sneak up on us." Commonly, people give other reasons for why they are having certain problems and do not initially attribute them to stress. Use the following tool to pique your awareness to different areas of your life, considering how stress may be affecting you in each of those areas.

Physical/Medical:

_____

_____

Emotional:

_____

_____

Spiritual:

_____

_____

Romantic Relationship:

_____

_____

Relationship with Friends:

_____

_____

Relationship with Children (consider each relationship separately):

_____

_____

Financial:

_____

_____

Work/Ability to Perform on the Job:

_____

_____

Other:

_____

_____

Living a Balanced Lifestyle

It is well established that living a balanced lifestyle can play a significant role in reducing vulnerability to stress and other negative emotions. While there is certainly a need for treatment of symptoms once they occur, a refreshing movement toward preventative measures seems to be gaining some momentum. The following set of tools will walk you through some areas that have been demonstrated to be helpful in this regard.

TOOL 12.3: THE PHYSICAL FITNESS

Stress has an undeniable and reciprocal relationship with our physiology. That is, stress can affect our bodies negatively in many ways; and, on the flip side of the coin, we can proactively do things physically that reduce our vulnerability to stress.

Some examples include walking, running, swimming, bicycling, canoeing, or other traditional physical exercise. Yoga, tai-chi, and other "alternative" practices or disciplines have been gaining momentum. Studies have even shown different types of breathing exercises to have effects on biology that have been previously unknown. Taking vitamins, supplements, and traditional medications as prescribed can all fit in this category related to being proactive in terms of one's physiology.

Use the following tool to think about and record exercises or practices you could initiate on a daily basis to be proactive about maintaining physical well-being as one means for reducing your vulnerability to stress.

TOOL 12.4: SLEEP AND STRESS

Doing what is within our power to get quality sleep is another thing we can do to be proactive about decreasing vulnerability to stress and other negative emotions. Many people continue to live under the misnomer that sleep is 100 percent about biology and completely out of our control. Sleep researchers continue to discover this notion to be untrue. The following tool highlights a few areas pinpointed by this research. Use it to explore potential changes you can consider making to improve your sleep patterns.

I typically get _____ hours of sleep per night.

I know that I need _____ hours of sleep per night to function well.

Possible factors influencing my ability to sleep include (put a check in all boxes that apply)

_____ Lying in bed worrying   _____ Caffeine or sugar before bed

_____ Use of alcohol before bed   _____ Room temperature/light

_____ Keeping devices in bed   _____ Habits of people I live with

_____ Noise in the house   _____ Things I am doing before bed

_____ TV, music, or other stimulation in the environment

Some activities that are calming, soothing, distracting, or pleasurable (but not arousing) I could try to use to replace any of the items listed above are:

_____

I would like my new bedtime routine to look like:

_____

Tips for Sleep Hygiene

Do	Don't
• Monitor room temperature • Go to bed at the same time daily • Get up at same time daily • Use bed for only sleep and sex • Keep bedroom quiet while sleeping • Take sleeping meds *as prescribed* • Establish bedtime routine • Go to bed when you are tired	• Use alcohol or drugs not prescribed for you by a doctor to sleep • Eat heavily before bed • Participate in overly stimulating activity before bed • Drink caffeine/eat sugars close to bedtime • Watch graphic movies or morbid TV shows close to bedtime • Take another person's sleeping pills • Lay in bed for over 1 hour if you can't sleep

TOOL 12.5: SPIRITUAL WELL-BEING

Evidence continues to mount that religious involvement and spirituality is associated with better physical and emotional health. Use this tool to consider how you might use your faith to combat stress and increase contentment in your life.

To me, God is...

_____

_____

To me, spirituality is...

_____

_____

Practices, disciplines, and activities in my life that contribute to my peace and contentment include:

_____

_____

People in my life that encourage my connectedness to my faith are:

_____

_____

People/situations that present an obstacle for me staying connected to my faith or spirituality include:

_____

_____

My plan for staying spiritually fit to combat stress in my life is:

_____

_____

In a study that identified, according to the authors, the 10 most stressful life events a human being could go through, eight of them had to do with relationships. The following version of this tool is designed to help you identify what relationships contribute to your stress, as well as what relationships can help decrease your stress. First, use the circles to identify current significant people in your life. If you read chapter 5, you know that we often call these "intimacy circles" with clients, and that we define intimacy as "Into-Me-See"—the degree to which we let people see into us. So people in circle 1 are the closest people in our lives. We might let them "see into us" completely—having no secrets. People in circle 5 are people we would not let "see into us" at all—sharing almost nothing personal. Circles 2–4 are for those people in between. Evaluate the relationships in your life, complete the circles to represent how close you perceive the relationships to be, and answer the following questions related to stress.

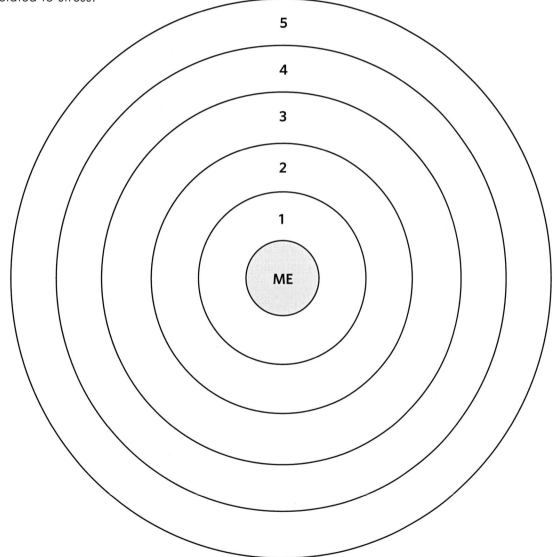

Adapted from *Group Treatment for Substance Abuse*, Velasquez, Maurer, Crouch, and DiClemente, 2001

STRESS CIRCLES QUESTIONS

Think about your circles ... if a stressful situation arises with another person this week, who is that likely to be:

_____

The person I am in tense interactions with most often is:

_____

When I get stressed, my behavior toward others tends to change in the following way(s):

_____

_____

People in my life who help me remain calm or manage the stress I am under are:

1.

2.

3.

Steps I can take to increase the frequency with which I have contact with helpful people are:

1.

2.

3.

Steps I can take to decrease my contact with stressful people in my life are:

1.

2.

3.

Steps I can take to better deal with stressful people I do have to interact with are:

1.

2.

3.

TOOL 12.7: STOP "SHOULDING" ALL OVER YOURSELF

As has been mentioned, stress is a subjective experience. Biological, environmental, and cognitive factors all play a role in influencing why a situation that is stressful to one person is not to another. This tool addresses a significant cognitive factor.

Albert Ellis is largely credited with pioneering the work chronicling many problems with "should" thinking. As was noted in the initial description of cognitive distortions (chapter 1), we can have these "should statements" toward ourselves or others. Chapter 7 denotes that when we "should" other people, the primary emotional response is anger (e.g., "He shouldn't have cut me off in traffic!").

But what about when we "should" ourselves? Since I am known as the "practical tools guy," I would be remiss if I did not mention that I am aware that what I am about to say sounds a little nerdy to most people. But stick with me. The cognitive specificity here is important.

Here goes. It is often helpful to break these "should statements" toward ourselves into two different categories:

1. Past-tense "shoulding"
2. Present-tense "shoulding"

This distinction is vital because it produces completely different emotional responses. When we "should" ourselves over something we believe we should have done in the past, the emotional response is *guilt*. Regardless of the perceived degree of the offense, this thought process is the same. Examples might include:

- *"I should never have said that—I think it hurt her feelings."*
- *"I should have stepped up and said something when my supervisor asked. I think I missed my chance."*
- *"I should have been there more for my kids when they were growing up."*
- *"I should not have driven home after I drank."*

These are all thoughts of people I have worked with recently. You might note that whether they are "shoulds" or "should nots" does not matter. Their commonality is more important: insisting that they should have acted differently to change some aspect of their past. This type of mindset leads to guilt 100 percent of the time.

So, this is not the mindset primarily involved with stress (although continuing to beat ourselves up over past wrongdoing can create its own kind of stress as well). Present-day stress is influenced by present-day "should" that can be characterized by putting *mental pressure on ourselves that other people (who experience stress differently) do not.* Examples include:

- *"I should clean the house today."*
- *"I should help out at the church."*
- *"I should do what my boss asks me to."*
- *"I should help, because they are family."*
- *"I should be able to do this perfectly. I should not make mistakes."*

Each of these types of distorted thinking comes from our beliefs. But to identify the beliefs behind the "shoulds" is more clinical work and less necessary in coaching. At this level, it is most important to help clients recognize this mindset and to collaboratively work with them to stop putting this mental pressure on themselves. Use the next tool to help work with clients around their present "shoulds."

I am most likely to put pressure on myself in the following areas:

_____

_____

Some "should" thinking I catch myself in often is:

_____

_____

If I don't accomplish what I think I "should" in the way that I "should" in the time frame that I think I "should," how could things turn out better than I believe they will?

_____

_____

Examples from the past where I put pressure on myself and it ended up being unnecessary include:

_____

_____

Use the thought log to identify and then challenge your "shoulds."

Present Tense "Should" Toward Self	Rational Responses/Challenges

TOOL 12.8: FOOD AND FEELINGS

Long before there was a book with this title, I contributed to writing a curriculum devoted to the topic of eating and feelings. Today there is an increasing awareness regarding the relationship between stress and emotional eating. If you use eating as a method of coping with stress, you are not alone. Millions of people across cultures report emotional eating to be a problem for them.

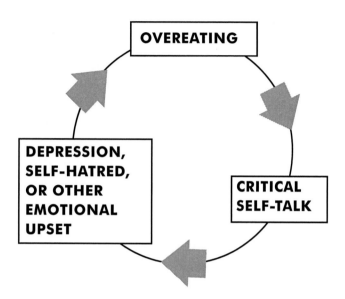

The diagram above represents the vicious cycle related to emotional eating. When experiencing stress, many people have thoughts about what food might do to alleviate it. These thoughts or beliefs influence overeating. Immediately following the eating "episode," most people then have critical thoughts toward themselves for the eating behavior. That mental beating one's self up then in turn causes more stress or other negative emotions. The questions in this tool are designed to help you think through where you can intervene in this cycle to overcome this obstacle if stress-related eating is a problem for you.

What steps could I take (from other tools or elsewhere) to manage my stress better in the first place so I am less tempted to engage in emotional eating?

_____

_____

The word "stress" is used generically by people to describe a broad range of specific feelings. What specific feelings do I experience most often just prior to emotional eating? (guilt, anxiety, anger, shame, other)

_____

_____

Three things I will do to increase my awareness of feeling this emotion sooner are:

1. _____

2. _____

3. _____

What beliefs/thoughts about food contribute to my stress eating?

_____ *"I can't stand this feeling! Food will help me not feel it."*

_____ *"Food is necessary to help me 'loosen up' for the party."*

_____ *"If I don't eat, I won't fit in."*

_____ *"Food is necessary for this celebration."*

_____ *"Food will comfort me in my distress."*

_____ *"Food is my friend—I can always count on it in tough times."*

_____ (Other) _____

Once I recognize and am able to name my feeling(s), three things I can do to tolerate my emotions rather than eat to change them are:

1. _____

2. _____

3. _____

After I eat as a way to cope with stress, some of the things I tell myself are:

_____ *"Food is bad."*

_____ *"Since I ate, I am a bad person."*

_____ *"Eating makes me a bad person."*

_____ *"Since I ate, I'll be fat and hate myself."*

_____ (Other) _____

Three ways I can reward myself for delaying gratification are:

1. _____

2. _____

3. _____

Reasons it is in my best interest not to emotional eat in response to stress are:

1. _____

2. _____

3. _____

It is helpful for some people to develop a list of affirmations to tell themselves "in the moment" when tempted to stress eat. "The urge will pass," "I want to be healthy for my grandkids," and "Running the marathon means a lot to me" are examples some of my clients have used. What affirmations might be helpful for you?

_____

_____

When I resist the urge to eat in response to stress, I feel:

_____

_____

The next time I am tempted to eat in response to stress, I can do/tell myself the following instead:

_____

_____

Food and Feelings Tips

Healthy Eating Includes:
- Eating what you enjoy
- Eating when you are hungry
- Eating that which sustains you
- Eating reasonable portions
- Eating regularly

Unhealthy Eating Includes:
- Skipping meals
- Binge eating
- Eating only sweets
- Overeating when angry/hurt
- Eating too much
- Eating too little

Results of Healthy Eating:
- Healthier
- More energy
- Longer life
- More physical comfort
- Doing what you want to do
- Better general quality of life

Results of Unhealthy Eating:
- Obesity
- Type 2 diabetes
- Anorexia
- Bulimia
- Anemia
- Social isolation
- Low self-esteem
- Self-hatred

TOOL 12.9: THE WORKPLACE STRESS ASSESS TEST

All of the "should" thinking addressed previously is relevant for dealing with stress in general. This tool is tailored to help you specifically with one type of environmental factor influencing stress: work-related stress situations.

Since stress in the workplace can come from a variety of situations, it is first important to identify what specifically is exerting stress on you. Place an X in the boxes of the situations you are struggling with:

_____ My workload is unmanageable.

_____ I feel like changes come at me out of left field.

_____ I don't have enough time to accomplish my work.

_____ I don't have the training I need to do my job.

_____ My coworkers make it difficult for me to do my job.

_____ I feel micromanaged. I wish I had more freedom.

_____ I wish I had more support when I have questions.

_____ I am not comfortable with how conflict is handled.

_____ I don't have a clear understanding of what my role is.

_____ I wish the organization would communicate more clearly.

For each of the X's you marked above, answer the following questions:

Describe the facts of the situation. Don't add your opinions or call names.

_____

_____

After running these facts by a trusted friend, colleague, or family member (not someone who will just automatically tell me what I want to hear), they recommended:

_____

_____

Now that I have clearly laid out and discussed the problem from my perspective, it is time to switch from problem to potential solutions. My proposal(s) for what might help resolve the situation is/are:

_____

_____

What is my role in the situation? What could I change in my mindset or behavior?

_____

_____

What issue could I bring directly to a coworker?

_____

_____

What might I need to take to a supervisor?

_____

_____

What might I need to take to human resources?

_____

_____

If none of the above can move toward resolution, I will know I might need to consider quitting when:

_____

_____

My plan for improving my workplace stress is:

_____

_____

TOOL 12.10: MY STRESS STRATEGIES

Now that you have a better understanding of the kinds of things that can prevent, create, maintain, and alleviate stress, and since different tools work for different people, you now get to develop your own individualized stress strategy tool. Use this final tool to take a big picture look at your stress and develop a strategy to combat it.

The stressful situations I am currently dealing with in life are:

_____

_____

My thinking or choices that might be contributing to maintaining my stress are:

_____

_____

Preventative habits I wish to continue to cultivate that might decrease my vulnerability to stress include:

_____

_____

My personal "Top 10" list of strategies for dealing with stress is:

1. _____

2. _____

3. _____

4. _____

5. _____

6. _____

7. _____

8. _____

9. _____

10. _____

CHAPTER **13**

Dealing with Difficult People

People don't often behave the way we think they should. And as Greg Lester puts it, "everyone behaves badly at times. And some people behave badly a great deal of the time."

However, since there are a number of different ways to "behave badly," nothing works all the time. That's why most self-help books are fatally limited. They teach things like "assertiveness" as if it is always a good thing. I am reminded of my client who once told me "I remembered what you taught us about being assertive in group, but it didn't work very well when I used it with that cop who pulled me over!"

Assertiveness, as with every other "tool" taught in this book or any other, is helpful in some contexts, and unhelpful in other contexts. Just because a tool "works" in one situation, doesn't mean it will in others. And as many coaching and therapy clients need to hear, just because a tool doesn't work in certain settings doesn't mean it might not work in others, so it is still worth trying!

Since we can't apply the same skill in every situation, the key is being able to know which tools to use with which people and in which contexts.

The Secret to Understanding ALL People
The ability to handle difficult people well is a requirement for navigating through any challenging situation in life. And there is a secret. But contrary to what some celebrities try to tell us, it is *not* "think it and we will manifest it." The secret is understanding the power that comes in recognizing human patterns of behavior—because people behave the way they do based on their learned patterns of behavior, *not* on the way we think they should behave. And once we (1) recognize the pattern of behavior in the person we are interacting with, and (2) accept that they will behave that way regardless of what we think, we are halfway there already. Why? Because we no longer expect disloyal people to keep our confidence, self-centered people to look out for our best interest, or people without a spine to stand up for a principle. Once we know what to expect based on their established patterns of behavior rather than our desires, the policies of the organization, the well-being of certain people, or the norms of society, we can devise a strategy to deal with that particular person more effectively.

What Makes People Difficult
It is not just that people are difficult or they are not. You probably know people who are a little bit self-centered, and you know people who are completely narcissistic. You likely know people who are mildly suspicious, and chances are you know someone who is all-out paranoid. The reality is that all human beings have personality traits on a spectrum. This is one of the problems with the *DSM-5*'s historical classification of personality disorders. It is not that we have a trait or we don't. We all fall somewhere on a spectrum with any number of traits. It is not that we are attention seeking or we aren't. We are more or less of any number of traits. That is not to say that there is no such thing as "normal," or perhaps a better word is "adaptive" personality function. John Oldham defined such as "the magnificent variety of non-pathological behaviors." Difficult people lack the capability to exhibit this variety in behavior appropriate to the circumstance life is calling for primarily for three reasons: extreme thinking, inflexible behaviors, and lack of awareness.

A quick review of the cognitive model of coaching and therapy clarifies what this looks like:

Event ➜ Thoughts ➜ Feelings ➜ Actions ➜ Results

In response to events in life, the more "difficult" a person is, the more extreme thinking they are going to have, thus the more intensely they will feel emotions, and the more inflexible their behaviors will be. The final piece of this is that they will have poor awareness as to how their actions contribute to their results.

Extreme Thinking

Difficult people have extreme thinking. In our clinical CBT parlance, we call this "black-and-white" thinking. If you are a therapist doing clinical work, these are people who typically require long-term schema or belief modification work. If you are a coach or someone working with these people in non-clinical settings, it is simply important to recognize this and be able to respond appropriately. Perhaps the easiest way to recognize this thinking in people is to look for hyperbolic language in their speech. Anytime you hear words like "always," "never," "best," "worst," "loves," "hates," etc. this is an indication of extreme thinking.

Inflexible Behaviors

At the actions stage, you are looking for responses that are disproportionate to the situation. Intense emotional responses, frequent disagreements, overreactions, and an inability to compromise are common manifestations of the difficult personality.

Lack of Awareness

While extreme thinking and inflexible behavior are challenging enough to deal with, this final characteristic is perhaps the most frustrating. Difficult people have little ability to recognize how their choices are contributing to troubling circumstances. Furthermore, situations that are troubling to those around them are many times not bothersome in the slightest to the person engaging in the behavior. This phenomenon makes motivation a challenge as well, and perhaps is the biggest factor in why dealing with difficult people can be such a challenge. Additionally, these people are more prone to behave in ways that assure they will get exactly what they don't want from others. What has become known in some circles as the "self-fulfilling prophecy" only strengthens these patterns over time if not subject to intervention.

While these three characteristics are present to one degree or another in *all* "difficult" people, they can take different forms. It is important to identify the type of person that you are dealing with. In my upcoming personal and professional development book I identify a number of types of difficult people. Five of those are "The Bully," "The Drama Mama," "The Yes Man," "The Eggshells Employee," and "The Overanalyzer." Below is a brief snapshot of each.

The Bully Continuum

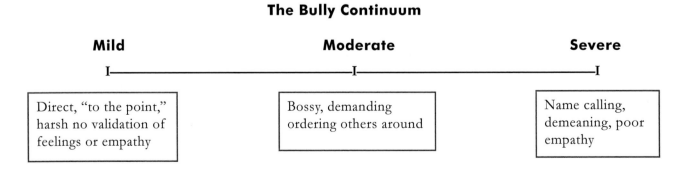

Mild	Moderate	Severe
Direct, "to the point," harsh no validation of feelings or empathy	Bossy, demanding ordering others around	Name calling, demeaning, poor empathy

Mindset
"Do what needs to be done, even if a few sensitive people have to be collateral damage."

Common Behaviors
Ordering others around, yelling, telling others what to do, name calling

As stated above, all of these characterizations are extreme manifestations of personality styles that have both strengths and weaknesses. In clinical terms, the "Bully" often has narcissistic traits. This represents an overdeveloped version of the "D" prototype on the DISC personality profile. When kept in check, these traits make for excellent leaders. They know how to take charge. They are excellent decision makers. They are determined, resilient, and productive. They make things happen and get the job done.

On the downside, their intense drive for accomplishment can influence them to be overly direct, sometimes demanding and punitive, and ultimately insensitive to the feelings and needs of others.

The Drama Mama Continuum

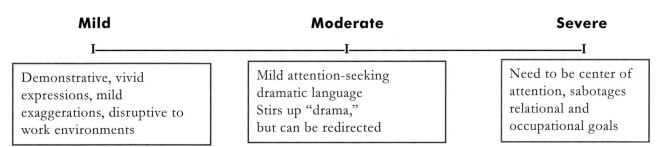

Mild	Moderate	Severe
Demonstrative, vivid expressions, mild exaggerations, disruptive to work environments	Mild attention-seeking dramatic language Stirs up "drama," but can be redirected	Need to be center of attention, sabotages relational and occupational goals

Mindset
"Life was meant to be a party. Make it one! (even if things don't always get done.)"

Common Behaviors
Spontaneous behaviors, dramatic displays of emotion, attention seeking

In clinical terms, the "Drama Mama" often has histrionic traits. This represents an overdeveloped version of the "I" prototype on the DISC personality profile. When kept in check, this type of person can be a lot of fun. They can be the life of the party and help others enjoy themselves. They are inspiring, spontaneous, and energetic. They can help make even the most mundane of projects or requirements seem fun.

On the downside, there are situations in life that require seriousness. They are prone to losing focus and missing deadlines. When unnecessary drama is inserted into serious contexts or situations, it can pose risk to required accomplishments and even compromise safety at times.

The Yes-Man (or Yes-Ma'am) Continuum

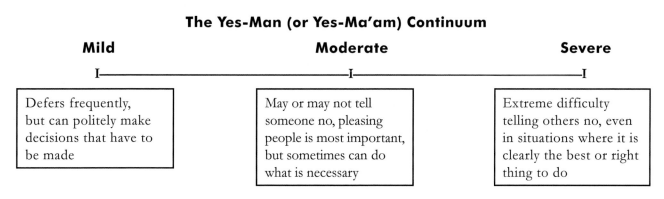

Mild	Moderate	Severe
Defers frequently, but can politely make decisions that have to be made	May or may not tell someone no, pleasing people is most important, but sometimes can do what is necessary	Extreme difficulty telling others no, even in situations where it is clearly the best or right thing to do

Mindset

"Even if I don't accomplish what I need to, everyone must feel comfortable."

Common Behaviors

Nurturing, sacrificing, and caretaking behaviors. Saying yes when it is in their best interest to say no.

In clinical terms, the "Yes-Man" often has dependent traits. This represents an overdeveloped version of the "S" prototype on the DISC personality profile. When kept in check, these traits make people feel comfortable. These individuals are all about relationships. They are social. They are loyal, friendly, and sacrifice their needs for the well-being of others. These traits can make them great spouses, friends, and teammates.

Many wonder how a person who is all about *avoiding* conflict and uncomfortable feelings associated with it makes a list of "difficult" people. While this is a good question, the downside of this style is that people with these traits often have trouble saying no when they really want to. Saying yes when no is best in a given situation can result in finding themselves with poor partners or friendship groups, compromising their moral values to fit in, or not meeting a deadline at work due to being pulled away at someone else's request. In fact, many supervisors will report their biggest "headaches" are not people who push back. At least they know where they stand. Rather, many will report it is those who tell them yes to their face, yet don't complete the given task more often than not.

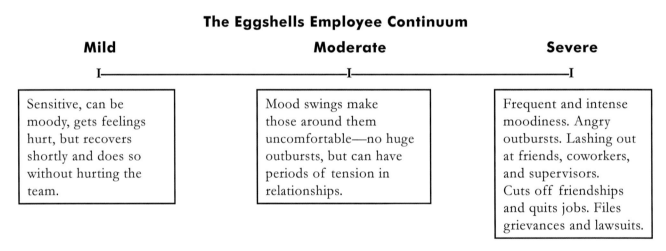

The Eggshells Employee Continuum

Mild	Moderate	Severe
Sensitive, can be moody, gets feelings hurt, but recovers shortly and does so without hurting the team.	Mood swings make those around them uncomfortable—no huge outbursts, but can have periods of tension in relationships.	Frequent and intense moodiness. Angry outbursts. Lashing out at friends, coworkers, and supervisors. Cuts off friendships and quits jobs. Files grievances and lawsuits.

Mindset

"I hate you but don't leave me." "Forget the project if I don't feel like it."

Common Behaviors

Difficulty being or working alone, glamorizing a person or situation, enlisting others to come against someone they dislike or are upset with.

In clinical terms, the Eggshells Employee often has BPD traits. The name is taken from the international best-seller *Stop Walking on Eggshells*. This also largely represents an overdeveloped version of the "S" prototype on the DISC personality profile, however elements from the "D" and "I" can also be seen in different people as well. It that sense, the profile of this person is slightly more complicated.

When kept in check, these traits can enhance powerful dynamics in personal relationships and make for great team members. People with these traits can be passionate, creative, and intelligent. They usually love working with people, as long as they are people they like.

On the downside, they are often known as the "overly sensitive" one on the team as they can be easily "set off" when comments hit them the wrong way. They can also come to dislike people they previously thought highly of, and at times, quite quickly. This person can then become a target of blame in the Eggshell Person's life, and the resulting intense emotions can make for uncomfortable and tense work environments. At times they even get punitive and can be known for their grievances and lawsuits.

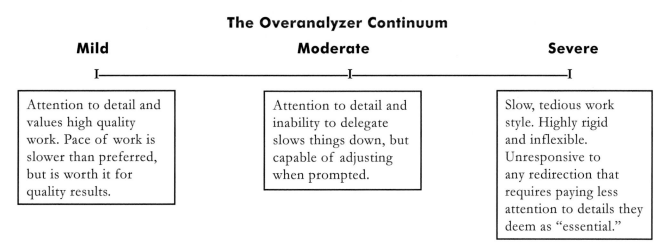

The Overanalyzer Continuum

Mild	Moderate	Severe
Attention to detail and values high quality work. Pace of work is slower than preferred, but is worth it for quality results.	Attention to detail and inability to delegate slows things down, but capable of adjusting when prompted.	Slow, tedious work style. Highly rigid and inflexible. Unresponsive to any redirection that requires paying less attention to details they deem as "essential."

Mindset
"Do it right, or don't do it at all. Don't quit until it's perfect."

Common Behaviors
Over-rehearsing, putting off starting things, inability to quit until "the time is right," and other perfectionistic behaviors.

In clinical terms, the overanalyzer often has obsessive-compulsive personality traits. This represents an overdeveloped version of the "C" prototype on the DISC personality profile.

When kept in check, these traits that emphasize paying attention to detail can serve companies and organizations well. Over analyzers are usually highly intelligent. Their cerebral nature can balance out the intensity of the bully, the drama mama, and eggshells employee. There is certainly a role in most industries for people who are analytical, thoughtful, and thorough, who value quality work. Even for companies that offer products or services that aren't typically associated with those features, every business needs an accountant (and if it has any online presence, it needs a tech person).

On the downside, people with this style are typically not the most efficient, and they often have difficulty getting things done. This is partially because the "analysis to paralysis" thing influences them to overthink and underperform. If something has to be absolutely perfect and thought out nine times before taking any action, this can certainly slow things down. Additionally, people with this style have difficulty delegating due to a fear that "others will just screw it up—to maintain an adequate standard I need to do it myself." While they perform the highest quality work, they also can have trouble seeing the bigger picture or vision. It is challenging to understand the scope of the whole forest for people with these traits who are so intently focusing on the nearest tree.

Some Fundamentals of Dealing with Difficult People
Understanding the type of difficult person you are dealing with is half the battle. Once you know the style of the person with whom you are interacting, you can be strategic about how to approach them. It is important to know why you are doing what you are doing in addition to knowing what to do.

The next chapter addresses the specifics of how to talk so people will hear you; that is, how to strategically alter what we are saying in a way that "hits the target" with different types of people. However, before addressing specific language, use the fundamental tools to help manage the difficult people in your life. Remember, different types of tools may be more helpful with different types of people. But as you learn a wider range of tools, your effectiveness in dealing with different types of difficult people will be enhanced.

Tools

This section outlines some fundamental tools for dealing with all difficult people. Because those using these tools likely have a variety of roles in the difficult person's life, tools will come in two categories:

1. Change-based strategies - for the practitioner working with the difficult person to help develop awareness and facilitate long-term change.

2. Situation management strategies - for the supervisor, employee, committee member, etc who is is not necessarily focused in the long-term change, but rather is simply needing tools to help navigate through day to day situations more effectively.

If you have been reading this book, you are familiar with these relationship circles. These circles can be used for many purposes. For the purpose of this exercise, use the circles to identify significant people in your life. If you have never seen this exercise, people you are the closest to go in your circle 1, people who have some place in your life (whether you like it or not), but with whom you have no trust and would share nothing personal go in circle 5, and the middle rings are for people of varying levels of closeness in between. Notice specifically the ones you view as "difficult" as you will soon be asked to identify their style. Remember to include personal relationships, work relationships, and people from any other context in your life that may include difficult people you will be required to deal with. Then answer the questions that follow.

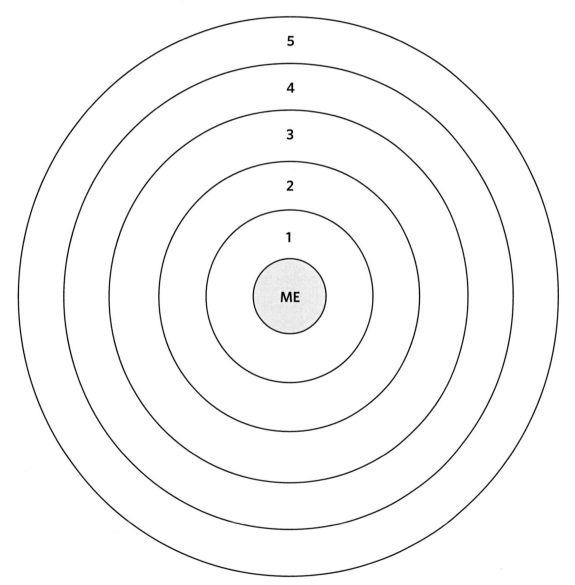

Adapted from *Group Treatment for Substance Abuse*, Velasquez, Maurer, Crouch, and DiClemente, 2001

Now that you have identified the people in your life, make a list of all your clients, potential clients (if you are in sales), and people in your personal life, as well as their styles you have identified. This will help your thinking in terms of how to interact with them moving forward.

Name   **Style/Type**

1. _____   _____

2. _____   _____

3. _____   _____

4. _____   _____

5. _____   _____

6. _____   _____

7. _____   _____

8. _____   _____

9. _____   _____

10. _____   _____

TOOL 13.2: IDENTIFYING RED FLAGS

The first step in effectively managing a difficult person is recognizing when you are dealing with one. A great number of people describe getting "sideswiped" by one of these individuals. I can't tell you how many times I have heard "It came out of thin air" or "He completely changed." Almost never is this the case. Almost always "red flags" were there from the beginning, but for one reason or another they were overlooked, minimized, or completely ignored. Use the continuums for each type of difficult person and identify the potential red flags for particular people you are dealing with, problems with your mindset that could influence you to overlook them, and to develop a plan to move forward.

The potentially "difficult" person in my life I am dealing with is:

_____

_____

My relationship to them is:

_____

_____

I would put them in the following category of difficult people:

_____

_____

Traits on the extreme end of the continuum I have observed that have me concerned are:

1. _____

2. _____

3. _____

I have seen these traits play out in the following interactions/situations:

_____

_____

Excuses I have told myself that these are not such a big deal include:

_____

_____

One trusted person I will run these by is:

_____

_____

TOOL 13.3: CONNECTING

Psychotherapy research has demonstrated time and time again the importance of the therapeutic alliance. It has been associated with decreased dropout rate, client comfort level, and overall positive outcomes. In addition to these clinical factors, we all do better in relationships that we trust. The ability to connect with other people may be the most important factor in romantic relationships, friendships, and business relationships just to name a few. Connecting is the ability to relate with people and identify with them in a way that increases your influence. Use the following tool to think about some ways that you can connect with the difficult person in your life.

The person I want to connect better with is:

_____

I want to connect better with them because:

_____

_____

Some things I have in common with them I can use to begin to develop a rapport include:

_____

_____

Regardless of what I might disagree with or not like about them as a person, when I really listen to them, I hear that their true desires and needs include:

_____

Positive attributes I can genuinely compliment them for include:

_____

Assumptions or biases of mine I need to fight to not have negative feelings toward them include:

_____

One safe way I can be vulnerable with them to lay the groundwork for them opening up to me is:

_____

_____

One way I can build them up daily is:

_____

_____

TOOL 13.4: GAINING BUY-IN (EXAMPLE)

As highlighted earlier in the chapter, one hallmark quality of what makes someone "difficult" is a lack of awareness. That is, their actions become problems for other people they interact with before they realize they are creating problems for them. For this reason, it can be necessary (depending upon your role with the person) to help them develop some buy-in before assuming they are ready to work on a particular problem. This tool asks clients to identify if anyone in their life has voiced any concerns with certain behaviors and, if so, why. Finally, it asks them to make an attempt to put themselves in the other person's shoes to see if they can see any validity in their point of view.

Sometimes this type of exercise can generate motivation in people who were previously not thinking about a particular area of life or a behavior that might be hurting them.

See the example below to help get you started, and then complete the blank tool that follows with your practitioner. Remember that reasons could include medical, financial, relational, spiritual, emotional, occupational, and legal areas just to name a few.

Person	Concern	Reason
Boss	Critical of other team members	Could hurt our team, could jeopardize my ability to move up in the company
Mom	Yelling at my kids	Could negatively affect my kids' self-esteem. Could damage my kids' trust in me.
Husband	I am always telling him what to do and getting angry if he doesn't do things my way	It could affect my marriage.

Concerns I give validity to include:
My bosses saying I criticize my team members

One behavior I could benefit from giving up to improve my chances at success is:
I will try to be more accepting of what my team members do. I will try to recognize when I am having critical thoughts and work on biting my tongue. If I think something still needs to be said the next day, I will run it by one co-worker before saying something to the whole team.

TOOL 13.4: GAINING BUY-IN

Person	Concern	Reason

Concerns I give validity to include:

_____

_____

_____

One behavior I could benefit from giving up to improve my chances at success is:

_____

_____

_____

TOOL 13.5: DEVELOPING AWARENESS

This tool aims to amplify any awareness you might have gained from the previous tool. Awareness is an area that most people believe they are better at than they are. We as humans can quite easily slip into "autopilot" mode where we just go through the motions without really paying attention to what we are doing. This can be particularly harmful if what we are doing is causing us harmful consequences. All people have some blind spots. But difficult people have more than their fair share.

Sometimes when attempting to develop awareness, it can be helpful to start with observing a behavior that you do not wish to change, such as how often you yawn, smile, or go to the bathroom. Once you get better at noticing those, then you can start working to pay attention to behaviors you do want to change. The first part of this tool will ask you to pay attention to a behavior and simply record how often you catch yourself doing it over a one-week period. The second part then is amplifying possible consequences of these behaviors.

Part 1

Behavior:

_____

_____

Day of Week	Times Engaged in Behavior
Sunday	
Monday	
Tuesday	
Wednesday	
Thursday	
Friday	
Saturday	

Conclusions:

_____

_____

Part 2

Behaviors Others Have Voiced Concern Over	Areas this Could Hurt Me
Behavior 1	**Physically:**
	Emotionally:
	Relationally:
	Spiritually:
	Financially:
	Legally:
Behavior 2	**Physically:**
	Emotionally:
	Relationally:
	Spiritually:
	Financially
	Legally:

TOOL 13.6: INCREASING FLEXIBILITY

All people have personality traits. Actually, all people have traits in each of the five problem areas addressed in this chapter.

For instance, the "Bully" is an extreme version of the "D" on the DISC profile and typically has narcissistic traits. However, what about the "D" who is not on the extreme end of the spectrum? This style also consists of, for instance, thinking highly of one's self. If you have actually acquired training or knowledge in a particular area, and you have developed some expertise, then it is appropriate for you to see yourself as an expert in that area and feel confident in that. However, narcissism becomes a problem when people *view themselves as experts in areas that they actually are not, take on arrogant attitudes, and show low empathy for others.*

Another example would be the "Drama Mama," which, as pointed out, is an extreme version of the "I" on the DISC and possesses some of the traits of *Histrionic Personality Disorder.* This diagnosis is characterized, in part, by overly flirtatious or sexualized behavior and dramatic speech or behavior. Having some histrionic traits may be helpful if one is single and trying to attract someone to date, a motivational speaker, or in theatre. Being "dramatic" in those specific contexts enhances their ability to inspire others and achieve their goals. But this becomes obstacle behavior if one is having sex with people at work who are married to someone else, singing in the middle of a prayer at church, or engaging in loud and impulsive outbursts at the committee they are serving on out of their need to be the center of attention.

We could do this with each of the other three types covered in this chapter. To reiterate, we all have *some* of these traits. However, most of us are able to "turn these traits on and off" depending on what is appropriate for a given context. We need to be able to behave differently when we are at a comedy club than we do when we are at a funeral.

The more extreme a person's thinking and rigid their behaviors is, the more difficult that can be. Use the following tool to help you identify traits that you have as well as areas that they could be *helpful* to you and areas they could be *hurtful* to you. Many people feel relieved to hear they do not have to get rid of these parts of themselves. However, the more flexible they can become, the more strategically they will be able to channel them productively in situations that will serve them well rather than pose problems. Consider the following example, and then do your own.

Trait	Helps Me	Hurts Me
Critical Mind	Analyze what's wrong with cars brought into the shop	When criticizing my wife and kids at home
Emotional Intensity	Passionate in relationships, when things are good they are really good	Get my feelings hurt and get angry too easily with people

MY FLEXIBILITY TOOL

Trait	Helps Me	Hurts Me

One change I will make this week to minimize the way my traits have been hurting me is:

_____

_____

One change I will make this week to maximize the way my trait can help me is:

_____

_____

TOOL 13.7: FOCUS ON THE POSITIVE

This often sounds like the simplest of the tools. However, using this "in the moment" is much different than posting a frou-frou meme about positive thinking on social media. Although it is challenging in practice, it can make a powerful difference in helping you to survive tense moments.

The person in my life I am working to handle more effectively is:

_____

_____

Three positive personality traits I admire in them are:

1. _____

2. _____

3. _____

Three of their accomplishments I admire are:

1. _____

2. _____

3. _____

The most positive thing about the person from my perspective is:

_____

_____

Themes in times when they are most difficult are:

_____

_____

The next time they are being difficult, I will make a conscious effort in the moment to focus on:

_____

_____

TOOL 13.8: SETTING BOUNDARIES

A boundary is a line of demarcation that separates where one thing ends and another begins. Boundaries can be geographical, physical, emotional, relational, sexual, and spiritual just to name a few. In terms of dealing with difficult people, boundaries describe limits that we set with one another in relationships. In terms of the circles exercise, boundaries determine how close we let people be in our circles.

Difficult people often don't respect boundaries. However different types of difficult people may push boundaries for different reasons. For instance, the Over Analyzer may work many hours of unauthorized overtime. His need for perfection or the right stopping place may compel him to work many more hours than he was given permission to. This is a boundary violation with respect to limits the company has authorized employees to work. In some ways, this is very different from the Bully who barges into your office without knocking in spite of being told numerous times, or the Eggshells Employee who calls you to ask for help 15 times in one day. While they are different types of problems, they are all problems related to boundaries.

People with extreme thinking and rigid behaviors don't like to be told what they can and can't do. But maintaining proper boundaries is essential for working with these people. You may have heard it said that *we teach people how to treat us*. Every time we answer the phone during times we said we wouldn't be available, fail to impose consequences for breaking down our doors, or have no repercussions for verbal abuse, regardless of what we said we required of people, we continue to send the message "I really didn't mean what I said; you can treat me (or the team) however you please." Use the following tool to consider how you might use boundaries more effectively at work to deal with difficult people.

The person in my life I need to consider setting firmer boundaries with is:

_____

_____

Reservations I have had that have kept me from setting boundaries sooner include:

_____

_____

The message I have continued to send is: _____,
without realizing it has been: _____.

I know it is time to set a limit because:

_____

_____

One boundary I am now willing to set and enforce that I previously was not is:

_____

_____

If the boundary is violated, I am prepared to take the following action:

_____

_____

Boundaries Tip Sheet

People with Healthy Boundaries

- Interact with people effectively
- Frequently get what they want in relationships
- Know what they will and will not do
- Know what they will and will not allow others to do
- Can set limits and still love
- Do not violate the personal space of others
- Do not take on responsibilities of others
- Can be responsible to others without feeling responsible for them
- Feel safe and secure
- Have healthy "circles"

People with Unhealthy Boundaries

- Frequently have difficulty in relationships
- Have difficulty getting their needs met in relationships
- Trust too easily and share too much personal information with the wrong people
- Trust too little and don't have people that they can open up to
- Violate the personal space of others
- Ask inappropriately personal questions of people they don't know well
- Feel responsible for other people's behavior and feelings
- Often are driven by guilt
- Choose actions based on what will please others rather than their convictions
- Tolerate unhealthy or inappropriate behaviors from others
- Feel unsafe in relationships
- Have unhealthy "circles"

TOOL 13.9: THE LEVERAGE

By now we are moving into the territory of last resorts. But extreme thinking and behavior sometimes calls for extreme measures. This tool is often most useful with the Bully but can work with any type discussed. One such measure is enlisting an invested significant other. This person is an individual who has some vested interest in the difficult person's success but is also in a unique position to have influence over the person's behavior that most do not have. It is often a spouse who is considering divorcing them, a supervisor who is considering firing them, or a parent who has some financial or other form of influence. This approach involves being upfront with the difficult person about what you are doing. Specifically, it includes collaboratively identifying obstacle behaviors to target as well as success behavior to increase, and then enlisting the invested significant other to compassionately confront obstacle behaviors as they arise and provide accountability. Use the following tool to begin this work.

The difficult person I am dealing with is:
_____

Obstacle behaviors I am working to decrease in them include:
_____

Success behaviors that would be in their best interest to increase are:
_____

One person who has influence over them that I could consider enlisting to apply leverage and accountability is:
_____

Behaviors I would want them to compassionately confront and report to work on include:
_____

Meaningful consequences they could impose on the difficult person include:
_____

Even though the difficult person has agreed to the process, when confronted "in the moment" initially, they will not respond well. Strategies for the invested significant other to employ in response to these reactions include:
_____

_____

I will know the leverage strategy is working if:
_____

_____

TOOL 13.10: ASKING FOR HELP

Finally, when all else fails, ask for help. And don't feel bad for doing so. Dealing with difficult people often requires a team. Enlist team members, management, or personal friends or family, depending on the situation. As you do this, be clear about your motive and intent. Go out of your way to let them know previous attempts you have made to solve the problem. Finally, it will be more appropriate and effective to bring in different people depending on the situation, Use the following tool to help you work through the process of asking for help.

The person in my life I am considering asking for help in dealing with is:

_____

_____

My interaction with this person is in what setting?

_____

_____

My previous attempts to solve the problems with this person have included:

_____

_____

Would it be in my best interest to tell the person ahead of time I am consulting someone else? Why or why not?

_____

_____

Reasons I have not asked for help sooner include:

_____

_____

I know it is now time to ask for help because:

_____

_____

People that I think would be best to bring in to consult in this situation include:

_____

_____

TIPS FOR DEALING WITH DIFFICULT PEOPLE STYLES

The Bully

- Work to develop authentic connection.
- Compliment them frequently and genuinely regarding their leadership or accomplishment.
- Choose your battles.
- Be direct when necessary.
- Submit when it doesn't cost you.
- Identify common goals—make it clear to them you will fight to accomplish goals they value.
- Apply leverage when necessary and possible.
- Enlist support/ask for help when necessary.

The Drama Mama

- Work to develop authentic connection.
- Compliment them frequently, genuinely, and publicly.
- Convey to them ways they really do inspire you.
- Find a way to make things fun for them.
- Provide accountability to help them stay on track.
- Demonstrate flexibility by being open to their spontaneous suggestions when reasonable.
- Gently point out how their "drama" is creating an opinion of them contrary to what they desire.
- Convey your desire for them to be though well of.
- Look for adaptive fits that harness emotionality as a strength.
- Enlist support/ask for help when necessary.

The Yes-Man

- Work to develop authentic connection.
- Validate their feelings.
- Use a friendly and nurturing tone.
- Validate their appreciation for others' feelings.
- Look for opportunities to allow them to work on teams.
- Confront problem behaviors by conveying that their inability to complete their task is negatively affecting their relationship with you.
- Give multiple positive strokes for jobs done well.
- Enlist support/ask for help when necessary.

The Eggshells Employee

- Work to develop authentic connection.
- Validate their feelings.
- Role model stability.
- Learn their "hot buttons."
- Avoid pushing buttons if possible, or do so without negative consequences.
- Compliment them frequently and genuinely.
- When they are upset, genuinely request explanation of why.
- Clearly convey your intent if something was perceived in a way that you did not intend it.
- Validate intense emotions without condoning behaviors that cannot be condoned for the sake of the relationship or the work environment.
- Give them permission to not believe you in the moment. Try not to get frustrated or argumentative. After you have conveyed your intent in the statement and your affirmation for them as a person, be ok walking away even if they are still not pleased with you in the moment. Likely they will feel different tomorrow.
- Enlist support/ask for help when necessary.

The Overanalyzer

- Work to develop authentic connection.
- Verbalize appreciation for the quality work.
- Validate that most others don't value detail as they do.
- Point out the value that style has in your relationship or your organization.
- Look for opportunities to harness perfectionistic qualities to better your relationship or your organization.
- Have the "forest for the trees" discussion when necessary. Point out the value of their attention to detail and also the consequences in that particular situation. Point out negative effects on the company, loved ones, or themselves. Make clear actual consequences if they continue inflexible behavior regardless of what they think "should" be the case.
- Enlist support/ask for help when necessary.

CHAPTER **14**

Belief-Based Communication

Understanding the role that beliefs play in differences among people is perhaps the most powerful information we could have. The final step involves harnessing that information and using it in a way that helps us communicate more effectively with people based on the belief systems that are involved. The following tools can help you begin to do just that.

TOOL 14.1: COMMUNICATION QUESTIONNAIRE

To me, communication is:

_____

_____

For me, the biggest obstacle to effective communication is:

_____

_____

One situation/relationship that has gone bad in my life as a result of communication problems was:

_____

_____

The person/people I have the most difficult time communicating with is/are:

_____

_____

My theory on why it is harder with them is:

_____

_____

"Drilling Down" on Communication

Did you develop any insights from completing the initial communication questionnaire? That was just to get you started thinking about this final topic.

There are seemingly thousands of approaches to go about addressing communication skills. This last chapter puts forth a model rooted in a cognitive behaviorally informed understanding of beliefs.

First, you may be familiar with the old adage that communication equals a message sent plus a message received. For some people, it even helps to visualize it as a formula:

Communication = Message Sent + Message Received

In his book, *Everyone Communicates, Few Connect, New York Times'* best-selling author John C. Maxwell points out that the average person speaks 16,000 words per day! If you transcribe those words, it would fill up a 300-page book every day!

But how often does it feel like we are wasting our breath? How often do our words actually hit the mark?

On the flip side, how often do we hear what others are truly intending to communicate to us?

Think about how many hurt feelings, damaged relationships, and miserable work environments could be saved with this secret? This chapter aims to point us in the right direction down that road.

First, we must keep in mind that communication can break down when messages are sent in unhelpful ways or received in unhelpful ways. What many people fail to recognize is that our beliefs influence the sending as well as the receiving of these messages. It is also important to remember that we are on *both* the *sending end* and the *receiving end* of these messages in our multiple interactions throughout a given day. Let's take a look at how this can play out.

In my role as director of outpatient services, I was responsible for approving my staff's time-off requests. Although they were all asking the same question, consider the differences in the approaches of four of my different employees.

Employee 1:
"Dr. Riggenbach, I was wondering, if it's not too much trouble, if there would be a time that is convenient in the next month for me to take a couple days off? I know everybody is working really hard, so I almost hate to ask...but I am really starting to feel run down."

Employee 2
"I have carried this team for three months. I put a request in your box to take off five days starting tomorrow."

Employee 3:
"I think I've worked three times more than anyone else this week. What would you think about giving your favorite employee a little time off before this little lady crashes and burns?"

Employee 4:
"Hey Boss, I know we are in the middle of an audit, and I want to be sure that I have gone through my final spreadsheet to be sure that all my charting is in place. It might take me a couple of days to double-check progress notes, treatment plans, and Medicare review sheets. But once I go all over those again, do you think I can have a few days off before we start the next program development?"

What did you notice? They all asked the same question, but used drastically different words, right? If you are a coach who is familiar with the DISC model of human behavior, you likely would have noticed that my first employee was an "S," (social type) my second employee was a "D," (domineering type) my third employee was an "I," (inspiring type) and the last employee was a "C." (cautious type). If you have a clinical background but no familiarity with the DISC, none of that means anything to you; however, you might have observed that the first employee likely has self-sacrifice beliefs, the second employee may have a more entitled disposition, the third employee (who believes she is "noteworthy") exhibits a mildly dramatic style in her speech patterns and her behavioral style, and the fourth, (who values "completeness") has some obsessive-compulsive personality traits.

Use the message sent illustration handout that follows to notice how the different beliefs affect the "Message Sent" part of the equation.

TOOL 14.2: "MESSAGE SENT"

Person	Disc Profile	Belief(s)	Language
Employee 1:	S	Self-Sacrifice	"Dr. Riggenbach I was wondering, if it's not too much trouble, if there would be a time that is convenient in the next month for me to take a couple days off? I know everybody is working really hard, so I almost hate to ask...but I am really starting to feel run down."
Employee 2:	D	Entitlement	"I have carried this team for three months. I put a request in your box to take off five days starting tomorrow."
Employee 3:	I	"I am Noteworthy"	"I think I've worked three times more than anyone else this week. What would you think about giving your favorite employee a little time off before this little lady crashes and burns?"
Employee 4:	C	"Completeness is Necessary"	"Hey Boss, I know we are in the middle of an audit, and I want to be sure that I have gone through my final spreadsheet to be sure that all my charting is in place. It might take me a couple of days to double-check progress notes, treatment plans, and Medicare review sheets. But once I go all over those again, do you think I can have a few days off before we start the next program development?"

Do you see how the beliefs served as a filter that influenced the language that was used to make the request? With this in mind, the following areas can be helpful to keep in mind as you communicate more strategically.

Know You

None of these four employees presented their request to me in an *intentional way*. They were just speaking from their natural communication styles. Learning to talk so that we know we will resonate with others requires that we understand our own beliefs and how those influence our natural communication styles. A later tool will facilitate altering our style, but if we aren't aware how we naturally come across, we don't understand what we are altering from. Knowing ourselves is the first step.

Use this tool to examine a recent interaction *you* had, specifically noting the role a belief of yours played in the language you used. If you think a different belief other than the four utilized above was involved in influencing what you said, refer back to chapter 1 for a more comprehensive list of beliefs.

TOOL 14.3: MY "MESSAGE SENT" (ME)

Situation:	
Belief:	
What I said:	
How my language could have impacted the outcome:	

TOOL 14.4: "MESSAGE RECEIVED" HANDOUT

Know You

I was the person on the receiving end in the examples of the vacation requests above. However, different supervisors obviously have different beliefs. Once we understand how we naturally send messages, it is important to consider what "filter" our words will be hitting; that is how is the "receiver" going to be prone to hear it. For the sake of simplicity, in this exercise, review the "Message Sent" Tool to consider only how employee number one's request might have been received by four different department heads.

Request off from "S" Personality Style	Supervisor Style/ Belief	Message Received by Supervisor
"Dr. Riggenbach I was wondering, if it's not too much trouble, if there would be a time that is convenient in the next month for me to take a couple days off? I know everybody is working really hard, so I almost hate to ask...but I am really starting to feel run down."	Domineering/ Entitlement	"Why doesn't she get to the point? If I don't need her during that time and she has earned it, I will give her the time off. That was 30 seconds of my life I will never get back!"
	Inspirational/"I am Noteworthy"	"Sure, she can have it off now. We can wing it without her!"
	Social/Self-Sacrifice	"Oh dear, she really does sound worn out—I want her to be ok. I better just give it to her now. I can work extra hours while she is out if I have to cover."
	Cautious/ "Completeness is Necessary"	"I will need to check the schedule to see when we might have some breaks in projects and when other staff has requested off. Then I can consider her request with all the other factors involved."

Now that you have seen an example of how beliefs affect the receiving of the messages we send, use the following tool to analyze a personal example where you think this was involved in keeping something you said from hitting their mark.

TOOL 14.5: MY "MESSAGE RECEIVED" (THEM)

Message Sent (What I said)	His/Her Beliefs	Message Received (How he/she "heard" what I said)

His/her filter changed the original meaning of what I intended to say in the following way:

_____

_____

TOOL 14.6: MY "MESSAGE SENT" (SOMEONE ELSE)

Now that you have examined your role in the sending of the message (being cognizant of your words *and* the "receiver's" filter, now it's time to put yourself in the shoes of the receiver. Use a modified version of the Message Sent Tool (14.3) to analyze a situation in which you believe someone else's beliefs and corresponding language influenced how they said something to you.

Situation:	
Belief:	
What I said:	
How my language could have impacted the outcome:	

Now use a modified version of the Message Received Tool (14.5) to consider the role *your* filter played in interpreting that language the other person used and thus your ability to "hear" it.

Message Sent (What he/she said)	My Beliefs	Message Received (How I "heard" he/she what said)

My beliefs/filtering changed the original meaning of what was intended to be said in the following way:

_____

_____

That skewed interpretation influenced my feelings and responses in the following way(s):

_____

_____

TOOL 14.8: CHALLENGE YOUR "RECEIVING"

Describe a situation. Use only facts:

_____

_____

What did the person literally say?

_____

_____

What did I hear?

_____

_____

How could I realign what I heard to be more in line with the facts?

_____

_____

If what was actually said still seems hurtful, are there any other possible explanations?

_____

_____

Even though they actually said _____, could they have meant anything else?

_____

_____

Even if I am convinced that they really intended the message to be as bad/mean/hurtful as I took it, what are the most helpful ways I could think about this moving forward?

_____

_____

Fact-checkers have become all too common during election cycles in the US. Their job is to follow candidates around the campaign trail and fact-check claims they make during their speeches. This is a good idea in theory. The problem is that many of these so-called "fact-checkers" have agendas as well; that is, they are biased by their perceptions.

Similarly, when testing our "receiving" of messages, it can be extremely difficult to weed out bias and get facts. Asking others what they really meant can be one helpful way to do this. Although when doing so, some people believe others will tell them the truth when in reality they do not. And on the flip side, sometimes others do not believe someone is telling the truth and the reality is that they are.

No tool works all the time. But it can be helpful to fact-check when trying to tease truth out of our perceptions.

TOOL 14.9: COMMUNICATION FACT-CHECK

I know it might be a good idea to fact-check my perception when:

_____

_____

When I consider the source that made the statement, it can change my thought process in the following way(s):

_____

_____

Are my feelings still hurt? Am I still bothered the next day? If so, how badly?

_____

_____

What is the nature of my relationship with the person who made the comment? Is this someone I have to continue to be in relationship with (i.e., Do I work with them, serve on a committee with them, go to church with them, have children in activities together?)

_____

_____

What do I potentially have to lose if I choose to fact-check?

_____

_____

I have decided to/not to check it out with _____ because _____.

Fact-Check Card

"I'm not sure if this is what you meant, but the other day when we were discussing _____, it felt to me like you were saying _____.

Is that what you really meant by that?"

TOOL 14.10: UNDERSTANDING OTHERS

Now that you have examined how your beliefs affect both your sending and your receiving of messages, it's time to do a little sizing up (even if you have to guess) of the person you are dealing with.

The person in my life I am trying to deal with is:

_____

My guess is that their personality type is:

_____

_____

My guess is based upon the following behaviors in them:

_____

_____

Knowing their style, I know the following information about them:

_____

_____

I think the following beliefs/thought processes are driving their behavior:

_____

_____

With this knowledge, I understand that they are motivated by:

_____

_____

Knowing this, if I want to get through to them, I will need to adapt my communication in the following way:

_____

_____

Strategic Communication

Once you understand yourself and understand the other person, here is where the interaction dynamics come into play. When you know (1) how they receive (filter) information, and (2) how you tend to send information, you can (3) know if and how to adapt your approach to communicate strategically to that particular person. I always hear people say things like "Nobody else in the world would have taken it the way they did! Why should I have to alter my approach?" And my answer is always "because you are the one dealing with them who seems to care about the outcome!"

The good news is, armed with the information laid out above, you now know how to do this! Based on your natural tendencies to "send" and their natural tendencies to "receive," strategically change the "sending" to ensure that the message is received as it was intended to be.

TOOL 14.11: ALTER YOUR APPROACH

Use this tool to facilitate your thinking about how you might alter your approach strategically to communicate more effectively with the difficult person in your life.

The person I am wanting to communicate with is:

_____

_____

They have been difficult to deal with in the past (for me or others) due to:

_____

_____

I would describe their personality style as:

_____

_____

Based on their beliefs, they will be prone to receive information in the following way:

_____

_____

What do I really want in this situation?

_____

_____

What is the best way to ask them given what I know about their personality style?

_____

_____

This will require altering my natural communication style in the following way(s)?

_____

_____

TOOL 14.12: COMMUNICATION SUMMARY

Sum up your learning and develop some specific communication-related takeaways.

The people in my life I have the most trouble communicating with are:

_____

_____

The core belief most often influencing my "sending" of messages is:

_____

_____

I will work on altering my language when communicating in the following way:

_____

_____

Since non-verbal's are 90 percent of communication, I will be mindful of my non-verbals in the following ways:

_____

_____

The core belief that most often influences my "receiving" of messages is:

_____

_____

Based on what I know about that belief, I will be on guard for what type of misinterpretation on my end?

_____

_____

If I do allow someone to push my buttons and get upset, I can use the following challenges to calm down quickly.

_____

_____

The first person I will practice this with is:

_____

_____

REFERENCES

For your convenience, purchasers can download
and print the tools from www.pesi.com/CBT2

Abelson, J. L., Liberzon, I., Young, E. A., & Khan, S. (2005). Cognitive modulation of endocrine stress response to a pharmacological challenge in normal and panic disorder subjects. *Archive of General Psychiatry*, 62(6), 668–675.

Ameli, R. (2014). *25 lessons in mindfulness: Now time for healthy living* (1st ed.). Washington, DC: American Psychological Association.

Antony, M. (2009). *When perfect isn't good enough: Strategies for coping with perfectionism.* New Harbinger Publications.

Antony, M., & Norton, P. J. (2008). *The anti-anxiety workbook: Proven strategies to overcome worry, phobias, panic, and obsessions.* Guilford Press.

Beattie, M. (1986). *Codependent no more: How to stop controlling others and start caring for yourself.* Hazelden Foundation.

Beck, A. T. (1967). *The diagnosis and management of depression.* Philadelphia, PA: University of Pennsylvania Press.

Beck, A. T. (2000). *Prisoners of hate: The cognitive basics of anger, hostility, and violence.* HarperCollins.

Beck, A. T. (2015). *Cognitive therapy of personality disorders* (3rd ed.). Guilford Press.

Beck, A. T., & Clark, D. (2011). *The anxiety and worry workbook: The cognitive behavioral solution.* Guilford Press.

Beck, A. T., Rector, N. A., Stolar, N., & Grant, P. (2011). *Schizophrenia: Cognitive theory, research, and therapy.* Guilford Press.

Beck, A. T., Rush, A. J., Shaw, B. F., & Emery, G. (1987). *Cognitive therapy of depression* (1st ed.). Guilford Press.

Beck, J. S. (2005). *Cognitive therapy for challenging problems* (1st ed.). Guilford Press.

Beck, J. S. (2011). *Cognitive therapy: Basics and beyond* (2nd ed.). Guilford Press.

Burns, D. D. (1999). *The feeling good handbook.* Plume.

Cloud, H., & Townsend, J. (1992). *Boundaries: When to say yes, how to say no to take control of your life.* Zondervan.

Connors, G. J., DiClemente, C. C., Velasquez, M. M., & Donovan, D. M. (2004). *Substance abuse treatment and the stages of change: Selecting and planning interventions* (2nd ed.). Guilford Press.

DeRubeis, R. J., Siegle, G. J., & Hollon, S. D. (2008). Cognitive therapy versus medication for depression: Treatment outcomes and neural mechanisms. *Nature Reviews Neuroscience*, 9(10), 788–796.

De Shazer, S. (1985). *Keys to Solution in Brief Therapy.* Norton.

Edwards, D. J. A. (2014). Schemas in clinical practice: What they are and how we can change them. *Independent Practitioner*, 34(1), 10–13.

Edwards, D. J. A. (2015). Self-pity/victim mode: A surrender schema mode. *Schema Therapy Bulletin*, 1(1), 3–6.

Ellis, A., & Harper, R. A. (1975). *A new guide to rational living.* Wilshire Book Co.

Ellis, T. (Ed.). (2006). *Cognition and suicide: Theory, research, and therapy.* American Psychological Association.

Gilbert, P., & Leahy, R. L. (2017). *The therapeutic relationship in cognitive behavioral psychotherapies* (1st ed.). Routledge.

Greitens, E. (2016). *Resilience: Hard-won wisdom for living a better life.* Mariner Books.

Hackman, A., Bennett-Levy, J., & Holmes, E. A. (2011). *Oxford guide to imagery in cognitive therapy.* Oxford University Press.

Hayes, S., & Smith, S. (2005). *Get out of your mind and into your life: The new acceptance and commitment therapy*. New Harbinger Publications.

Kahl, K. G., Winter, L., & Schweiger, U. (2012). The third wave of cognitive behavioural therapies: What is new and what is effective? *Current Opinion in Psychiatry*, 25(6), 522–528.

Kuyken, W., Padesky, C. A., & Dudley, R. (2009). *Collaborative case conceptualization: Working effectively with clients in cognitive-behavioral therapy*. Guilford Press.

Leahy, R. (2003a). *Cognitive therapy techniques: A practitioner's guide* (1st ed.). Guilford Press.

Leahy, R. (2003b). *Overcoming resistance in cognitive therapy* (1st ed.). Harmony Books.

Leahy, R. (2006). *The worry cure: Seven steps to stop worry from stopping you*. Harmony Books.

Leahy, R. (2019). *Emotional schema therapy*. Routledge.

Leahy, R., & Gilbert, P. (2018). *The jealousy cure: Learn to trust, overcome possessiveness, and save your relationship*. Guilford Press.

Lester, G. (1995). *Power with People: How to handle just about anyone and accomplish just about anything*. Ashcroft Press.

Linehan, M. (1993). *Cognitive behavioral treatment of borderline personality disorder*. Guilford Press.

Linehan, M., Goodstein, J. L., Nielsen, S. L., & Chiles, J. A. (1983). Reasons for staying alive when you are thinking of killing yourself: The reasons for living inventory. *Journal of Consulting and Clinical Psychology*, 51, 276–286.

Ludgate, J. (2009). *Cognitive behavioral therapy and relapse prevention for depression and anxiety*. Professional Resource Press.

Makinson, R. A., & Young, J. S. (2012). Cognitive behavioral therapy and the treatment of posttraumatic stress disorder: Where counseling and neuroscience meet. *Journal of Counseling & Development*, 90(2), 131–140.

Maxwell, J. C. (2007). *Failing forward: Turning mistakes into stepping stones for success*. Thomas Nelson Publishers.

Miller, W. R., & Rollnick, S. (1992). *Motivational interviewing: Preparing people to change addictive behavior*. Guilford Press.

Miller, W. R., & Rollnick, S. (2012). *Motivational interviewing: Helping people change* (3rd ed.). Guilford Press.

Moody, T. D., Morfini, F., Cheng, G., Sheen, C., Tadayonnejad, R., Reggente, N., O'Neill, J., & Feusner, J. D. (2017). Mechanisms of cognitive-behavioral therapy for obsessive-compulsive disorder involve robust and extensive increases in brain network connectivity. *Translational Psychiatry 7*, Article e1230.

Navoco, R. (2007). Anger dysregulation. In T. A. Cavell & K. T. Malcolm (Eds.), *Anger, aggression, and interventions for interpersonal violence* (pp. 3–54). Routledge.

Neenan, M., & Dryden, W. (2013). *Life coaching: A cognitive behavioural approach*. Routledge.

Neehan, M., & Palmer, S. (2012). *Cognitive behavioural coaching in practice: An evidence-based approach*. Routledge.

Padesky, C. A., & Mooney, K. A. (2012). Strengths-based cognitive-behavioural therapy: A four-step model to build resilience. *Clinical Psychology & Psychotherapy*, 19(4), 283–290.

Perlis, M. L., Jungquist, C., Smith, M. T., & Posner, D. (2008). *Cognitive-behavioral treatment of insomnia: A session-by-session guide*. Springer.

Porto, P. R., Oliveira, L., Mari, J., Volchan, E., Figueira, I., & Ventura, P. (2009). Does cognitive behavioral therapy change the brain? A systematic review of neuroimaging in anxiety disorders. *The Journal of Neuropsychiatry and Clinical Neurosciences*, 21(2), 114–125.

Prochaska, J. O., Norcross, J. C., & DiClemente, C. C. (2010). *Changing for good: A revolutionary six-stage program for overcoming bad habits and moving your life positively forward*. HarperCollins.

Ramy, H. (2020). The biology of cognitive behavior therapy. *European Psychiatry*, 41(S1), s637.

Reis de Oliveiria, I. (2015). *Trial-based cognitive therapy: A manual for clinicians*. Routledge.

Riggenbach, J. (2013). *The CBT toolbox: A workbook for clients and clinicians* (1st ed.). PESI Publishing.

Rohn, R. (2005). *Positive personality profiles: D-I-S-C-over personality insights to understand yourself and others!* Personality Insights.

Scrimali, T. (2012). *Neuroscience-based cognitive therapy: New methods for assessment, treatment, and self-regulation* (1st ed.). Wiley-Blackwell.

Segal, Z. V., Williams, J. M. G., & Teasdale, J. D. (2018). *Mindfulness-based cognitive therapy for depression* (2nd ed.). Guilford Press.

Seligman, M. E. P. (2006). *Learned optimism: How to change your mind and your life.* Vintage Books.

Sokol, L., & Fox, M. (2009). *Think confident, be confident: A four-step program to eliminate doubt and achieve lifelong self-esteem.* TarcherPerigee.

Thoma, N. C., & McKay, D. (2015). *Working with emotion in cognitive-behavioral therapy: Techniques for clinical practice* (1st ed.). Guilford Press.

Velasquez, et.al (2001). *Group Treatment of Substance Abuse: A Stages of Change Model.* Guilford Press.

Warren, R. (2012). *The purpose-driven life: What on earth am I here for?* Zondervan.

Weisinger, D. (1985). *Dr. Weisinger's anger work-out book: Step-by-step methods for greater productivity, better relationships, healthier life.* William Morrow and Company.

Wells, A. (2011). *Metacognitive therapy for anxiety and depression.* New York: Guilford Press.

Wells, A., & Matthews, G. (1994). *Attention and emotion: A clinical perspective.* Psychology Press.

Whitmore, S. J. (2017). *Coaching for performance: The principles and practice of coaching and leadership.* Nicholas Brealey Publishing.

Young, J. E., Klosko, J. S., & Weishaar, M. E. (2003). *Schema therapy: A practitioner's guide* (1st ed.). Guilford Press.

Young, J. E., & Klosko, J. S. (1994). *Reinventing your life: The breathtaking program to end negative behavior and feel great again.* Plume.